CLEAR PICTURES

REYNOLDS PRICE

CLEAR PICTURES

FIRST LOVES, FIRST GUIDES

NEW YORK

ATHENEUM

1989

Parts of this memoir appeared, in earlier forms, in *Kenyon Review*, *The Leader*, and a limited edition published by North Carolina Wesleyan College Press.

ATHENEUM
Macmillan Publishing Company
866 Third Avenue, New York, N.Y. 10022
Collier Macmillan Canada, Inc.

Library of Congress Cataloging-in-Publication Data
Price, Reynolds, ———
    Clear pictures.
    1. Price, Reynolds, ———   —Biography.
    2. Novelists, American—20th century—
Biography.   I. Title.
PS3566.R54Z465   1989   813'.54   88–34395
ISBN 0–689–12075–3

Macmillan books are available at special discounts for bulk purchases for sales promotions, premiums, fund-raising, or educational use. For details, contact:

Special Sales Director
Macmillan Publishing Company
866 Third Avenue
New York, N.Y. 10022

10   9   8   7   6   5   4   3   2   1

Printed in the United States of America

FOR

KEVIN HELLIKER

CONTENTS

CLEAR PICTURES

FOREWORD

ONE OF THE stranger days of my life came in March 1987, when I passed the age at which my father died. He lived for fifty-four years and forty-two days; now I'd exceeded him. Few men will doubt that such a passage might cause long reflections. In me those thoughts sparked two brief poems, but mainly they stirred an old idea. For years I'd thought that someday I'd write a memoir. As early as my junior year in high school, I began a verse autobiography. It covered a few shining moments of childhood and the agonies of adolescence; then it ran out of fuel and skipped unceremoniously to my resurrection from the dead. And in my last year of college, for a course in psychoanalytic theory, I wrote a self-psychoanalysis—as solemn and absurd as most. Once it won me a grade, I burned it.

In all the years since, I've mostly resisted written memories. Aside from a few short stories and poems in which I've dealt candidly with personal history and feeling, I've done little more than keep a daily log of appointments, visitors and phonecalls. After I abandoned the steamy diary of my pubescent years, I've had slim luck with regular journals. More than once I've tried—and for a period of nearly two adult years, I managed—a daily narrative record of events.

Even then however, I hated recording the latest thoughts and feelings, knowing from old experience how hopeless my Great Thoughts sound in hindsight, and eventually I quit. It's hard work enough, surviving the acts and responses of a day, bad or good. But reliving it all that night on paper is painful overtime. I've also felt that the commitment to keep a journal makes me even more analytic and manipulative of myself and others than I naturally am. It's my observation with journal-keepers that they often seem to live for their journals. Maybe they're barely conscious of the motive, but I often detect an inward grin as they think "Do *this*; it'll sound so fine in my journal tonight."

So I kept the long-stored memories back, on into my fifties. Then in the summer and fall of 1984—when surgery, radiation and steroids had grounded me—I was idle at home for five months. I had a third of a novel finished (it would later be *Kate Vaiden*), but I couldn't touch it yet. I managed a few short poems, and I reverted to the first acts of making in my life. I sat in a chair, day after day, and drew picture on imaginary picture. They were all brush drawings, and most of them were guesses at the face of Christ. With world-excluding headphones I'd sit a whole day, listening to a Cavalli mass, a Vivaldi *Gloria*, Bach's orchestral suites or a Handel concerto. It was mostly Renaissance or Baroque music. That live but looping and twining order was healing; the Romantics and the great majority of twentieth-century composers were far too self-absorbed and strenuous for help (though oddly I listened to a lot of Mahler).

Those friends who knew me well enough, and some who didn't, began to concern themselves with my doldrums. There were many suggestions of projects for me, but a single idea kept returning. And it often came more or less like this, "You always remembered so much more than the rest of us. Why not take this time at home and write it all down?" It wasn't the kind of foolish idea most people give writers—"Let me make your first million: I'll tell you my story, and you write it down." But I had to smile at the mixture of implications—*Do it for the sake of doing something; do it before it's past too late*—and I couldn't begin.

Worse than foolish, the idea repelled me. With all the misery of inaction, I heard what my friends meant—*The clock's running out*. And I was damned if I'd use a gift, that might still be buried somewhere in my keeping, and bow to the approach of a death that I didn't want or, in my best hours, think imminent. I understood the odds against my gamble on endurance, though I was lucky not to know how grimly the doctors viewed my chances. And I saw how plainly I was enacting the common deathbed refusal to make a will or the reluctance of some artists to finish a work whose completion they associate with death.

At least as clearly, I saw how hard the job would be. In the past when I'd thought of memoirs, I'd known I was betting on a long life and wouldn't begin till late in the span. And I knew there were two strong reasons for that. First, since early maturity I'd seen how much my external actions were like those of most workers. Internally mine were laced with uncanny indications of design (elegant or awful Cat's Cradles of order and intent, insisting upon the unseen presence of a maker). But as the meat of narrative, most of my days were tepid broth.

For the visible events of my adult life have consisted mainly of work, years alone in silence at a desk or companioned by students in a classroom. There have also been stretches of family love and duty, much friendship, much travel and passionate episodes—most of them happy but more than one disaster. Disasters in general make better reading than happiness. But most of my pleasures and all my serious wrongs have involved persons who are still alive, most of them still my friends.

With a single exception I'm in regular touch with every person I've loved, to speak only of the living. They've given to me richly, in agreeing to love me or accept my love. And I have no wish to violate such trust, now or ever, by describing their gifts in imprecise words that even a sympathetic reader couldn't hope to weigh fairly. The continuing popularity of whores' memoirs only deepens my refusal (whores can be anything from ex-White House employees to the spurned mistresses of rock stars). Likewise I resist another common memoir—a gripping-enough narrative in which the writer changes all the warmer names, juggles places and dates and otherwise lies his way through events that he's secretly intent on distorting or veiling.

Till the spring of 1987, the thought of a memoir was still far off. Then two doors opened. I agreed to speak to the annual meeting of the Friends of the Duke University Library. I'd attended Duke as an undergraduate from 1951 to 1955. I returned to teach in 1958, taught full-time till 1961 and have lived nearby and taught for half of each year since, with the usual leaves. The membership of the Friends includes many colleagues I've known from boyhood, so I decided to recall for them the more amusing and important public memories of my student life.

The act of finding the history and setting it down filled an easy few days. And though I've always had a fair memory, this time I managed to surprise myself. I'd write down a fact—say, the location and dimensions of my freshman room in 1951—and the measured space would prove to be, not an isolated spot in my mind but the visible nub of a hidden string that, pulled on gently, unreeled itself as yards long, invariably branched and hung with more stored pictures than I'd known I possessed.

Or better maybe, I'd make a list of hard facts—teachers, courses, the names of lost friends. And once set down on the page before me, they'd prove to be only the exposed glints of abundant veins. Quickly I knew much more than I could use, unless I meant to sedate my friends (not an uncommon result at such dinners). I pruned back ruthlessly and read the speech. My audience took it with apparent interest and corroboration; and several of them asked for more. By then, after three more surgeries, I appeared to be good for longer than my doubters had expected; so the urging sat lighter on my mind than before.

When classes ended a few weeks later, I turned instead to finishing a collection of thirty-three years of critical and personal essays. Simultaneously in the hope of easing back pain, I began ten weeks of training at Duke Hospital in the techniques of biofeedback and hypnosis. My hypnotist was Dr. Patrick Logue; and he spent a good part of our first meeting in assuring me of the benign nature of hypnosis. I was able to assure him that, because of an enjoyable adolescent trance, induced by my tenth-grade biology teacher, I had no fears and was eager to start.

In the remainder of that first hour—with only the doctor's level voice and his ample stock of verbal images for serenity, trust and the imaging of painful areas—I entered a quarter-hour state in which I was literally ecstatic, standing in high pleasure outside my usual mind and body yet thoroughly *in* them. My experience of hypnosis bears no resemblance to the common notion of a deep sleep in which the subject surrenders judgment to the hypnotist. My states are more closely related to the kind of half-sleep we enjoy in a cat-nap—telling ourselves we're awake and in fact hearing the clock tick or a friend in the kitchen but drifting by the moment into a welcoming harbor, the peace of which can endure for hours after returning to the world.

When I returned to normal a few minutes later, I was startled to find my three-year pain diminished by more than half. Better still, the relief lasted for the three hours Logue had estimated. The sensation was so powerful that I felt as if I'd whiffed a potent drug; I was even disturbed by the newness. But as I worked at home with a tape of Logue's voice, the strangeness passed. And in the next month, we met weekly and worked with the same methods and good new images to speed my entry on a calm acceptance of benign suggestion and the distancing of pain. Then we turned to the business of weaning me, first from the doctor's presence, then his recorded voice. The goal was that I relax myself, in my office or a crowded airport lobby, with only the trained ability to shut out distractions and return myself to a state in which I could again convince my mind to discontinue its alarm and grief at a past physical assault it could no longer warn against or repair.

Most serious workmen learn in time how gladly the unconscious faculties will accept respectful curbing and guidance and give us the work we need. I'd practiced such useful routines for years, but another aspect of the hypnotic experience proved even more rewarding. In that first hour of assurance, Logue had told me that the possible ill effect of hypnosis was its potential for uncovering repressed traumatic memories—a scene of childhood abuse or an early witness of violence. He'd gone on quickly to say however that since we wouldn't attempt memory regression, the chance of such a shock was most unlikely.

Still he'd aroused my curiosity; and at the end of our sessions, I asked about the possibility of a memory search at a later time. I told him that recently I'd grown curious about the first two years of my life, a time from which I've kept only a few quick visual memories. It was also a time when my parents and I often lived in the crowded quarters of single rooms and when our poverty was further harrowed by the waning days of my father's alcoholism and my mother's fears. I'd begun recently to wonder if I might have witnessed some awful act between them.

Logue reminded me that children often witness sexual exchanges between their parents and store those memories as loud and hurtful. He also told me a startling thing I should long since have deduced. When we recover a buried early memory, it returns in the form in which it was stored, without later adult revision or taming. A two-year-old's experience of a family quarrel is likely to be stored as a far darker threat than his parents intended. So a hunt for buried memory is more than dangerous; it can be shattering.

When I told Logue that my interest continued, he proposed an immediate trial. In a lighted room and without inducing hypnosis, he simply said "Where did you live when you were three years old?"

"In Asheboro, North Carolina—Graystone Terrace Apartments on South Elm Street."

He said "Where was the main entrance?"

"A white door in the center of the two-story red-brick building."

"Good. Now open the front door, and tell me what you see."

I said "A hall running straight through the ground floor, mail boxes on the right. Two-tone gray walls, darker below and lighter above." By then I'd begun to surprise myself with the hard detail of apparent memories I'd never known I had.

"Where are the stairs?"

"Halfway back on the left, black rubber treads on the steps."

He said "Good. Where's your apartment?"

"Upstairs. You climb the steps and our apartment is straight ahead of the landing, on the right-front corner of the building."

"Good. Enter your own door now, and what do you see?"

And so on through the furniture and floorplan of our small quarters— the gold-painted radiators, pictures on the walls, the position and color (chartreuse) of a laundry basket in the bathroom.

Each of Logue's questions tripped immediate precise answers till finally he said "Now what don't we know?"

"Whether anything I've seen is correct."

He said "Exactly, though my guess is—considering your confidence— that some part of what you've seen is accurate memory."

As we'd planned, our sessions ended that day, though the pain-calming benefits of hypnosis continue to grow. With obvious relief my mind accepted the message we sent it. Imperceptibly but with no hard resistance, it discontinued more than a few of the phantom alarms on its ruptured circuits. Only at times of tension or fatigue does it now crank up the old firebells. Given the tumble of apparent memory during that trial run though, I postponed maybe forever a full-dress exploration of earlier memories that may be unusably clear, harsh and unconfirmable. But the bite of that wide-awake excursion on the look of an apartment building, which I left at the age of four, only deepened.

In the next few weeks, as I worked alone at the pain and as it receded, a trickle of good memory began to replace it. Numerous early scenes and speeches seemed literally to crowd the time and space vacated by pain. And the memories didn't—it's important to say—come in self-hypnotic states. I was more than respectful now of buried scenes; and in my daily home sessions, I continued to concentrate on relaxation and the distancing of pain. But the memories would crowd in at all other times. Maybe the same inner voice that was taming the pain was bringing me memories in recompense. I think I was now in intimate touch with my deep resting mind, and it chose to serve me in more ways than one.

At first the memories came from far back, early childhood; then from nearer, youth and young manhood. The returning scenes were filled with the faces of people who'd borne my weight on crucial stretches of the road from helpless infancy. I was glad to get them and made no effort to stem the flow. And late in the summer, as I began to feel the gathered force of so much past, I turned to write a story I'd planned but had never begun.

A friend had asked me to contribute a novella to a British-American series he was editing. Such unexpected requests have often triggered interesting work. So I thought the invitation might be a chance to look back at a distant experience I'd enjoyed but had never touched in my fiction. I'd write a story that fed on the summer I spent in 1953, as a cabin counselor in a boys' camp in the mountains of North Carolina. If the memories proved fertile, I might secrete a story that fell within the hundred-page maximum my friend had set.

I began with little more than a place, two central figures and a squad of subordinates. The action and the characters luckily invented themselves as new things, bearing little or no resemblance to the events of my uncomplicated summer at the camp (none of my campers had a complaint worse than constipation or chigger bites). But the atmosphere, pleasures and worries of those ten weeks returned in an unexpected rush. I wrote the first draft in two weeks, with time out for a trip. And when I was done revising, I had a novel, not a novella.

As in the talk to the Friends of the Library, once I tapped on my memory, it rolled open a long file-drawer whose existence I thought I'd forgot—the weather, the plants and beasts of a place and time, the local songs and jokes, the dining customs (even the way we raffled extra desserts), the laughable but finally moving solemnity of a unique and near-vanished American institution and my own twenty-year-old self as receiver, censor, curator of it all. I even reached the point where I could lie at home in the dark of 1987 and be my young self in a canvas upper-bunk thirty-four years ago, with my pre-adolescent charges breathing loudly in deep sleep below me, all trusting my protection while on every side a charged wilderness pressed toward us loudly with a staggering beauty, pure air, rattlesnakes and panthers.

That much lost time had reassembled itself so nimbly and into such interesting new shapes that, when I finished the last revision, my mind fell through a sudden hole in its floor. I experienced a post-partum sadness of an intensity that let me gauge the heights of pleasure I'd walked in those four weeks of rampant memory. The polar differences of joyful work and desolate completion were as dramatic as if, one moment I'd been a strong young man striding through his first tested maturity and the next, a gray-haired man unable to walk. Luckily the fall lasted only a few days. And like much pain, when it vanished it left no visible scar.

But the pleasure of such work in the mines of the past lingered powerfully and called for renewal. After three weeks I began an even more direct expedition on the deeper veins. I'd set down a series of childhood memories. They'd somehow portray that swarm of faces I was triggering still. I made a short list of the indispensable adult names. Then I took a few days to write myself a long informal letter, asking preliminary technical questions and sketching the possible answers. Soon I'd reduced my concerns to a working principle. Since the visible events of my childhood are no more interesting than most, I wouldn't attempt a straight-through narrative from birth. And in any case I'd look at others more than at me.

I'd see my early life, not as a road or a knotted cord but as a kind of archipelago—a ring of islands connected, intricately but invisibly, under-water. And I'd study each of the islands in separate chapters that examined one or more of the few adults who proved crucial to my early tries at trust-ing myself and others. I took a beginner's confidence in the certainty that each of my instructors was varied and interesting enough to watch.

I'd look at each of those vital relations without significant omission or disguise. And whenever natural or possible, I'd stop at the point where I moved beyond easy reach of those teachers (I've never outstripped their shadows). That point was reached at their deaths or on the late summer day when I left home to go the twenty-odd miles that constituted a world away—college and its exotic life. That day I entered a huge new contest for which I'd brought no usable shields, a serious game that promised to ask for strengths I hoped I had or could get. It was also a place in which—from the first week—I began to meet, merge solitudes with and love those friends I've mentioned.

As the chapters drew one another onward, the principles held. Five times I altered an important name rather than risk the uneasiness of a survivor with whom I've lost touch. But a common sadness of those my age—that most of my childhood intimates are dead—made the hewing to fact easier than I expected. Since my life began with them, I began with my parents. They brought me at once to my mother's sister Ida, the weightiest anchor of my childhood. Ida's life and home brought on the chief of many important black men and women. One black man's solitude suggested my bachelor cousin Macon Thornton, who—unaware—set me an example far more bankable than the money he also provided. Then on to the villains and fears of the vulnerable time before puberty, then the abstract forces and those who led me toward them, and last to my father in his final days.

The longest chapters look at my relations with two of the less per-sonal realities, the arts in which I've worked from the age of three and the unseen creator of all that I know or guess at and doubtless more. Though numerous adults and a few contemporaries were involved in each case, my relations with those two things soon became exchanges whose power exceeded the force of single persons or groups; so I've taken the chance to focus more nearly on myself toward the end.

I've said that everywhere, my first concern was to portray the facts and any resulting truth, as clearly as I can see them. In no case have I consciously invented memories when I had none. On the contrary, some readers may regret the number of times I define the richness or absence of my recall. But loyalty to the surviving memories, or the transformations that my memory worked, was paramount.

At times I quote direct speeches, even conversations. I'm confident that many of the short speeches are given verbatim. They were repeated at family meetings till their rightful order was stamped on our minds. That's, after all, half the purpose of oral history in any culture, the perfect transmission of a few right words through time's malicious will to ambush the whole of our past and blank it. In the case of imagined speeches and exchanges, I've worked toward the most vitalizing form of resurrection. I try to keep faith with those special rhythms and gestures that summon the hungry dead once more to their own vivid lives—if for no more time than the length of a patented phrase or verb, the hobbled strut of a joke or plea.

More than once I claim memories that go further back than most of my friends can credit. In the years I taught Freshman Composition, I regularly asked my students to excavate their earliest memory, if only the color of light on a crib rail, and then to convey it without embroidery in prose. Almost invariably they evoked a quick image or a lingering sound from late in their third year or early in the fourth. The only student who shared a recall as early as my own was in the first class I ever taught—September 1958, a sixteen-year-old woman who became the novelist Anne Tyler.

I even claim persistent images from what seems uterine memory. I've met no one else with similar recall of that dim light, muffled sound and trusty harbor, though I'm told by an eminent psychiatrist that such images are not unheard of in the analyst's office. And I've heard physicians say that there's no known physiological block to such recall. Again I'm convinced of the validity of every memory I claim. Whatever a sound-and-sight documentary would show of my past, each picture I claim here has hung in my head for long years now—my buried archive: true or false, for good or bad.

I'm also aware of, and a little guilty about, the occasional tone of upward-and-onward struggle toward the light—little Reynolds, born at last. But aren't most men and women irresistibly the heroes of their memoirs, even of their daily tales and complaints? Much of my early industry and peace is the passive result of being an only child till a brother joined me when I was eight. He soon became a winning and complementary partner in household transactions. But before his appearance I lived with two mainly tranquil but fragile adults. Like so many children I knew that their continued calm hinged scarily on my own careful virtue, my dependability as a weight-bearing pillar of the household. And again like most children, I bore the load unquestioningly. So my chances for early mischief were reduced. I take some refuge in the hope that, if my memories often illuminate young Price with a rosy traveling spotlight, at least his story may be more watchable than the familiar ground-licking of avid self-haters. I've tried to acknowledge my plentiful early failures and absurdities.

But an unavoidable fact about most middle-class American childhoods of my time—1933 to 1954, when I turned twenty-one—is their innocence. Our likeliest crime was a misdemeanor on the order of soaping car windows on Halloween or minor pilfering. In my first attempt at Halloween mayhem, we stopped all traffic on our street with a rag-hung rope, raised across both lanes as any car reached us. We managed a number of screaming, near-coronary stops before the police lights hove into view. Then all of us fled in craven terror, and I remember huddling with Cleo Spencer in a nest of garbage cans till the cops were gone. My only try at theft came when I lost the inflating needle for my football and tried to pocket one from the dime store. I went to the aisle where the new balls were kept, with their tempting needles tucked in the lacing. But my hand refused to make the reach.

I'm aware of matters here that may baffle well-meaning readers. I'll mention only two. Several times in my thirties and forties, I was accused by friends of being too analytical, too ready to hold acts and emotions in tongs at a safe distance for study. For years I denied the charge—it was always a charge—and I'd reply that there are no safe distances. As I've worked at these memories though, I begin to scent the trait. But obtrusive as my pebble-by-pebble archeologist's hunt for groundwork may be, it's unavoidably a trait of all students of time and behavior—

psychologists, psychiatrists, priests, confessors, writers and other narrative artists. Such introspection is the greater part of the motive force of memory.

I hope the trait seems less chilly here than it sometimes seemed in more intimate rooms. Still a patient reader may encounter moments when he feels I've found a pattern that's too neat or self-serving. In reply I could only grant that I may have over-read the evidence. But isn't that also a human need—the endless dig for meaning, justification and forgiveness? Another week or year I might find different explanations and designs; these are the ones I found as I wrote them. If I don't insist upon their eternal validity as history, I do offer them as faithful to present memory and, for me now, as emotionally logical.

I've said that one of the patterns I watch longest here is the ceaseless and unknowably intricate figure woven at the heart of my life, and the world's, by what I've called the *unseen power*. I use that potentially spooky term as an occasional substitute for *God* because I'm maybe too aware that some of my friends find my belief foolish or at best a forgivable anachronism, much like my insistence on writing comprehensible English when many of my younger academic comrades are bent on full-time careers as jargon-huffing murk machines. By using synonymous but fresher terms for tarnished counters like *God* or *faith*, I'm attempting to suggest, not the gassiness of New Age speculation or TV evangelism but the naked force of realities long-studied in our civilization and always acknowledged by our grandest minds. They are realities that thrust themselves early and unsought through the ceilings and unroofed spaces of my life and that I've mostly trusted.

La Rochefoucauld said that most people would never have fallen in love if they hadn't known such a thing existed. I'll risk a similar thought about some of my young friends, even my kin—they'd fall for God if they knew he existed. Most of my younger acquaintances are not so much antagonistic to a thoughtful faith as they are uninformed about any but the televised brands of Christian guilt, hypocrisy, concealment and the hate that fuels them all.

Yet most of my annual raft of students for a course in the poetry of Milton arrive with a spiritual dryness that quickly ignites in the presence of the hugest God-haunted and -questing mind in Western letters. To me a mature indifference to one of the oldest concerns of the human race—one that actively concerns a continuing majority of Americans—is as baffling as knowing that sex exists but seeing no reason to glance its way, much less have a go.

I say here later that the gravest sin, after cruelty, in either of my parental families was self-absorption and its inevitable boredom. I've tried to honor the family morals and have worked to be honest, entertaining and useful in whatever time a reader gives me. Yet whoever the performer and wherever the stage, some member of the audience can be counted on to yawn and nod. Even in the blaze of light at York Minster, at a Billie Holiday club-set or watching and hearing a Leontyne Price build Paradise on the empty air with nothing but a voice and a face like the prow of an archangel oaring our way through dawn, there's at least one snorer to chasten pride. I don't quite claim such stainless credentials, but I still imagine my row of yawners. *Sleep well. I hope you* borrowed *this book.*

I hope other readers feel paid for their time by an honest try at charting the lines of food and care, lure and defiance, that brought one creature through the mines of childhood, out of the house and into the world. I'd like to guarantee, here at the start, a whole new thing unfolding throughout, a usable guide. I was almost done with the job however, a job that felt so new in my hands, when I saw I was trying one more time to make the thing I've tried since childhood—at least a room of tall clear pictures that look like the world and are mainly worth watching.

Will Price and Elizabeth Rodwell near Macon, North Carolina. Since he's dressed for church and is free in afternoon light and since she displays the onyx ring on her right hand but hides her left, I estimate that the time is a Sunday afternoon in the early winter of 1926—no wedding ring yet. They will marry in January 1927; six years later, they will be my parents. As a child I was puzzled by the apparent absence of my father's left leg and by his and mother's strangely merged shadow; but from early on, it was my choice image of the love that made me.

1

THREE USEFUL LESSONS

WILL AND ELIZABETH PRICE

I'M LYING IN DRY SUN, alone and happy. Under me is a white blanket. I'm fascinated by the pure blue sky, but Topsy the goat is chained to my right—out of reach they think. The sound of her grazing comes steadily closer. I've sat on her back, she pulls my cart, I'm not afraid. Suddenly though she is here above me, a stiff rank smell. She licks my forehead in rough strokes of a short pink tongue. Then she begins to pull hard at what I'm wearing. I don't understand that she's eating my diaper. I push at her strong head and laugh for the first time yet in my life. I'm free to laugh since my parents are nearby, talking on the porch. They'll be here shortly, no need to cry out. I'm four or five months old and still happy, sunbathing my body that was sick all winter.

That scene is my earliest sure memory; and it poses all the first questions—how does a newborn child learn the three indispensable human skills he is born without? How does he learn to live, love, and die? How do we learn to depend emotionally and spiritually on others and to trust them with our lives? How do we learn the few but vital ways to honor other creatures and delight in their presence? And how do we learn to bear, use and transmit that knowledge through the span of a life and then to relinquish it?

I've said that all but one of my student writers have located their earliest memory in the third or fourth year. My own first memory appears to be a rare one. The incident was often laughed about in my presence at later gatherings—the day poor Topsy went for Reynolds's diaper, got a good whiff and bolted. So I might have built a false memory from other people's narratives. But I'm still convinced that the scene I've described is a fragment of actual recall, stored at the moment of action. If it wasn't I'd have embellished the scene further—adding clouds to the sky, a smell to the grass, the pitch of my parents' voices. What I've written is what I have, an unadorned fragment that feels hard and genuine. And the only trace of emotion is my lack of fear, my pleasure, both of which produced my first awareness of dependency—the goat won't eat me; help is near.

From the presence of Topsy, I know I'm in Macon, North Carolina. She was born, the same day as I, on my Uncle Marvin Drake's farm up near the Roanoke River. My father has had a small red goat-cart built, big enough for me and one child-passenger; and Topsy is already strong enough to pull us. Since we left Macon before I was a year old, then the memory comes from my first summer in 1933. That February 1st, I'd been born in the far west bedroom of my mother's family home in Macon.

Macon was then a village of under two hundred people, black and white. Because it was an active station on the Seaboard Railroad's Raleigh-to-Norfolk line, it had grown north and south from the depot in the shape of a Jerusalem cross—a north-south dirt street, an east-west paved road parallel to the train tracks and a few dirt streets parallel still to both axes.

There was a minuscule but thriving business district—three grocery and dry-goods stores, a gas station and a post office. There were two brick white churches, Methodist and Baptist, and two frame black churches, one on the west edge and one in the country. There were fewer than forty white households, mostly roomy but unpretentious frame houses, no pillared mansions. A few smaller black houses were set in the midst of town with no hint of threat or resentment; but most black families lived on the fringes of town—some in solid small houses, some in surprisingly immortal-seeming hovels. And on all sides, the sandy fields of tobacco and cotton lay flat and compliant, backed by deep woods of pine and cedar and big-waisted hardwoods.

Almost every white family employed one or more black women, men and children as farm hands, house servants, yardmen, gardeners and drivers. With all the deep numb evil of the system (numb for whites)— slavery and servitude did at least as much enduring damage to whites as to blacks—those domestic relations were astonishingly good-natured and trusting, so decorous that neither side began to explore or understand the other's hidden needs. When they'd granted one another the hunger for food, shelter and affection, their explorations apparently ceased; and the ancient but working standoff continued.

Yet a major strand of the harmony of all their lives consisted of the easy flow of dialogue expressive of mutual dependency, jointly sparked fun and the frequent occasions of mutual exasperation. There were even glints of rage from each side; but in our family homes at least, there was never a word about the tragic tie that bound the two peoples. And if a cook or yardman mysteriously failed to appear on Monday morning, even the kindest white employer was sure to foment angrily on the blatant no-count ingratitude—no trace of acknowledgement that a bone-deep hostile reluctance might be fuming.

Since the family trees of strangers are high on anyone's boredom scale, I'll limit the following to what seems bare necessity if I'm to track these mysteries. My mother Elizabeth Martin Rodwell was born in 1905 and reared in Macon in the oak-shaded rambling white seven-room house built by her father in the mid-1880s. He was John Egerton Rodwell, station master of the Macon depot. He'd grown up in a big nest of brothers on a farm, some four miles north, between Macon and Churchill. His mother Alice Egerton, whether she knew it or not, could have claimed descent from the English family that commissioned John Milton to write his masque *Comus* in 1634 to celebrate the elevation of John Egerton, Earl of Bridgewater, to the Lord Presidency of Wales (the leading player in *Comus* was his daughter Alice Egerton, age fifteen). While the memory of such a standing was retained by a few of the deep-country farmers my Egertons had become, after two centuries in slaveholding Virginia and North Carolina, they seldom bragged on their blood.

My mother Elizabeth's mother was Elizabeth White—called Lizzie, even on her gravestone—from the oldest continuously settled part of the state, Perquimans County in the northeast corner, eighty miles east of Macon. Lizzie's mother had died in Lizzie's infancy, and she had been reared by her storekeeper father and an agreeable stepmother. On a visit to friends in Macon, she met blackhaired, brown-eyed funny Jack Rodwell; and she married him soon after. She was all of sixteen, mirthful and pleasantly buxom (a later problem), not pretty but widely loved for her good talk, her endless self-teasing and much ready laughter.

She was fated to bear eight children in twenty years, seven of whom survived her. One boy died in his first year; the other three left home early, in the common Dickensian fashion. They packed their small belongings, kissed their parents (all my kin flung themselves on kisses with the recklessness of Russian premiers), flagged the train and headed up the line for railroad jobs in Norfolk, already a teeming port of the U.S. Navy. Of the four daughters, my mother Elizabeth was the youngest. Lizzie used to claim that Elizabeth was conceived because, well after Lizzie thought she was done, the Seaboard added a four a.m. express. Its window-rattling plunge through the heart of Macon would wake Jack nightly and leave him with nothing better to do in the dark than turn to his mate.

My father William Solomon Price was born in 1900 in Warrenton, the small county-seat five miles from Macon. Before the Civil War, the town was a social and political center of the state (a local statesman Nathaniel Macon was Speaker of the House of Representatives in the presidency of Thomas Jefferson). As such it was the home of wealthy slaveholding planters, many of whose elegant houses have lately been refurbished, though Warrenton now shares the sad lot of all bypassed farm towns—its children leave.

Will's father—Edward Price, a famed dry wit—was a son of the town carriage-maker, of Welsh and Scottish stock; Edward's mother was a Reynolds from Perth, Scotland. Barely out of boyhood and balked by Reconstruction poverty from his hope to study medicine, Edward avoided the family business and clerked for the remainder of his life in the county's Registry of Deeds. Will's mother was Lula McCraw, also of Warrenton and the descendant of Scottish, English and French Huguenot immigrants. One of her third-great-grandfathers was James Agee, a Huguenot whom we share with our Tennessee cousin, the writer James Agee. Lula Price was small, with a bright voracious mind, watchful as a sparrow and capable of winging a startlingly ribald comment from behind her lace and cameo with such swift wit as to leave the beauty of her face unmarred. Her short narrow body bore six strong children, all of whom survived her; yet she found the energy to run a ten-room house generously, almost lavishly, on her husband's modest income with a strength of mind and hand that, again, her white-petal beauty belied.

My parents met six years before their marriage. The meeting was in 1921 when Will was twenty-one and Elizabeth sixteen. They'd each gone to a dance at Fleming's Mill Pond, with other dates—Will with Sally Davis, Elizabeth with Alfred Ellington. Elizabeth's date introduced her to Will; and despite Sally Davis's beauty and wit, an alternate circuit at once lit up. First, both Will and Elizabeth looked fine and knew it, within reason. Second, they were both storage batteries of emotional hunger and high-voltage eros. And third, their short pasts—which felt like eons—had left each one of them craving the other's specific brand of nourishment.

Will had graduated from high school four years earlier and had since held easy jobs, none of which required him to go more than a few hundred yards from his family home, while continuing to sleep and board with his parents. His two elder brothers had gone as far as was imaginable then, to Tennessee; but all three of his witty and unassuaged sisters were still in place—the eldest having left her husband and returned unannounced at the age of twenty with a young son to live for good in the shadow of her father, whom she loved above all and whose deathbed pillows were found in her cedar chest at her own death, more than fifty years later. Both Will's parents were in hale, testy, often hilarious control; so the house contained eight Prices in five bedrooms, plus at least one cook and a handyman.

I can hardly think how a healthy young man, between the ages of seventeen and twenty-seven, can have stood to inhabit such a crowd of watchers and feeders—and stood them, day and night, for ten years after finishing high school—but stand them he did. As the youngest son, Will was his mother's "eyeballs." And later evidence suggests that she uncon-

Will Price in 1918. He's eighteen and wears a National Guard button. He thinks he will soon be shipped away to the trenches of France and cannot know that the armistice of November 11th will save him. Unclouded yet by drink or care, his gray eyes burn with the hopeful fervor he'll fight to reclaim, fifteen years from now.

sciously mastered his growing dependence on alcohol to keep him close to an all-forgiving bosom (Elizabeth told me, late in her life, that "Will's mother would ride with him to the bootlegger when no one else would go").

For whatever reasons, Will's extrication from the grip of such a rewarding and demanding mother—and from his fondness for Sally Davis—took him six long years of fervent courting. And once he and Elizabeth had steeled themselves, they married as far from Warren County as they could go and still be sheltered by kin. Elizabeth's next-oldest, and favorite, brother Boots gave her away in Portsmouth, Virginia; and in Warrenton, Will's sisters rose at dawn to set all the clocks in the Price house an hour ahead. Then at "noon"—as the distant vows seemed imminent and their mother announced her imminent heart-spell—they could say "Just calm yourself, Muddy; it's too late now. Will and Elizabeth are a whole hour married and on the *train*." And so they were—the Orange Blossom Special, in a "drawing room" suite (courtesy of Elizabeth's Seaboard brothers) and bound for Florida, one of the gorgeous ends of the Earth in those grand days.

Elizabeth's parents had died young. When my mother was eleven, Lizzie's kidneys failed; and Elizabeth was led to her mother's deathbed—surrounded by galvanized tubs of ice to cool the fierce heat—for a final goodbye. Three years later, sitting on her own porch, Elizabeth looked up the dirt road to see a mail cart from the depot roll toward her. It bore her last anchor—Jack Rodwell her father, dead of his second stroke at fifty-eight.

From the age of eleven, Elizabeth and her sister Alice, called Britsy and five years older, were mothered by their kind sister Ida. Ida was eighteen years older than Elizabeth; and with her came her then-volatile husband Marvin Drake and their three boys. Though they were Elizabeth's near-contemporary nephews, they quickly became her surrogate brothers, foster sons and chief playmates.

The Drakes had moved in at Lizzie's death to keep house for Jack and the girls; and once Jack died, they stayed for good. Ever after, Elizabeth's feelings about the years of at-home orphanhood were understandably mixed. She was grateful for the chance to remain in her birthplace with

mostly well-intentioned kinfolk. But on rare occasions in my own childhood, I'd see her ambushed by sudden resentment. In those short forays,
she'd glimpse the worst—she'd been dispossessed in her rightful place by
an interloper with a cold eye for gain, a brother-in-law (who would ultimately purchase the Rodwell children's shares in the home and will it
and all its Rodwell contents to his Drake heirs). In a few days though,
I'd hear her say "Let's drive up home and see Ida and Marvin." In her
best mind, my mother knew they'd kept her alive.

Will and Elizabeth were reared then in classic, though healthily honest, family situations where blood-love, or at least loyalty, was the bind-
ing principle of a majority of the by-no-means happy populace. As an
inevitable and paradoxical result, my young parents were primed for another love, private but transcendent, that would lead them out of the
blighting shadows of their homes into the glare of their own graceful
bodies in one another's hands, worked as they were by aching need.

The repeatable public stories of their courtship were among my own
favorites from their long repertoire. There was the night when, returning
from a performance of *The Merry Widow* in Henderson, Will left his
Model A Ford for a moment to buy cigarettes; and Elizabeth, still too
well-mannered to mention a body-need, was forced to lift the floorboard
and pee quickly on the hot gear box. It reeked mysteriously through the
rest of Will's evening. Or the time the same car got bogged in quick-
sand and almost sank them. Or the hard days of Will's terror when Elizabeth suffered a ruptured appendix, twenty years before the discovery of
antibiotics, and was rushed in agony from Macon to Norfolk on a
stretcher in the baggage car of a train—the only place she could ride
flat—for six weeks of desperate but successful remedies. Or Elizabeth's
happiest memory of her strongly ambivalent mother-in-law—the time
they were driving alone together, struck a turkey, killed it neatly and
brought it home to eat. Or the lovers' own mutual fits of jealousy and
their laughing reconciliations, alone in the woods by the sandy creek in
Macon or at big late dances in the open pavilion at Fleming's Mill Pond
or a place in the woods called Largo.

Well before I was in school, I came to realize that they'd been together twelve years before my birth—six years of courtship and six of mar-

Elizabeth Rodwell in 1926, before her marriage; she's twenty-one. The original is hand-tinted and was probably made in Norfolk, Virginia, where she often visited her favorite brother Boots, a doting bachelor. Her eyes will never lose this unabashed warmth. And she'll keep her hair short the rest of her life, going always to men's barber shops, never a beauty parlor; but she'll soon retire the vampish curl.

riage. And with that realization came a kernel of bitterness that I'd missed so much of them, that they'd had so much without me. Knowing nothing of the mechanics of reproduction, I lamented my absence from so much fun and from all the magical snapshots in their albums. Why hadn't they wanted to bring me in sooner?

The kind of merciless consolation available only to children and mad-men came in my realizing simultaneously that those twelve years broke into two pieces, good and bad. The courtship was happy, though subject to the clouds I've mentioned (Sally Davis took a long time resigning her hold on Will, and Elizabeth ran an unpredictable sideline in other beaux). But the six years of marriage before my birth were all but tragic. Will's boyish taste for bootleg liquor—the fuel of so much of his early fun—became a nightmarish and paralyzing thirst.

The drunkenness, and all the missed work-days, led to aimless dan-gerous roving with his bachelor best-friend and fellow-soak, whom I'll call Alec, while Elizabeth waited—sober and wretched in whatever room they'd rented that month. And all round, the troubles of an always-poor state grew as the Great Depression plummeted. Even Will's sisters, two of whom by then had suffered disastrous marriages, told Elizabeth that they couldn't fault her if she left for the sake of her own self-respect and sanity. She later admitted that, in their courtship, she drank her own share of bathtub gin, especially at Boots's nonstop party in Norfolk. But now, avid as she was for her own chance at life but devoted to Will in his pitiful baffling thirst, she was sober in earnest. And she stayed. Long after his death, she said to me "The thing was, he always came back late to me, so sick and helpless, saying I was all he had. I wanted to doubt him, but I knew it was true."

With all their other troubles, living near their families in a fruitful farming county, they never went cold or hungry, though I've heard Mother say "With one dollar bill you could pack the car with groceries; the only trick was finding that dollar." More than once she was forced to down her pride, approach her solvent brother-in-law, who owned the local feed-and-seed store; beg for a dollar and endure his asking "Why in the world?—to buy Will's liquor?"

Will's constant worry, beyond a drunkard's guilt, was jobs and in-come. Like his father and two older brothers, he'd never really thought of college; and he was skilled in nothing more saleable than wit, charm and a generous heart. As a boy and a youth, he'd sold newspapers, clerked in the freight office of the Warrenton Railroad's depot. He even rode as conductor on that lightly traveled, remarkably short line—less than five miles out to Warren Plains and back. The only job I recall his mentioning from those first married years was door-to-door life-insurance sales. At least it wasn't office work. With his own Ford, and without the cold-eyed scrutiny of a boss, Will could roam the backroads of Warren and Vance counties, canvassing hard-up farmers. I never heard tales of his drinking at work but he must have. For whatever reason, the jobs were short and unambitious; and he and Elizabeth moved restlessly from rented room to rented room, all within a fifteen-mile radius of their family homes.

Pictures of Will Price in youth show a strong upturned face with a radiance almost better than beauty, a heat centered in the gray eyes that burn with what seems fervor—where does it come from; what fuel does it take? A few years later, the courtship pictures still show him as a trim dapper man with splendidly live eyes, an upright carriage of his medium frame and with always the threat of a smile on his mouth. But I've found no pictures of him from those hard first six years of marriage; and surely that gap in the record can't be accidental (thirty years later when I got a home-movie camera, he was openly fascinated with his own walking likeness; and he often said he was going to buy a whole reel and get me to use it all on him, though sadly he never did).

It's only with my birth that he appears in the albums again, holding me with the winning edginess of a fledgling member of the bomb-disposal squad. But by then, in his early thirties, he's taken on weight. It looks like bloat and, worse, there's a blurring glaze on the once-hot eyes. Half-smiling still, thoughtful and protective as he is, by now there's a presence in his life even more demanding than his wife and first son.

I also have no pictures of Elizabeth from those six years. But her long absence from the record of an eagerly snapshooting family is also eloquent, though I recall only two occasions when she mentioned the slow pain. In 1961, seven years after Will's death, I was living in England and working on an autobiographical story called "Uncle Grant." It was about a black man who worked for us in those early years; and I wrote to ask Mother if Grant, in his devotion to Will, had ever drunk with him. She answered quickly; no, Grant "never took a drink with Will that I know of." And then, for the only time in all her relations with my writing, she hinted at a possible suppression—"I don't know, but maybe 'twould be better not to bring in the drinking days, they were so horrible" (that instinctive slide into the poetic *'twould* still sounds its desolation). When she reappears in my baby pictures, it's clear that she's fared much better than Will. In her late twenties now, she's lost her baby fat but is still a good-looking woman ("a well set-up girl, I can tell you," as Will might have said). Whatever pain those dark eyes have eaten has left no trace, not yet.

In the face of their own problems, and the economic world-maelstrom in which they were helpless floaters, it's hard to guess why in early May of 1932 they conceived a first child. Once I was grown, Will told me of the pains he took in those years to preserve a single washed condom in a box of powder for numerous uses, but he didn't connect the fact with my conception. I may have been an accident, and few of us want that; but it feels at least possible from here that Elizabeth, justifiably leery of childbearing, arranged to conceive as a last hope of braking Will's rush to drown. She'd tried every other way she knew. Maybe a child would get his attention where all else had failed; he had seemed to enjoy his nearest nephew and niece.

Physically, the pregnancy was uncomplicated. They were living in Henderson as the day approached, again in a rented room with a cranky widow who monopolized the bathroom. The intention was, though, that I should be born in Elizabeth's home in Macon. I've said that it was her birthplace and that of her brothers and sisters; it had also seen the deaths of one of her brothers and both her parents. No Rodwell or Price of their generations had yet been born or died elsewhere. Will's boyhood friend Dr. Pat Hunter supervised the pregnancy; and when Elizabeth felt contractions in the late afternoon of January 31st, she and Will lit out for Macon. (Earlier in the day Adolf Hitler had assumed dictatorial powers in Germany, but they wouldn't have known or cared.) Elizabeth's water broke before they arrived; but she walked from the car into the house, to find Ida and Marvin playing rummy with friends. There was no telephone; a cousin drove to Warrenton to fetch Pat Hunter; someone else went for Betty Lyons the black midwife. And soon after they arrived, labor set in.

In the living room Marvin, Will and the friends tried to wait it out. They scrambled eggs and played more cards by the hot woodstove, though Will was far too scared to concentrate. By midnight nothing had come from the bedroom but cries from Elizabeth. The friends left; Marvin tried to sleep. But Will lurked helpless at the edge of the hardest birth ever suffered on the place.

It was remembered as that, even by the other women present—black Betty Lyons with Ida and Cousin Joyce Russell, who administered ether on a clean cotton pad till she herself was nearly unconscious. By the time I began to listen, that night was one of the epic family tales, a ghastly double-death turned back as cold morning broke. In the far west room on a white iron bed six feet from a woodstove, Elizabeth worked for twelve hours.

I was breeched—turned backward, stalled defiant—in the womb; and since antibiotics were twelve years off and a caesarean was all but unthinkable, Pat Hunter struggled to turn me. No luck. Near day when Will peered in again, Pat looked up and said "I'm losing them both." It was all Will needed. More than once in later years, I watched him hear the story of his next act from others; but I never heard him tell it. Even for a narrator as driven and dazzling as he, it was far too weighty for public performance.

He fled the house in the freezing dawn, went out to the woodshed; and there he sealed a bargain with God, as stark and unbreakable as any blood pact in Genesis—if Elizabeth lived, and the child, he'd never drink again.

By the time he was back in the house, Pat had finally turned me, clamped forceps to my pliant skull, braced his feet on the rail of the bed and pulled me out by main force. My rubbery skull was dented, and one ear was torn; but once I'd wailed and been handed to a revived Joyce for bathing, Pat went to tell Will. Elizabeth was alive, exhausted but safe. And plainly I was there too, the first of their sons.

No one recalled, in my presence, what either Will or Elizabeth said to Pat or to one another, nor did anyone say when Will told her of his solemn deal. Likely the first words, after endearments, were my name—

Edward for Will's dead father, *Reynolds* for his Scottish grandmother. Will's elder brothers had so far produced three girls and a boy, none of whom bore their grandfather's name. My guess is that it meant much to Will to go to his mother with the news of a boy named Edward Price—again. There seems to have been no question of a name from the Rodwell side, though Elizabeth often told me "Will put his foot down— you couldn't be a junior." That was saved for another boy years later, when Will may have loathed his own name less.

He must have told Elizabeth his hopeful news soon because, obedient to medical wisdom at the time, she spent the next three weeks in bed (or near it) and would have needed cheering. For the remainder of his life, he teased her about the long rest—"I thought we'd have to hire a damned steam shovel to get you up. You were that scared of touching your foot to the floor." She had been badly torn and would need surgical repair years later.

God had kept his half of the bargain. The family myth had it that Will Price kept his half. The fact is, in time he did but not at once—and no wonder. In the upper South in the 1930s, the help available to a drunk who hoped to quit was no more unusual than prayer and no more imaginative than the standard injunction to buck up, be a man and do the manly thing. Professional help was limited to small private clinics for the discreet sobering up of drunks who could pay for weaning, "vitamin" shots and a dollop of scoutmasterly advice; but one and all, the clinics were notoriously unsuccessful in long-range help. It's now conceded that the majority of enduring recoveries in America are achieved through membership in Alcoholics Anonymous, but A.A. had not been organized in 1933. It was one year off and nearly twenty years before its groups appeared in the smalltown South.

So Will was all but on his own. His mother and sisters were slim help; the middle sister was involved in her own sad marriage to a charming drunk who would soon kill himself, leaving her and a young daughter to return to the Warrenton home. Both Will's brothers, by then in Tennessee, were also drinkers—as were all three of Elizabeth's and ultimately all her nephews. Whether or not Will's mother unconsciously fostered his thirst, there's no doubt that in his cups he often resorted to the tiny

The Rodwell house in Macon, built by my maternal grandparents, John and Lizzie Rodwell, in the mid-1880s—the birthplace of all their eight children, including the youngest, Elizabeth in 1905. The far left window opens on the bedroom where she bore me in 1933. Before and after, this porch heard thousands of hours of splendid talk.

glistening face of his mother, so ready to forgive and provide what an interloping wife was baffled to find.

The interloper though was the stronger prop, the wife he'd courted so hard for years. Elizabeth was no more a trained alcoholic counselor than anyone else in the South of those days; but she was passionately ready to help, to nurse him in his sickness and to wait in hope. Once she told me "The help was seldom more than waiting, then fixing him soft-boiled eggs with butter in a glass." Years later Will also acknowledged the spiritual guidance of Robert Brickhouse, his Baptist minister in Warrenton; and he had the bald enormous fact of a mortal deal with the God he never questioned. If Will Price couldn't keep his half of the bargain, then in his mind the unquestioned corollary was that God had every right to reclaim Elizabeth and Reynolds. And given the Old Testament tally of God's response to such defaults, the corollary surely stood cocked and ready to seize its double blood-due.

I stress that I never heard my father mention the deal and its terrors; he was no chattering fundamentalist but a silent wrestler in the scalding dark. In the first two years of my life, we continued to camp out—first in Henderson, fifteen miles southwest; then around Warren County with relatives and in rented rooms; so I spent many hours in the close company, not only of my housewife-mother but with Will. I remember frequent bearhugs and the scrape of a beard that could never quite be shaved; I can see flashes of my first Christmas; I have a glimpse of his delight when I took a first step on my first birthday. But I have no memory of seeing him high or loud or abusive.

Will and Elizabeth were long dead and I was in my forties before I learned from Lulie, the sister nearest Will in age, that Will concluded the deal more gradually than legend records. Admitted, at once he began to quit or *taper off*, as drunks still say. There were no more long nights of aimless driving through the county, no more work-days missed as he slept comatose at home or hid beside the loyal Elizabeth in self-hating self-pity. There was nonetheless still a fair amount of beer. According to Lulie, the real end did come suddenly but not till I was three.

Those first three years were dogged by illness—allergic rashes so severe that Mother pinned my arms to the sheets at night to prevent gouging, a winter-long bout of whooping cough and then a mysterious succession of frightening seizures. Without warning, my fever would soar; and in a matter of minutes, I'd rush into racking board-stiff convulsions. Only fast plunges in cold water and quickly administered enemas appeared to help. The doctors were helpless; maybe I was allergic to egg. (By age five however, I was eating egg with impunity. All my life I've been subject to sudden allergies that vanish as suddenly; but I now strongly suspect that in infancy I was showing first signs of the often congenital type of spinal tumor that would not fully manifest till I was fifty-one.)

Whatever the cause, everyone agreed that my seizures were dreadful to watch. Elizabeth would spring into purposeful action; Will would stand by, anguished and unmanned. At their height I appeared to be dead; when they passed I would sleep exhausted through whole days and nights. And all that I later knew of Will Price affirms that, early in the course of my afflictions, he'll have sighted the link between their threat and his continued cheating on a dead-earnest deal.

In 1935 he got the first good job of his life, as a salesman of electric appliances for Carolina Power and Light Company; and we moved forty miles to the small mill-town of Roxboro where finally we had a rented house to ourselves. An imperious surviving letter from Will's mother—clubbing him, in a potent tall script, for negligence and ordering him to see that she got "toe pads" before the week was out—suggests how short a hyphen fifty miles could be, even in slower days. But at least he wasn't in five-mile reach of that brand of vampire whim.

The year I was three, his oldest sister Mary Eleanor was visiting us. Late one afternoon she and Will walked up the slope behind our house to a neighborhood curb-market for a loaf of bread. While there, for whatever reason, Will chose to drink a bottle of beer. When they ambled down to the house twenty minutes later, I was in the grip of the hardest seizure yet. Elizabeth had failed to reach Dr. Gentry, so she'd called the black doctor, but he still hadn't come. And with all their efforts, I was borne further off—eyes rolled back white, skin purple, hands clenched so tight my palms were cut. Lulie said "Will knew you were dying, he knew he had caused it, and he quit then and there."

Such a mortal dare would have come at Will as no shock at all, no

Will and I in the summer of 1933. Though his struggle with drink has begun, Will's face is still bloated; and I've assumed the unknowing but apt solemnity that marks so many of my early pictures. The Model A Ford is used by Will in his unsuccessful effort to sell life insurance to poor farmers, made worse by the Depression.

ambush. He trusted, and his sons do, that even a life as low to the ground, as wasteful and destructive as his own, was of serious weight in the hand of God. In his own head then, he earnestly swore to redeem his pledge.

In half an hour both doctors were gone, I was cool and sleeping, and Elizabeth could finally start cooking supper. According to Lulie, it was my last seizure. In any case, Will Price lived another eighteen years and never again drank so much as a spoonful of alcohol. His quitting was as graceful as his jokes. He could watch kin and friends drink with no apparent temptation, and he always kept a pint of bourbon far back on the top pantry-shelf (and a four-ounce bottle in his suitcase)—for emergencies with the heart he believed to be weak, though it beat like a perpetual piston through the worst of his end at fifty-four. Even more importantly, I suspect, the stored bottle was also an emblem—the old demon, captive and harmless on a shelf.

I have no conscious memory of those dangerous times in my own beginning; but they too entered the family treasury, and some of my good memories are of listening to the tellings. As with so many of our perils, my seizures were soon recounted as comical—the farcical actions of Will, Elizabeth and others in the critical moments when I went stiff as an iron bar. There were tales of how they blundered into one another with tubs of cold water and assorted collapsible rubber goods to wrest young me, one more time live, from another death; of how many new dresses and shoes were ruined in the drastic baths and enemas (not to mention the tale of that afternoon when they'd gone to Richmond for Ida's operation and left me with Aunt Britsy, who couldn't swim a stroke. She took me wading at the country-club pool; but as she was shepherding me toward the bathhouse, I broke away laughing, clambered to the diving board and flung myself to the bottom of the deep end. To the end of her mind, Britsy loved the climax—"Your big old head just sank like a *rock*! I was dressed to the nines in a pink dress, with white brand-new summer pumps. I hollered for help and nobody came, so nothing to do but get to the bottom of twelve feet of chlorine and haul that head out the best I could. The simpleton lifeguard finally came; by then I'd learned to swim somehow, and we were both safe. The shoes were ruined").

What I prized from the tales of my near-brushes was better than any direct memory. I heard beneath their affectionate laughter a thing all children, and adults, hope to hear—I mattered mightily to them. And when they feared for my life, they gladly let themselves be fools in the hope to save me. What I also heard, unconsciously at first, was the secret mate to the message of love—I was not the only thing they loved. In saving me, they were saving the proudest license they owned: their own good names as load-bearing struts in family and town.

I began that early to sense how much they depended on me, as a thing outside them to tend and serve. I was both a serious toy and a temporary household god, stocked profusely as a pomegranate with all their seeds and absorbing their world with the parched senses of a desert monk. The degree to which I depended on them was hid from me. Maybe I was far more independent than they guessed; I hoarded secrets early. But full knowledge of my helplessness would have stove me in, like a baby plunged through ten thousand fathoms. Like most sane children I felt both free of all support and alone as a hawk in the winter sky. I needed that delusory space to grow in.

If I'd known so early for instance that I was, for my father, an actual hostage given to God—an Isaac to his Abraham—I might not have understood or borne the weight of the office. Luckily, that knowledge and my understanding of its clandestine but vital role in my growth, was not leaked to me till the age of five when, high himself, Elizabeth's oldest brother Skinny taunted Will to join him in just one little drink. When Will smiled and refused, Skinny broke the story in the room before me with a careless salting of fat-man laughter. I blamed him all the rest of his life.

But no, Will's bargain was sealed. And for all I know, I may yet be a piece in a larger game than I can see or begin to guess—some continuing test of Will Price's deal or of my own worth to be his son, the life for which he sacrificed a stronger prop than I may ever have proved to be.

Despite my brain's refusal to store painful early memories, or its burial of them, my first sustained recall does come from the two years we lived in Roxboro. I remember waking one morning before my parents. Since they were sleeping late and had told me not to wake them, it must have been a Sunday. I lay and watched sunlight press on the window shade. Something in the meeting of yellow sun and the shade's white cloth made me think of a hula skirt I'd seen in a movie. (I'd already seen a good many movies, in the afternoons with Elizabeth or with her and Will at night. The first I recall was *Ramona* with Loretta Young in 1936.) I was in a crib with tall iron bars, but I managed to reach the top of the bureau and find my scissors. Armed, I stood up, slid the wood rail from the bottom of the shade and sliced the cloth into my first version of a hula skirt. Then beside the window, on the cool tan plaster, I drew a huge head from the funny papers—a chinless Andy Gump. Then too proud of my work to wait any longer, I called to wake my parents for a viewing.

I can also see our black terrier, dead under the tree on a Christmas morning (the only explanation I ever heard was that Will dropped a laxative pill the night before and was unable to find it; but the dog succeeded, ate it, lay down to rest in the tree's cotton snow and died in the midst of my Santa Claus). I remember tumbling on a neighbor's freshly paved drive and coming up with a speck of black gravel visibly embedded in my elbow for life. And I see, with a clarity that's still jolting, my mother on a stretcher, bumped down the high rock steps of our house and into an ambulance (ambulances then were identical with hearses except in color, white not black). There's a big red stain on the covering sheet. She's in the throes of miscarrying her second child, a girl. She's hemorrhaging fast and is bound, at top speed, the thirty miles south on a two-lane road for Watts Hospital in Durham. There they'll save her, only moments to spare, with direct blood fed arm-to-arm from Sheriff Pinnell, coincidentally of Warren County—the only man on the hospital rolls with her rare type and in driving distance.

For a boy who was thought of as affectionate I have few specific memories of my parents' love. In my mind there are lingering atmospheres of childhood safety and pleasure, but they don't bring special incidents with them. I was born at a time when breast feeding was considered half-savage, certainly low-class and unsanitary. Elizabeth was always a tactile parent, not sticky with hugs and kisses but always there if touch was needed—as it was, many times a day. My infant mind stored up, as I said, a sense of the abiding halo of her tenderness but with no single narrative picture to prove it.

Even more strangely I have only dim memories of what, years later,

Topsy the goat, born the same day as I, hauls me and my cousin Marcia Drake through Macon in the winter of 1934. In my farmer overalls, I'm plainly un-amused to yield my padded seat to a guest.

Elizabeth would work at like an embedded splinter—my eagerness to join them in bed on the rare mornings when Will could linger. It never crossed my mind that I was intruding on an intimacy that long preceded me, that had caused me and might well wish to cause me a brother or sister. But after Will was dead, Elizabeth said out of the apparent blue one day "Once you managed to climb in between us, Will would never make you leave."

I heard no complaint in her voice, but why did she confess in such telling words and so long after? It was almost surely because, in her endlessly communicative family, no evidence of love or any of its woes was ever concealed. Whatever, the confession was hardly news. Like a normally watchful child, I could detect deceit on their faces at a quartermile. Will Price welcomed me beside him; and it was mainly him I joined, him I needed to tame and know. And early, I focused on his magic scar—the deep white dimple in the fat of his right hand where, in a childhood accident, he'd fired his father's revolver on himself.

The story that went with the scar was gripping. Will's father was at work, and Will hied two friends to follow him into his parents' bedroom. There the standard Southern household-pistol ticked like a bomb on the high mantleplace. On tiptoe Will managed to fetch it down and to sport it boldly at his much-impressed friends; then he heard his father's homecoming footsteps mount the porch. His short arms strained up to replace the pistol, and it fired through his hand. At the sound, everybody in the house ran toward him—sisters, parents, cook and dog. More scared than pained, he clapped his right hand over his heart and howled. His ever-fearful mother stopped in the doorway, saw his hand pressed on what was plainly a bleeding heart and fainted where she stood. It was months, of pus and drainage tubes, before he was safe—an undoubted hero to all his friends. But there in bed those lazy Sundays, as he told me the tale each time, he was grown and strong in my hands no doubt but somehow still a boy like me. Mother was with me all hours of the day; a safe resting father, a boy like me, was way too scarce a chance to lose.

Likewise I have no memories before age five of most other functions of our intimacy. Earlier there are none that involve food and family meals, though my parents were hearty eaters; and I gladly fell in line. There are no scenes from what must have been hundreds of hours of play

with Mother, Father, the cook and with other children or alone; no
pictures of favorite toys, except a garish and soon broken plaster elephant
and a yard-high Easter rabbit. No tears or raised voices, not to speak of
abuse; and before five, no trace of all our journeys back home.

Many times a year, with only brief stops at the Prices' in Warrenton,
we headed for Macon and the deep-breasted, laughing open-hearted and
manic-depressive Rodwell family and all its outriders. The Price family
by then consisted entirely of women—Will's three sisters (two of whose
marriages had ended in tragedy), his mother and his maiden aunt Sis
Belle. They were wittier, certainly smarter than most of the town and
county; and they were great readers, when the Rodwells of Elizabeth's
generation (though rich in horse-sense) read nothing but the newspaper
and *The Upper Room*, a Methodist daily-devotional booklet. But except
for occasional outbursts of regret—that his sons were more Rodwell than
Price—Will too homed toward the Macon house and Ida's bountiful
table. There he avoided his mother's demand, his sisters' envy and the
drunken ghost of his recent past.

Macon remained firmly *home* till we at last bought our own house in
Raleigh in 1947. Will said at the time that he intended to die there. He
almost did, just up St. Mary's Street at old Rex Hospital. But he was
buried from the house. And Elizabeth spent her last conscious moment
there, after a stroke, on the floor of the den—actual home.

Unlike some students of memory, I've never felt that narrative memory
is random. On the evidence of many years' storage, I'd say that my mind
keeps what it needs or ever hopes to use, plus acres of likable background
decor—radio commercials and dumb pop-songs of the late thirties and
forties and the names and exact wardrobes of a few grade-school classmates, never seen again. A friend or relative seldom comes up with a
surprising memory involving me; once reminded, I can usually call up
the file and add to their version.

So I'm all the luckier that the first sustained memory of my life—a
memory that covers more than a few minutes of the past—has kept long
stretches of a warm evening alone with my parents, probably late in the
spring of 1936. We'd finished supper and, to give the house a chance to
cool, we left all windows open and awarded ourselves that peaceful pleasure of roomy prewar America, "going to ride."

Elizabeth likely suggested it. More than most things, she craved the sight of people—people doing anything. She'd sit in the baking car in a parking place on Main Street, with me more fretful by the minute, and just hungrily watch people passing, ordinary homely citizens. There seemed to be more deaf-mutes visible in those days; and without knowing a word of sign language, Mother could watch their coded gestures with rapt dark eyes that barely blinked; and she laughed when the mutes laughed. Maybe she had a passion for witness deep in her that came to me in her blood and made me the writer she never thought of being but had many skills for.

Whoever the instigator, in that warm spring dusk we drove out aimlessly to the open country that lay no more than a quarter-hour south of our house—flat fields of wild grass that I see as almost gray, no later than early May then. Planted like dummies in the grass, real cows gazed at us as if we were some entirely new creature. We stopped at the creamery for Dixie cups of vanilla ice cream. Then we sat in the creaking car, in the graveled parking lot, and ate slowly from the quarter-pint cups of waxed cardboard with wood paddle-spoons that tasted as good as the cream (you could also rub them pleasantly on gums swollen with the buds of new teeth).

It was a time in America when you never thought of phoning your friends to ask if a visit was welcome; you just drove up. If it was inconvenient, they either said so or hatched a white lie, "We'd love to see you; but right this minute, we're headed to see Uncle Foy at the clinic—not expected to make it through the night, they say." You knew it wasn't strictly true (you used similar tactics), but you sent love to Foy and got out cheerfully.

So next we cruised past Margaret and Ray Jackson's—Ray worked with Will—but saw no one on the porch. We turned at the end of the street and tried again—a tap or two on the horn, nobody. They must be at Margaret's mother's, Mrs. Wilkerson's. No, we won't bother them there; let's mosey on back. So we wandered home, or at least to the last whole house we'd occupy for three more years, slowing only once to wave back heys to Doretha Bumpass, our young blue-black maid who waved and laughed in our blue exhaust.

Sometime in the ten-minute last leg of that ride—before we stopped in the drive by the white rock steps of our house on the hill on South Lamar

Street, there on the rough cloth of a back seat—I knew for the first and
final time that we were all married: Elizabeth, Will and Reynolds. We
were now in this car, in all the world and in all our lives from here out,
three people who'd trust each other for good; and that trust would last
on every side.

Why the revelation came at that moment in my life and theirs, I still
don't know. Ignorant of any syllable of news about my harrowing birth
and Will's ordeal, I watched this knowledge open inside me like a sudden strong flower. I knew that this thing here in the car with us was what
both Will and Elizabeth meant by a word they used several times a day
and begged to hear from me. I'd heard the word hundreds of times and
never thought to wonder at its meaning, *love*. In general, I thought I
could tell it was good. But best of all for one who was growing a little
bored with the powerlessness of childhood, I saw that it gave me a job.
From this night on I must do as much to love and help them as they
were daily doing for me.

Obviously I didn't have anything like the powers of logic or language
to lay the proposition out so clearly. But even a casual watcher of pri-
mate behavior knows how a nonverbal mind can steadily consume the
visible world and transform the data into unspoken decisions of great
complexity, wit and even benevolence for the creature's own safety and
pleasure and for those of his tribe. So my present mind has no trouble in
affirming that—on a particular night, silent on a back seat behind my
parents—I deduced a fact: Will and Elizabeth and Reynolds were one
thing and would stay so.

In the past I'd gone straight to one or both of them with all my inventions, but now I kept silent. Maybe I thought they'd always known
or had learned like me in the last two minutes. Maybe I thought it was
my secret, like whatever secret they kept from me when they took their
Sunday afternoon naps behind a shut door, an exclusion that I can't recall minding. Anyhow in the front seat, they were talking to themselves—
something they glimpsed on the ride, some joke.

Nothing we'd seen or said in the past hour would have proved interesting to anyone else in the world, only the quiet here and now of a lazy
town becalmed by spring and the oncoming dark; but I saw it as light
and heard it as grand, and it changed my life. Without their knowledge

it also changed theirs. Without ever saying so, they let a child help them. We had another five years to work our triad, till Will and Elizabeth gambled again and started another child, one that would live.

As soon as she knew she was pregnant, Mother told me briefly what to expect in the coming months. A new baby was growing inside her the way I had. Soon I'd have a playmate. Since we were living in the country with few other children near, the prospect excited me. But I also recall that it was during the pregnancy that I began to recover or invent persistent and powerful uterine memories. They were purely visual, no sound whatever. I was suspended in a straw-colored fluid, staring out at the feeble light which barely seeped through Mother's skin, if she stood in bright sun. I've never heard similar memories from anyone else; and I suspect their reliability for several reasons, mainly because they feel more than a little like the self-reward of a child about to be joined by an unknown equal—*someone else is in there now, but I was there first, and I remember how it was.* Still the images have stayed strong with me for more than forty years. This instant I can see the slow rose light at it sifts through Mother's flesh, blood and water; I can enact a stillness so dense it seems like unearthly music and a safety so total that again I know why I turned my butt to the outer world and very nearly refused to be born.

The coming months were uncomplicated, and Mother's labor was reportedly clamorous but much less difficult than with me or the dead girl. A friend named Kitty Headen and one of my adult cousins had stayed at home with me through the Sunday-afternoon wait; and though I don't remember worrying, I did phone the delivery room more than once and ask the nurse for progress reports. And after dark the cousin took me in to Mother's room where she and Will and I beamed at my thoroughly substantial ten-pound, ten-ounce brother, young William Solomon Junior—Bill.

In a week they were home where I could check the continued strength of Mother's loyalty and, satisfied, watch and touch my brother. Despite the odd uncertain or desolate moment, I yielded quickly to the realization that, if the triad had grown, then in compensation my loneliness had ended. One of my epic uncertainties entered the family treasury at once—the day Reynolds dislocated Bill's shoulders. Bill was lying on the floor, we were playing, I extended my forefingers, he held on with grinning trust, I kept lifting till Bill was upright—all his weight on infant arms—and both of his shoulders suddenly dislocated: screams, a rush to the clinic and everyone's laughing assumption that I'd intended jealous harm. I doubt my knowledge of baby anatomy extended so far. I can recall once biting his fingers as he gave me a generous bite of his toast. Despite such moments, I can taste even now the fresh delight of learning the boy's open face, his early laughter, prevailing geniality and the immediate presence of a watchful mind, ready to learn every trick we could teach and to thank us steadily with stunts of his own.

Yet with all his eagerness to grow and join us, his first year was as hard as mine—a severe strep-throat infection, still before antibiotics, that nearly finished him; then at age two, an emergency tonsillectomy. I was ten when I saw him wheeled back from surgery, unconscious and blue with a scary long tongue stretched out on his cheek. I thought he was dead, and any lurking trace of rivalry dissolved on the spot. The coming years would see us in rare territorial skirmishes, but at least from the time of that hospital sight—fresh from surgery and all but dead—I silently opened the triad and worked him in.

The resulting rectangular family, as strongly as it was braced, seldom climbed to the old intensities of the triad; but if I look back honestly, I have to guess that by then I was ready for a seismic change. I'd already stolen glimpses of the skyline of puberty (the bodies of adolescent boys in the pool bathhouse, the fragments of sexual code I stored from family jokes and other children's stories). So I was half-longing for that sweet promise to thrust me a few steps ahead and away—a loss, I foretold, and a welcome liberation.

But our Roxboro evening has a half-hour to run. We are still a triad. And we waited in the drive. Will and Elizabeth gave their patented chuckles, which I couldn't match; then they reached for the doors and looked back at me. I hope I managed to touch them somewhere, the sides of their necks or the rising line where jaw meets ear. They welcomed touch till the day they died and generally thanked me. The fact that I don't remember acts or words after my moment of understanding—our leaving the car or climbing steps to open the front door that we never locked—must mean I was drowsy, maybe already nodding, maybe carried by Will.

In my own room a few minutes later, I was awake again in my bed— still a high-sided iron bed, all but too small. Mother had left me and the room was dark, but a hall light was on and would shine through the night. I knew any minute my father would come in to kiss me once and say "Said your prayers?" I had the vaguest notion of what prayers were but I usually nodded.

Then I heard a quiet singing voice in the hall, a song I also knew and had asked about—"When I Grow Too Old to Dream." I'd asked Father recently what "too old" meant. Now in the doorway stood a small old man with sloping shoulders; the voice was his. He stopped singing long enough to say my name, then started again and stepped to my bed. I was no brave hero, but I'd got a full share of both my parents' endless curiosity—who and what was this? His voice was weak and he wore old-fashioned pinch-nose glasses. Even as he stood at the rail of my bed to finish—"*When I grow too old to dream, I'll still have you in my heart*"—I didn't recognize this tired man with sparse white hair. He was silent a moment. Then he removed the glasses and said "It's me, darling. I'm too old to dream."

From cradle to grave, Will's practical jokes were the welcome scourge of his friends, kin and in-laws. In that less analytical time, nobody asked if a concealed hostility was at work in his impenetrable disguises, ruses, forged letters and convincing crank-phonecalls. If there was veiled anger in his motive, then it seems realistic to see also what an imaginative and entertaining way he found to vent it—our own home-theater, complete with regular catharsis. No one was ever so much as bruised; and no one ever expressed resentment, neither on the spot nor in after years. Those were tougher spirits in general then, not trained to expect kid gloves, day or night.

There'd be stunned moments as you, the object of the joke, faced this black-coated official of the U.S. Department of Agriculture, who was claiming you'd overplanted your tobacco allotment by two acres and must plow it under by sundown Monday. You'd call for your wife—"Oh, Molly! Come hear this news." And only when Molly's sharp eyes had come would you begin to guess that this preposterous bureaucrat, whom you'd seen step down from the train half an hour ago and walk your way, was your in-law Will Price who'd planned this flawless skit for weeks and boarded the train ten miles down the line to perform it with you. Then would come volleys of laughter from all and a cry of "Will, you *fool!*" from the victim, when *fool* was the last thing Will ever was.

And with trombones blazing, the story would enter the treasury to be told at most large family gatherings. Everyone was skittishly resigned to a turn as the object of one of Will's long-planned hoaxes. What removed all whiff of cruelty was his clear intention to amuse and everyone's delighted response, even the victims', and the fact that the victims promptly began to plot a turnabout, if he or she had the wits to catch Will unawares. In that crew of expert comedians, some did.

The singing old man was my first turn and, I now see, almost my last. (Three years later one evening, against Will's expectation, I opened the door on another strange-man disguise he intended for Elizabeth. He was wearing the pinch-nose glasses again, but this time a small derby hat rode high on his head, and he was draped almost to the ground in a black duster. I still didn't know him; but in too gruff a voice, he asked for the lady of the house. That alarmed me. I hooked the screen door and ran to warn Mother. To be sure, I thereby tipped her off and blunted the point of his joke—an attempt to enter and formalize the sale of a set of asbestos shingles she'd allegedly ordered.)

My memory of his "too old to dream" guise ends oddly at the almost unbearably forked moment of recognition—it was my father, he was still here young, someday he'd be old and dead. But Mother often told me how at that point I cried out for her to join us, not so much from fear but in an early flash of foresight. Surrounded as we were by aging kin in varying states of decline, I'd already asked more than one straight question on old age and death. They'd answered me frankly, as they mostly did; and now I saw the lesson, the second in a row.

Mother came quickly with a damp washrag. She rubbed the talcum powder from his hair; and there he stood young again, cheeks bright with fresh blood. I couldn't know I'd just undergone a primal scene in human emotion, the source of the richest moments in poetry—the lost kinsman found. I knew only the urgent thing. My young father, beaming down at me, would last to be my equal partner in our new triad. I was sitting upright on my narrow mattress. I know I didn't stand, but I also know I welcomed him back with a heart flung open in heedless welcome.

And curled in his long arm beside him now was the still younger mother I'd long since valued higher than happiness or my own life ahead. Given the chance, that moment there, I'd have chosen *Now, forever near them, young as this.*

With eyes so dark they barely glittered but drew all available light to herself, my mother watched us both—a far more tangled gift from fate than any her orphan heart can have begged.

The rest of her days she'd braid and loosen, and braid again tighter, our separate strands till at last she was half-blind, alone in a big house, in the grip of a pain so constant that she finally said to me "If I thought an icepick could find that nerve, I'd plunge it deep in my eye this minute and gouge till I killed it."

Safe in our spring night, none of us saw down that long shaft nor guessed how, a fast eighteen years farther on and forty miles south, I'd stand at another rail beside Will's bed and feel his heart's last beat with a hand still smaller than his and, eleven years farther still, how I'd take the wedding ring from Elizabeth's finger, still warm and soft.

But on that early safer night, sometime in the minute after Mother wiped his white hair and I saw him plain, Will Price leaned to touch my forehead with wide dry lips. Never, on any night I spent under the same roof as he, did he let me leave for anything risky as a full night's sleep without that rite—maybe in provisional farewell, maybe in self-reminder of his vow but surely in devotion and willed dependence or at least the care that never failed again in his life.

What I thought I'd discovered for good was part right, part wrong. In another few years I made the supplementary discovery—Will and Elizabeth had not only started without me; they had prior claims on one another, and those claims swam in powerful secret beneath our triad. If I felt deceived or locked out, then I choked the feelings and buried them deeper than I can now find. I remember liking the odd shut door on Sundays; the riddle of what they were up to intrigued me so much that I broached their secrecy only once. That was when I was nearly nine and

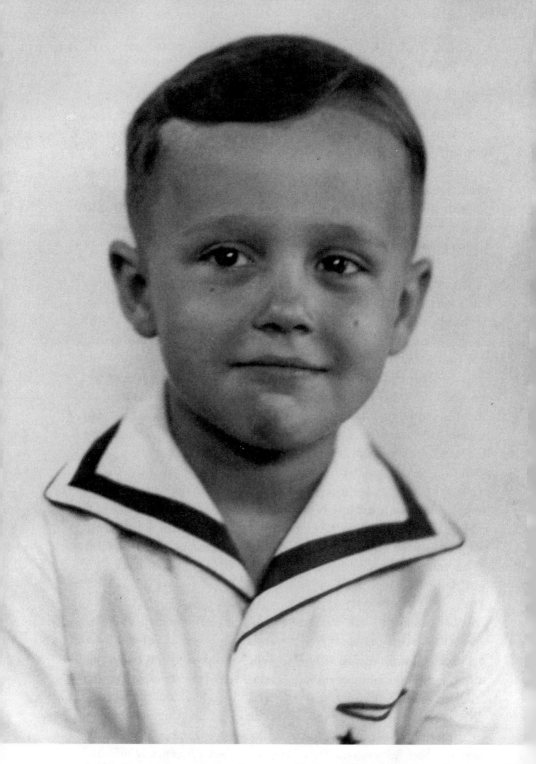

In Asheboro, July 1938. I'm five years old, dressed in one of the sailor suits that Elizabeth favored. With the curious smile, I mean to conceal my secret career as guide and defender of two young parents, helpless as babes.

left my funny papers on the floor by the radio to knock on their door and ask Will where Pearl Harbor was that the Japs had just bombed.

By then anyhow I was constructing a life of my own that was slowly walling them out, though the wall would always have big gates. Because we often lived on a road with few other children, I'd built myself an intricate set of private jobs and games, mostly secret—drawing and painting, reading and long fantastic games in the woods that had me extemporizing yards of plot and dialogue, soliloquies mostly or coded words of private joy to be alone, spoken to nothing more likely to hear than the scuttling crawfish in the creek behind our house. I'd also found, sooner than most boys, how my narrow body and still-hairless skin could reward itself time and again, a free and apparently harmless narcotic; and that was the highest wall of any.

Yet I cherished my father and mother more than anything else but the dim mirage of my future life. Any threat against them would set off desolating ground tremors—Will's suspected bad heart; Elizabeth's uterine problems, which fortunately I failed to realize were caused by mine and Bill's huge bodies, not to speak of our long-dead sister. After decades of listening to the confessions of others, I have to say that I spent a lot less time than most people in feeling anger or resentment toward my parents.

Not that we lived in a hushed bland world of becks and smiles. A whole day among us was more like the on-stage sounds and gestures of a tank-town opera house south of Naples. The waves and swoops, bellows and laughter, the threats of vengeance enacted with trick stage-knives were how we evaded mealy mouths and minds stoked to bursting with packed-down rage. That's not to hide a normal set of real wounds under comic wraps. Our excellent eyes and our yen for words meant we knew each other's tenderest flesh and could torment it quickly. I can't recall a whole night though when the verbal aggressor didn't beg the victim's pardon nor a pardon refused, however long the scar burned and showed.

None of that means we aimed at sanctity; no whole family has yet been canonized. And we were not even candidates, but we knew we were all unsparable parts of a vital shelter. Like all shelters, ours was subject to high natural storms within and without. But until Will and Elizabeth faced their deaths, the shelter turned most grades of weather. Much of its strength came from tacit agreement to claim it was permanent, not just a tent for a few thousand nights.

If it was a tent, then after all it was pitched on steel poles, longer lasting than even we suspected. I, and then Bill, were actual parts of the roof and sides, in ways that few children now seem to be. From infancy we not only threw a great steady stream of our strength into earning the care they gave us, unceasing as it was. We also accepted with zest our equal duty to raise the tone of any hour, not with pious sentiment or hymns of thanks but with watchful keen original jokes. Hard as we worked though, tired as we got, neither one of us doubted (or doubts today) that Will and Elizabeth—children far less wary than we, with homebred fears and yawning needs all dogging their heels—bore the greater load.

So I sit at this desk most days still, older than Will managed to be, in more or less steady thanks to them and a small clutch of others for basic training in independence, dependence, hunger, feeding, fireworks and damage control, awe at creation and its hid guardian. Maybe I see that the aim of their schooling was something as nearly impossible as *courtesy.* Courtesy in the broad continuous sense, not the merely polite—knowing where to look and what to see, when to bow or kneel, when to leave or stay, how to stay alone if death clears the room. Their vision of duty was harder than any combat marine's; and at times they failed it—loud short floods from their hot abundance, mishaps soon acknowledged and regretted. But none of their failures hobbled me. None of my failures is charged to them—and I've done harm, past their scope to do. Too young and agonized, they died brave deaths. They were calm and ready. Though I doubt they knew, it was their last lesson.

2

AN OPEN HEART

IDA RODWELL DRAKE

Bᴇ ᴛʜᴇ ᴛɪᴍᴇ I began to store long memories, I was feeling a strong need for solitude. At four I couldn't have named or described the urge; but since I was an only child for so long, since Will was gone from home all day and Elizabeth often left me with the cook, it was easy enough to go to my room, the depths of the yard or the woods and think whatever I needed. Most such time before adolescence was more nearly random than ordered and purposeful, but the solitude came with my nature and the family situation, and I freely indulged it. Elizabeth was mainly cheerful but was subject to patches of the blues; when she noticed my retreats, she understood and allowed them.

But in the few waking hours he was in the house, Will objected to my times alone. If I shut my door, he was quick to open it, ask if I was sick and then say it was too hot to stay shut up. If I went with him on a business call, which I always enjoyed, he'd keep up a stream of talk in the car—all new to me or funny at least—but if my eyes wandered or I missed a cue, he'd say "Let me see that tongue a minute, Ed" (the color of the tongue was still a prime health-index in the 1930s; and I've said that Edward was my first name, after his father; no one but Will used it, and for him it was a nickname). If I'd been unusually quiet, he generally thought my tongue looked suspiciously coated—"A good dose of magnesia tonight will take care of that."

After a dodgy first three years, my tongue was mostly pink and healthy; but I got the word. Though a hand's reach away, I'd left my father alone

Ida Lee Rodwell, born in Macon in 1887. She told my cousin Marcia, her granddaughter, that this was her engagement picture. Soon she will marry Francis Marvin Drake, the son of a Confederate major and five years her senior; they will be together, almost every day, for nearly fifty years. Though she can't be more than twenty here, the eyes already see her life.

too long; I hadn't been brought along for that. I already knew Will had daily needs for retreats of his own. Each night he knelt by his bed to pray, in plain view but with both eyes shut; and he spent long days on back-country roads, struggling alone to sell lamps, stoves and refrigerators. But he feared the same withdrawals in me. Maybe he thought I was planning some way to leave him, young as I was, when I was the thing that held him true to his vow not to drink.

Elizabeth then was the outlaw exception, but Will shared fully the ancient family dread of private time by any one member. I was too young to know or tell him; but what neither he nor the bigger part of my kinsmen noticed was how many children of their old ideal, even in our enormous family, were eventually driven to seek drastic solitudes—howling or dumb madness, querulous ill-wishers and suicides ghastly enough to punish the genial survivors to their own graves.

I lacked the mind or the words to think or say it; but I sensed near the start that if I was going to learn solitude, the raw taste for which had come in my blood, I'd have to find a training ground other than home. I'd need a place with one clean room and a door that shut; I'd need a long window onto the world and one understanding woman nearby. I found her early, the day I was born—the other lone soul in my mother's swarming family—and more than my parents, whom I loved maybe too much, that soul was the safest refuge of my childhood.

She was Ida Rodwell Drake, Elizabeth's sister but older than she by eighteen years. It was Ida, with her husband Marvin Drake and their sons, who returned to Macon at her own mother's death to keep house for her father Jack and her motherless young sisters, Elizabeth and Britsy. When Jack died suddenly a few years later, the Drakes stayed on and did an honorable job of raising the two girls to marriageable age.

Yet something, somewhere in the mix, was wild. Given Ida's goodness and Marvin's eventual forbearance, how was the family to explain the mystery when their three sons—all laughing charmers who'd give you their last red cent—revealed their long thirsts for drink? And though Elizabeth mainly loved and thanked her foster parents, there still were times when a harsh bafflement surged up in her and dimmed her affections—a harshness that, if anything, was stronger in Britsy and Louise, the eldest sister. The two youngest girls had seen their parents replaced in their bed, a hard-handed in-law had tried to command them. Elizabeth at least had rebelled hotly more than once, sometimes fleeing to her brother Boots in Norfolk—how could she trust in anyone's love; why should she live?

Fast as they came though, her orphan blues and grudges would lift. And by the time she was in midlife, and Ida and Marvin were old, her doubts seemed gone for good. Late in the night before the brain surgery that preceded and only slowed her death, Elizabeth phoned one person for a possible farewell and certainly for thanks—Ida, herself a widow by then.

I monitored the bafflement early; and since anything that troubled Mother's waters troubled me, I tried to understand. But I couldn't and my parallel love of Ida was by then so strong that it grew out of reach of anyone's harm. Ida was present, and working, through the long night of my birth, there in the Macon homeplace. Because Elizabeth was bed-ridden for nearly a month after labor, Ida took the chief part in my rearing through those primary days, when the first bonds are made. And by the time I was two or three, any visit to Macon required careful planning.

I had to be asleep at departure time, so far gone that I could be smuggled unconscious to the car; otherwise I'd never agree to leave—there'd be wrenching scenes of hysterical parting from Ida. If I was defiantly wakeful, they'd have to ease Ida out the back door—down to the garden or next door to hide, on the theory that if I couldn't see her, I wouldn't crank up my sobbing heartbreak. I clearly remember one such scene, in the orange glow of an old car's overhead lamp. Ida had stayed for our farewell; and Will and Elizabeth had to restrain me bodily from jumping out of the car. (By then I was calling Ida "Ducker," for reasons unknown. The Price sisters, with their verbal inventiveness, thought I'd formed it cleverly from the knowledge that a *drake* was a kind of *duck*. But that strains the ingenuity of even a Price child; in any case for me, Ida was "Ducker" the rest of her life.)

What I didn't know till adolescence was that I was maybe crucial to her life for one long stretch. At the time of my birth, she was only a month from age forty-six. Several years earlier, sabotaged by genetic inheritance or tripped by a late pregnancy and an early menopause, she had slipped into a profound depression that came near to ending her. I see now that each of the four Rodwell sisters—from Louise, born in 1885, to Elizabeth in 1905—was a victim of genuine recurrent melancholia; but none of the others appears to have suffered as intensely, as long or as mysteriously as Ida.

The bout through which she struggled in midlife came with an ugly twist. She believed she was pregnant. For nearly a decade, in the midst of a family that was not long on psychic subtlety, she knew a child was in her; and her anguish got little more than laughing denial from her family and friends. Even gynecologists ridiculed her; a uterine dilation and curettage were performed at a clinic in Richmond; and the surgeon's first words to Ida when she woke were "Mrs. Drake, if you're pregnant, I'm going to have a litter of puppies." A few minutes after, she turned to my mother and said "He hasn't so much as touched my body, much less scraped my womb." And despite her pain and weakness, she went home believing she'd been defrauded.

The horror deepened. For years longer she'd stand before the living-room mirror, measuring her waist—"See there, I'm bigger than yesterday. This child's coming here without a stitch to wear, and the house is cold, but you won't believe me." Elizabeth later told me that, when Ida was "low," Will could talk to her when no else could. Doubtless in his own depths, he'd learned the words he needed to hear and could give them to Ida. But any consolation burned off fast; and in her deepest trough, she confided to Elizabeth a terrible fear for her weak-eyed youngest son— "Please don't leave me alone with Wittie. I don't know what I might do to him."

Years after she recovered, more people than Elizabeth told me how Ida devoted herself to me so early when, damaged and weak myself, I arrived in her home at the low ebb of her life. It was she who'd taken me from Dr. Hunter's hands, and Mother said I welcomed Ida's arms. Whatever fears she'd confided about her own son, in that more innocent time, no one worried at her closeness to me. For all their own reasons, they were glad. And from that dawn forward, Ida found she could bury some of her pain in this boy—a new trusting thing, plainly untouched by her long dread, when her own patient husband and sons were helplessly mired in the torment with her. Did her young sister-daughter's birth pangs somehow purge Ida's own fear of labor (all her life she dreaded family weddings and births)? Did the new boy, torn and bruised by forceps and handed to her, become the child she'd long foreseen? The three known facts are that I was a thing she could freely choose to love, I had not torn her body or mind, and I didn't refuse her.

Since in short order I was caught in the happy but exhausting toils of love for my needy parents, I welcomed Ida as a parallel safer mother. She was fine to look at, quick to smile but no easy giggler. She was endlessly generous and always ready to treat me as an equal, when I acted the part; and with her I very rarely lapsed. She never condescended with childish talk or lax standards; and maybe again because she hadn't borne me, she was free of the hungers that made my parents press too soon on too young a child for more returns than he had to spare.

As long as we lived near enough for frequent visits, Ida improved. She still stayed mostly at home but was ready whenever we came to take my hand and quickly enter the world we were making, with no cross word, no single regret. When I was three we moved fifty miles west, then more than a hundred and Ida slipped again. I don't claim that my absence was the cause. Her despair preceded me and was too dark for simple explanation; but the simultaneous fact is that—when I was four or five, living three hours away—the hardest of her ordeals occurred.

She and Marvin were returning from the weekly five-mile shopping trip to Warrenton. The official story was that, as the car moved homeward at forty miles an hour, Ida discovered that her black coat with the modest sealskin collar was shut in the passenger door. She cracked the door open, a gust of wind caught it, sucked it outward; and Ida fell with awful force to the road. The head wound was especially grave; and even years later, her memory of the moment was awful. More than once, I'd ask for the story; and she'd relive it—"When I hit the pavement, I landed on my head and tumbled twice. That dark coat fell down over my face, and there I was on my hands and knees staring out at the dark and chewing cold sealskin. I thought I had already waked up in Hell."

Six months old in my sporty carriage in Macon, the summer of 1933. Behind the burdened and deceptively self-possessed face, I've already seized on Ida's love.

It was thirty years later; and she was dead of heart failure before I wondered if the fall was accidental or whether at last she might have seized a chance to end her torment.

Even the head wound slowly healed. I remember seeing her in bed, with a tall dome of gauze and tape but smiling lopsided. In the weeks of recovery, it slowly dawned on the adults that her long despair had also healed. She was back from whatever dark journey she'd made, or she'd reached wherever she was bound. In hundreds of hours of intimate talk, I never heard her mention the breakdown directly. Once when I was grown and told her that a young woman friend was hospitalized with profound depression and was receiving electroshock therapy, Ida looked away (no one I ever knew could look farther) and said "No living soul who hasn't walked through it can begin to imagine, the tortures of the damned."

In later years a few of the up-to-date relatives speculated that the trauma had amounted to a kind of ultimate shock treatment. Whatever the means, something saved Ida. Except for peculiar pains and tin-glings—she often spoke of her "foolish head"; and when she let me feel her scalp, I could trace the ridges of hard scar-tissue—she moved to the end on a mainly steady course.

Or so it seemed to us who looked in at intervals, though there was a mysterious episode with the foolish head late in the 1940s, serious enough to require a live-in practical nurse for some weeks. Generally we had only to phone and say we were thinking of driving up for the weekend, and she'd urge us to hurry. As we turned into the white sandy drive hours later, she'd be on the porch in her apron, waving. The four of us would spend a night or two, scattered in various hot or cold bedrooms, depend-ing on the season—the house was never centrally heated or cooled, and there was no indoor plumbing before I was ten.

Nephews, cousins and in-laws would hear of our arrival and gather at meal times. It was no chore apparently for Ida to serve a bountiful seated Sunday dinner, the midday meal, to fifteen or more. And on Sun-day evenings, she could invite the long porchful of guests to stay for supper, then rise and work her own loaves-and-fishes miracle with two dozen eggs, a few slices of ham, endless fresh tomatoes and the hundred rolls she'd laid out to rise on Saturday night.

On into the 1940s the feats were accomplished in what seemed effortless grace, without running water. Every drop was toted from the well and boiled on the woodstove at dishwashing time. Most days Ida had the strong knowing help of Mary Lee Parker, the black woman who worked with her as far back as I remember. But the planning, a fair amount of the cooking and all the serving and clearing were done by Ida, with various assisting kin who, in their delighted tribal chatter, were less help than bother.

Through that and much more, I never saw her angry or even exasperated. I never heard her chide or nag, though I saw her go silent more than once and stare out the window toward whatever unimaginably distant constellation calmed her. I never heard her voice raised except to call a far-off child or a wandering dog; and even in a packed house with fifteen mouths to feed and six or eight to bed down that night, she never showed a trace of reluctance. Yet by osmosis I understood early that she and I were mates. We cherished our kin but we needed time alone. I chose her as my guide in those first skills my parents couldn't teach; and before I started school, I was paying her long summer visits alone. That way we could taste the joys we shared with no dilution.

Our joys were simple and blameless. We played checkers and easy card games—fish, slap-jack, Authors, Old Maid. She tried in vain to teach me the dazzling Euclidian constructs she could weave from common string on nothing but her extended fingers; cats' cradles were the least of those elegant buildings. We'd go once more through her box of old photographs; and she'd recite the captions that I memorized behind her, "That's Mama in the awful hat she bought to wear on a trip to Portsmouth. Papa said it made her look like Aunt Theenie—Theenie was an old colored woman who lived down back of the cemetery and wore the worst hats. She could make a black hat out of most anything, and you always knew it was bound to be Theenie a good mile off when you saw a big black hat coming up the road. So when Mama got to Portsmouth, nobody could stop her. She had this picture made and mailed it to Papa. Look on the back now and see what she wrote." Before I could read, I would point to the tall handwritten words and say them with Ida, "See other side for Aunt Theenie."

We picked flowers in the morning—five brands of roses, sweetpeas, snapdragons, bachelor buttons. And a little later we went back for the boggling profusion of fruits and vegetables—strawberries, blackberries, cantaloupes, watermelons, onions, peppers, two kinds of squash, snap beans, butter beans, black-eyed peas, corn, lettuce, cucumbers and as many as fifty tomatoes a day (the screened back porch would often have a hundred tomatoes laid down in varying shades from yellow to red; and we'd sometimes go there with nothing but paper napkins and salt and eat four or five apiece, our chins streaming juice). After midday dinner we'd sit in the dark-green front-porch swing with my head in Ida's lap as she scratched my hair slowly and told me ghost stories or, better, stories from her own childhood.

Why do children in general especially prize stories from the childhoods of their grown kin? Is it just that *Homo sapiens* loves stories; or is the pleasure more specific, an assurance that this present child, unsure as he is, will last and grow to recall his youth with affectionate laughter? Whyever, I had a big favorite from Ida's past—the time her best friend spent the night with her. They retired to the same bed, stuffed their ears with cotton to keep out earwigs and finally tied their big toes together. In the middle of the night, the friend got up to pee in the slop jar. She forgot the tied toes and dragged Ida halfway out on the floor. Each time she'd tell it, the proffered picture of a young Ida yanked from sleep to the verge of falling—and the lovely thought of the old Ida admitting her absurd plight—would convulse me. I'd ask for the story on every visit; and accepting absolutely a child's comfort in endless repetition, she'd serve it up in the same exact words. If it was late afternoon, once we finished laughing, she was likely to say "Now let me make you a brown-sugar sandwich." For a late afternoon sinking spell, I still recommend them—two slices of good buttered bread with a liberal sprinkling of moist brown sugar.

I've yet to meet the child you can fool in matters of love. Children have foolproof radar for sincerity; one false eyeblink and you've lost them for good. And just as I never saw Ida show anger, I never caught her bored in my presence. If her interest began to lag, she would say there was something that needed doing and leave. I also learned early that asking her to read aloud was the same as giving her a shot of morphine. She seldom read for her own pleasure; faced with a whole page of type, she quickly slipped into hypnosis, then sleep. It was no good waking her; another two sentences and she'd nod off again. Like everyone around her, she was not a deep thinker; but how could she bear such long slow hours, not in baby talk or condescension but in serious mature conversation with a child? From here, it seems that she chose me to be the live receptacle of what she knew—the good things at least, the happy past, with brief excursions into family tragedy to anchor my instruction in the truth.

In later years I've known other women and a few men who are capable of a similar patience with child companions, but no one else has shown me a calm as unshakable as Ida's. Admitted, she lived in a quiet village where the worst external threat—to a white woman anyhow—was stepping on a nail; and the loudest sound was a through-train to Norfolk. But indoors all her life, the psychic weather could turn gray fast and linger overhead. So her calm in my presence was either her natural brand of grace or a perilously generated mask; or what was more likely in the years of her breakdown, the calm was an unselfconscious strategy for hunting what she craved. If only she could sit quiet enough, she'd attract the help her mind required. And help was either a time alone or the company of an undemanding other, another who craved uncrowded stillness and would share it with her. God knew I was one such; and there in the swing, I'd know in my bones I was pleasing her grandly, by the passing second. I knew, not because she told me so or thanked me; I could taste it in the air and drink it from every calm smiling glance, not one of them starved.

Yet maybe my equally calm adoration was a substance, a mineral her mind and bones had lacked far longer than she knew. In later years I often heard what a quiet listening child I'd been; and in one of the hard times of my adult life, a serene and wise girl-child named Katherine Ellis made me similar healing gifts. So maybe a light but steady attention was the thing I gave Ida. Marvin her husband was stone deaf and mostly beyond the reach of her voice, her sons were gone; and at the time of my childhood, all her grandchildren were girls when she was admittedly partial to boys. I was it then—the help she found in the house, at her feet.

For my part, the crucial attraction lay in my early understanding that

Ida and I shared more than one pleasure. In the pristine wordless clarity of childhood, I knew that, in vital things, we were the same age. We were both worn-down and needed rest; we needed time alone to mend, to plan our defenses before the loud family called us again. I'm speaking of the years when I was between three and eleven, 1936 to '44. What was wearing that young a child down and making him plan for long summer stays in Macon with Ida, weeks when I'd spend hours alone out walking the dirt roads or reading in the back room or napping in the scalding heat of August or planning circuses with Ann Bullock across the tracks (we staged at least three, to sizable village audiences; and my chief contribution was an umbrella-borne leap from Ann's four-foot stone wall)?

I understood the problem—my married life. I've stressed that, to the age of eight, I was Will and Elizabeth's only companion; and from the age of three I'd been intensely conscious of my importance to them and theirs to me. Their sufferings in the years before my birth, Will's struggle to dry out and my own early crises, far from separating us, had bound all the closer the sides of our triangle—one that, in my innocence, I saw as equilateral, with equal burdens and duties on all sides.

The strangest thing was not that a three-year-old came to such conclusions but that his parents shared them. Clear and merciless as we were, we were right. For the years until my brother arrived, we constituted not simply a marriage but a romance. I took no share of their sexual bodies, but each of us cherished the others' flesh; it was all we could see. And for that, if no more, we gave each other reliable care, though we took heavy tolls. So whatever the heights and depths of my home life, I was more than ready to take country rests in the shadow of Ida's cooler love.

Not once till years later, when I heard the stories of her depression, did I catch one glint of her private hell. Detained in the introspection of childhood, I asked only questions that touched on her and me together— tell me again what you did the morning I was born, tell about Joyce nearly passing out from ether, tell me how I looked and what you did with me, how will you feel when I go back home? However happy or sad the answers, not then or later did I ever see Ida weep, though the other Rodwell sisters were cataracts of easy tears; so I had no cause to ask if she hurt. The clear answer was, she didn't—not with me.

Ida and I at the Wright Brothers Monument, Kitty Hawk, in the summer of 1939. We've come with Will and Elizabeth to see an outdoor historical pageant, *The Lost Colony*. Though Ida is fifty-two and is only now surfacing from her long torment, this is the first pleasure trip she's taken since her honeymoon.

Yet she never leaned, never pressed too hard, never asked for more than I could give. Both my parents, especially Will, would laugh and ask a half-serious question, "Which one of us do you love the most?" When I hesitated to choose, he or Mother would teach me the Solomonic answer, "Both the same." That brand of hunger never showed its teeth in Ida, not even in laughter. She said more than once that she liked my eyes; she liked to scratch my knobby scalp. When we parted she'd generally say "I *love* you," but she never asked for a return declaration. Despite the normal hugs and pecks, our bond had no fleshly component. Aside from the afternoon scratching in the swing, she and I seldom touched. When she helped me bathe, she'd scrub away with firm dispatch. And when she washed and dressed, she'd move to the darkest corner of her and Marvin's bedroom to use the pitcher and washbowl.

There was no hint that she loathed her body or anyone else's, only the tacit request for privacy. Dressing, trips to the privy and the nights with Marvin were her only complete privacies in the times of my visits; and even then, their door was never shut. But as much as any possessed genius, Ida had the gift or curse of instant access to solitude. Even in the crowded dining room, her hazel eyes could roam aside or drift out of focus; and you'd know she was gone. If Elizabeth was present, she'd say "Come back, Ida Lee! Talk to the world"; and Ida would join us.

So I learned early to anticipate her needs. Sometimes in late afternoon we'd be in the living room; and I'd notice her answers slowing down, her eyes veering off. She never asked me to leave, but I knew to go—downtown for the mail or to my own room for a parallel rest. In twenty more minutes I might drift back. She'd be on the sofa, wide awake with maybe a Bible open beside her. Like her three sisters, she attended church and no doubt found some comfort there; but I can't recall her speaking of religion, certainly not to press her faith on one other soul, least of all to despise or judge. (As a Methodist woman in a small church, it was her occasional turn to prepare next Sunday's communion; and my earliest memories of the wonder of that sacrament rise from the times I'd watch her slice loaf-bread into tiny squares and fill the five dozen tiny glass cups with unfermented grape juice. Those, she told me, were "in memory of Jesus.") Most times her Bible was a filing place for verses she clipped from the daily paper, the usual lines of praise and thanks that have meant far more to the race than Dante. Mostly by then she was ready for company; she'd likely meet my eyes and smile—"You ready to help me? Let's go set the table." And we'd head off to fix the thirteen-thousandth supper of her married life.

In the triad of my home family, the only private moments were Will's prayers or his and Elizabeth's Sunday naps behind a shut door. Other times we lived in our own unconscious Eden. Will walked nude every chance he got, unabashed as the day-old Adam. Even when dressing, Elizabeth made no effort to hide the magnetic but repellent scar in her side, the legacy of drainage tubes in her girlhood siege of peritonitis. Before the age of twelve, my lean body had few secrets; and early I shared their indoor fascination with one another's bodies—the differing textures of skin, the length and curl of eyelashes, eventually and delicately with the central genitals (as strange as any wild creature in the woods). From the age of three though, my mind was pocked with its own black caves full of thoughts about my parents and me and a few young friends. I recall no fuming anger or pent-up rage but days of gradual speculation on a thousand mysteries and fervent hopes for everything from a live pet elephant to angelic vision and growing wonderment at my body's competence to please itself.

With Ida, again the bond was cooler. With a normal child's interest in the scars of damage-survived, I focused early on a surgical dimple in her right cheek, where a mole had been removed, and on the loose bluish skin on the backs of her hands. My only physical fascination was with her hair. Elizabeth's coarse black horsehair was short as my own, and she went to a men's barbershop for her biweekly trim. But Ida's fine brown hair came down below her shoulder blades. Each night she slowly combed it out and plaited it into one long switch; I was always asleep before then. But I tried to be on hand each morning after breakfast when she combed it free again with a wide-toothed ivory comb, plaited it tighter and coiled it into a hard bun that bristled with tortoise-shell pins.

I was still a stranger to the hair fetishism of puberty, though I knew many folk tales with long-haired princesses and shaggy dwarfs. And Marvin had sworn he was present at the exhumation of a woman long-dead. When they raised the coffin lid, there she lay—still perfect in beauty—and her lustrous gold hair had grown in the grave till it crowded the space. She'd been buried alive. All the men bent to look; but at the touch of daylight, she crumbled to dust that no man could hold. Yet memory tells me that there was not even the bud of erotic feeling in my absorption in Ida's hair. With all my chances, I seldom touched it; I know I never asked to comb it. Still the deft rite seemed a skill worth learning; most children will watch any visible process with rapt attention, sensing already how often the world demands odd skills when we least expect.

After that, Ida was ready for work. Mary Lee would be in the kitchen with midday dinner under way; but in that old and rangy house, there was plenty of work left. So my main job was to move aside. Those four hours then, from breakfast to dinner, were the first of my solitary times in the day. The house itself gave me little to pore over. It was honestly and solidly built; its contents and decorations were modest. There was no conspicuous bad taste, no stunning eyesore; but with the exception of a few good pieces of Victorian walnut and oak, a painting of a stag in snow, another of an angel walking on clouds (both by a girlhood friend of Ida's) and a forest of family photographs, there was little to distract me from private thoughts. Marvin kept a stack of recent issues of the monthly *Progressive Farmer*, the weekly *Look* and the daily Raleigh *News and Observer*; but there can't have been more than fifty books on the lot. Though the Drake's oldest son had graduated from Duke University, neither the Rodwells nor Drakes of the older generations felt the need for book-instruction, beyond occasional Bible verses, or for further vicarious life beyond their own dreams.

So I'd sit on the porch, reading the stack of books I'd brought from home (I prized a complete collection of *Classic Comics*, everything from the Bible to *The Last of the Mohicans* in cartoon versions). Or I'd draw and paint in my sketchpad. Even then I was mostly drawing "freehand" and from fantasy, seldom from life—like most Southern painters who have inexplicably been little-interested in the beautiful but steamy outdoors. I might wander back and check the garden, in hopes of seeing the blacksnake that had fought a hot duel with Marvin in the strawberry patch; but the goal of my mornings was the ten o'clock train with the second mail. A half-hour after it passed, I could cross the tracks and the Raleigh-to-Norfolk two-lane highway and check for mail. Even in the country, I still put a great head of energy into waiting for the mail. I was always expecting something I'd sent off for—a $2.98 cardboard micro-scope that had looked so professional in the ad, a supply of fake postage stamps with my picture on them or the latest returns from the dozens of autograph requests I mailed out to everyone from Franklin Roosevelt and Toscanini to the latest dim starlet.

With a frequency that I took for granted but that now seems incredi-ble, they almost all responded with photographs, autographed cards, oc-casional notes. Sometimes the notes mentioned my name; and seeing it—in a world-famed script like General MacArthur's, winged specially to me halfway round the Earth—was a whole new kind of luminous foxfire. But even the baldest signature was a beckoning chink of irresistible light to a life like mine, happier than I knew and already rooted in the ground of my work but guessing I stood as far from art and the core of power as any bird-sized porter in Asia.

Ida hadn't seen a movie since *Gone with the Wind*; and world news was of no real interest, unless it involved that part of the Earth where her middle son Marvin Jr. was a Marine writing funny letters home and wait-ing to invade Japan (I never showed her the picture of a naked girl from Okinawa that he sent to me). So it didn't worry me that she was benignly indifferent to my celebrity mail. I made it a part of my secret excitement. Those outsized figures of the actual world knew my name and address; they were waving me onward. I was waiting here till I knew how to meet them. But even their dazzling faces and names didn't mar the ease of my time in Macon. Life in the presence of Ida and Marvin, plainly so much older than my parents yet strong and genial, was helping me over one more tall hurdle—well before my adolescence, I was learning to be-lieve in a future. Gauging their height and their durable bodies, I knew I'd last and eventually grow to run my own self-justifying public life.

After dinner Ida would be free again till supper, and those early after-noon hours are when we sat again in the swing. We'd murmur and sway ourselves into an untroubled stupor that we'd fight off till finally she'd say "Isn't it about time for you to stretch out?" I'd go to the west bed-room—the one I was born in, the same iron bed—and lie for an hour, mostly open-eyed with yellow shades drawn against the hot sun, while Ida snored like a purring cat on the living-room sofa. That was the precious lonely time I'd come to find.

Again there were no pictures or books to guide my thoughts, only ink-blot-type water stains on the ceiling which I could study for imagery—one stain, I recall, was plainly a seal's head. And hot as the days were, with no air conditioning, I'd lie back on the stillness and think the thoughts about past and future that were hard to manage if my parents were near—Reynolds grown and running his own career, at a microscope or a painter's easel; Reynolds in Hollywood, as the screen son of Johnny Weissmuller or Greer Garson (I'd written to each with the proposition). But I never dreamed a Reynolds with his own home and family, just always alone and good at his work but never lonely.

Aside from Ida's purr, and sometimes a motorboat-snore from Marvin, the only sounds were distant—cars on the highway, black Pap Somerville's ox cart creaking toward town, the putter of black Ben Harrison's Model T (Ben was called "Dr. Pepper" and had been a bootlegger), the chink of the well chain, hornets building their gray paper nest big as a ham on Anna Thompson's neighboring window: nothing strange. And even in the room where I'd endured a birth that was the hardest trial of my life to now, I never hatched a thought of lurking danger, human or otherwise. For my mind anyhow Ida and Marvin in their perfect strength had woven that dense a safety net round the house.

So slowly I began the management of the dangerous taste I was born with. I could practice solitude—blank rest-time, strategic withdrawal from the work of love and nearness or concentrated serene meditation on the unseen world, a form of prayer. I've since watched dozens of children do it, but they mostly abandon the skill in adolescence. My own early flair for gazing at a spot on the wall long minutes, and courting calm like a Buddhist monk, stayed with me for good. Yet the gentle knocks and thuds of life, recommencing in the house at three, would also be welcome; I'd rush to join them. Painlessly too then, in Ida and Marvin's house, I learned when to end retreat in a glad return to the nearest trustworthy human.

That would mostly be Ida, back in the kitchen, beginning to assemble supper. After a walk to the post office or Russell's store and maybe another few minutes in the swing, we shared the light meal with Marvin and any chance guest. And then we'd have the evening fate sent us—there were seldom any plans, certainly no plans to "go out." Britsy and Herman (she'd married a Rodwell cousin) might drive up from Warrenton for two hours of talk; or we'd listen to the radio, with Ida and me sitting far back since Marvin would need the volume on high. Or our cousin Clyde Coleman might stroll up from two houses down the road with his Baltimore-bred and therefore exotic wife E. P., whom I liked precisely because she was from two states away.

Then the adults would play a few hands of setback or rummy with Ida and Marvin, while I read magazines behind them on the sofa or ransacked the photograph box again and told myself the stories she'd taught me—Marvin's young brother the year he drowned while trying to swim across the Roanoke River ("They were too far from home and Marvin couldn't swim. So nothing for him to do but stand there, helpless on the bank and watch his brother sink"), then Ida and Louise as country Gibson Girls with their hair up, Elizabeth barefoot and one-year-old laughing helplessly in a wicker-work chair and my cousin Marcia and I as babies (me bald as Mussolini in his prime), posed outdoors in the lily patch with Topsy the goat.

Also as I waited for the adults to finish and for Ida to bring out the tangerines or nuts, I'd drift back and forth between the bright living room and my dark and mildly scary bedroom. Though I can't recall ever being bored before age thirteen, already the talk of my family and their friends was beginning to amaze me—how could they sit for happy hours and speak of nothing but food and family, the weather, the war or Mrs. Roosevelt's latest ridiculous column (they were all staunch New Deal Democrats, but the peripatetic and meddling Eleanor was far from the beatified heroine she later became)? I wanted to tell them about my books, my drawings, my letter from General Eisenhower which had come that week from Allied Headquarters. And they'd glance my way with a grin and a joke; but all children at adult events were still assumed to be oblivious, safe in the muffling cocoon of youth. They thought we were no more alert or judgmental than their parked and cooling automobiles outside in the night.

Most nights after supper, we'd be alone. Ida by then would be a little drowsy, but Marvin would want a last cigar, and wide-awake me would join them on the porch. We'd sit at least another hour in the dark—Ida and I in the swing again, Marvin in a rocker—and talk the slow half-finished sentences that, to any outsider, would have seemed as pointless as an old dog's dreams. But in them I heard two urgent things—I was smart enough to talk to, even to hear; and two grown kinsmen in full possession of their God-given wits still wanted me close but would not compel me. It was that, and my pleasure in solitude, that kept me from ever being lonely in Macon. There were no other resident white or black boys my age who weren't at backbreaking work in the fields. Never mind—I was in an element richer than friendship; and luckily somehow, I never once doubted it.

Around nine-thirty we'd have finally exhausted the news of the day. Then Marvin would rouse from his deaf silence. He'd locate the moon, study its omens, guess tomorrow's weather and announce bedtime like an invention he'd minted that instant. I might even run out one last minute to catch lightning bugs in a mayonnaise jar with holes in the lid, skirting the black oaks wide enough to hide a crook or a hungry ghost. And even then the Drake wisdom held; they left me alone in all my play—no condescending modern attempts to squat at my level and reel time backward and crowd, with their guesses, a child who was happily hid in the mystery of his own mind, his clandestine play.

Then with hoot owls and coon dogs belling down the road in Mac Thornton's woods, Ida would lead me off to bed. She'd check my hair and limbs for ticks, then kiss me lightly on the forehead and leave with no insistence on soap and water. One of my favorite things about Macon was the scarcity of baths—the old country-rate of maybe two a week, with daily touch-ups. Even so, a much-told story records that one summer I arrived and convinced Ida that Mother had taken me to a dermatologist who said that I suffered from dry skin—me, a well-oiled brunette—and must not bathe often: one of my earliest works of fiction.

I'd enter the cool sheets, knowing that she and Marvin were in a high bed two rooms away with all doors open. If I woke in the sounding August dark, I could hear them turn in the high four-poster and know which was which by the depth of the creak. But the strangled gasps of their snoring said all I needed then, "If we can trust the dark this fully, then rest assured that you're safe too." And I could sink back, gone till day.

My parents moved us frequently—eleven times before I was twelve and twice more before I left for college—so I'd have just begun to tame a place and hear its secrets before Elizabeth would hand me an empty box and say "Pack your toys, son. We're moving tomorrow to a lot nicer place." Generally we improved our standing; but until I was fifteen, if I was at home and my parents went out and were late returning, I'd feel a spread of anxieties from unease to panic. The fear was as much for them as me. And the distant roar of the Second War only heightened my sense of the world's danger to their vulnerable bodies that had barely escaped destruction and were not guaranteed—hadn't Elizabeth's parents vanished before she was ready?

With Ida in Macon, in addition to sane hermitage, I learned more nearly to trust the world, not (like Will) to suspect it of constant malice. That I learned it in the shadow of a woman who was recently in profound distress, to the possible edge of suicide, is not the strangest paradox of a childhood set round with full-grown mysteries. Even harder to credit is the fact that, by learning independence beside her and in sound of her level voice, I came wholeheartedly to love a grown woman safer than my mother. And with that trust and my willed dependence, I contributed unknowingly to healing her mind for the three more decades she faced. I've said they brought her a personal calm, except for the permanent sadness of her sons (one recovered from drink but died young; another recovered after her death), the loss of Marvin ten years before her own death, the deaths of her brothers and then of Elizabeth, her young sister-daughter.

Our light romance cooled a little more when I was eleven, and we moved back to Warrenton for three years. That put us within ten minutes of Macon. I couldn't imagine summer stays in a house we were visiting almost every Sunday; and along with a rough rejection from my contemporaries in Warrenton, I was feeling the first strong tides of puberty—that undertow that draws us to our kind. All Americans know that, in those years, most of your childhood seems dumb, if not shameful;

Ida and Marvin in the late 1930s (she wears the dress she wore at Kitty Hawk). Pictures of them together are rare, but this one plainly states their relation—she holds a rose and watches gravely; he lurks in his hat but is near behind her. Only their clothes touch.

and you're in danger of disowning anyone who's likely to remind you that you didn't boil up full-grown and genitally competent from the wellspring of Eros.

And just as I edged into those years of near-insufferability, my brother Bill was an ebullient and open-armed three-year-old. Not only did he and I entertain the family with joint recitals of Christmas carols and such contemporary hits as "Don't Fence Me In" (Bill singing, I playing Ida's piano); he slipped easily into part of my old place with Ida. Yet again our nearness to Macon made long visits by Bill seem pointless. And despite the cooling, I never thought of my romance with Ida as childish. During the three years in Warrenton, for reasons I'll mention later, I was again without close friends; so I missed few of the family visits to Macon. And on through high school and college, I'd make occasional weekend visits and always for the old reasons—to float back on the serenity she fostered, especially as passion began to crowd my path, and to remind myself of the gift for self-reliance I'd learned in her house but often misplaced in early manhood.

In the second year of my collegiate English major, with a discovery of the Milton-Egerton connection, I had a new reason—Ida was the one older Rodwell who could give me the begats, our ancestors two generations back at least. And one of the happy nights of my life was spent alone in the west bedroom, reading in an unbroken stretch Hemingway's *The Old Man and the Sea* at its first appearance, in *Life* magazine. And right through Ida's death, whenever we were together or talking on the phone, we could quickly restore more than half our old care. Our voices would darken in reflex sympathy to signal the feeling, not sentimentality but knowing and merciful tenderness. Maybe we both knew silently that we'd got the best of each other, years past, and must now move on.

As we were on the verge of leaving Warrenton, in a new and precisely timed act of grace, Ida's youngest son Wilton and his wife Margery presented her with a first male grandson—a winning gentle boy, Rodwell Drake. From the first he was called Roddy and was said in the family to be much like me when new and unspoiled—watchful and eager to please. Before he could walk alone, he stepped into my worn shoes in Ida's heart. Since his parents had built their own white house in the Methodist church grove only a hundred yards west, Roddy and his near-twin-brother

Charles were soon underfoot all day. And before long Roddy was spending his nights there as well, asking the same urgent questions that all children ask and getting them answered with Ida's laconic good sense that granted your need in patient dignity.

She'd found a new receiver for the unstinting love she had to pour, a love that had somehow failed to save her sons from years of pain. For once, I was able to watch gladly as someone took an old place of mine and received, full-force, a gift I no longer needed. But again she and I never stopped showing we remembered our prime and could call it back. As proof of thanks, on one of my last high-school vacations, I spent a weekend at Ida's with her and Roddy and drew their smiling faces, brimmed with the secret trust they shared.

To my mind a saint is someone who—with however many faults, even crimes—eventually leads us by example, almost never by words, to imagine the hardest thing of all: the seamless love of God for all creation, including ourselves. By that standard Ida Drake is the one saint I've watched at close range. And I've never heard a live syllable of dissent, even from the daughters-in-law who sometimes wondered at her stoic calm in the face of her sons' long cycles of pain. (I need to say that, with all their sufferings, each of the sons at his usual best was an open-hearted, loyal and laughing part of the family's gatherings; and in the hard times, their wives and children were incredibly patient in their wait for joy.)

All my older family were innocent of the findings of modern psychology. Ida once said to me "I saw in the paper that now they think little things that happened in your childhood can affect you years later." The news may have given her food for long thought; she never spoke it though and I never asked. But the world knows what degrees of torment can be concealed beneath one pair of eyes. Ida suffered for her sons, suffered with them when they let her; but like the best doctors of the time, she was worse than helpless in the face of addiction. She could only meet the unspoken question of their chaos by working to live the kind of life she intended—selfless, free-handed and watchful, not of her own fine face in a mirror but of every *visible* need that passed—yet no one ever heard her praise herself, by direct claim or implication. Any compliment to her dignity, strength or her generous hands was refused with a frown and a shut-eyed "*Pshaw!*" which ended that.

Before her death I doubt I saw faults. By the time I was three, I had a list of my parents' wrongs but Ida escaped. Only later did I notice the central blindness she shared with every white man or woman she knew and with the large part of other Americans in her day. By the time I was in high school, I'd sometimes catch a quick hardness in her voice as she spoke with Mary Lee the cook—a woman of impeccable honesty and warmth and a delicate artisan in her work. The fact that Mary Lee had told Ida the name of her white father, a local gentleman, and that Ida believed her, in no way altered Ida's sense of the rightness of their separate social order. If you'd asked her "What's Mary Lee to you?" she'd have said something like "A good loyal cook and a trusted friend." And as far as she went, she meant it.

But Mary Lee worked six days a week, sometimes seven, to serve a table where she could never sit. She worked for the going low wage; and she worked more than twenty-five years, barring illness, with little time off—not that Ida had more. Most of the boundaries in the relation were those that have prevailed in the majority of all societies, those that sanction servant-master relations. Mary Lee worked for a decent family in a clean warm house; and she lived in one, not a mile's walk away. All the Drakes, the Rodwells and my Prices thought of her with thanks, admiration and affection. No one came to the house without spending time with Mary Lee in the kitchen or without slipping her a dollar or two at the end of a meal. Any one of them would have gone a long way to meet her needs, on the widely spaced occasions she spoke them. Given the time and the mind of the whole white country, Mary Lee could not have got better and she knew it; all my kin would have told you the same. They were right.

Worse still, the gulf between her life and ours was not only silent. To most white eyes in eastern Carolina by the 1920s, it was simply invisible—as unnoticed a part of the landscape as pinetrees. And from the end of Reconstruction till the 1960s (Ida's lifespan exactly), she would never have heard the gulf and its evil audibly protested, not in her world. And she never left it except to read a Raleigh paper, as blind as we.

From one standpoint it was a blindness bought cheaply. Though monumentally forbearing, Mary Lee would show her own edge on random occasions—when asked, say, to iron a shirt for Uncle Grant (the black yardman whom she openly resented) or when approached on the subject of surrendering her Sunday-off to a houseful of hungry company. She almost never refused though and never seriously complained, not in a way that Ida could hear. And if you'd challenged Ida, she'd have likely said "If Mary Lee were upset, she'd say so plainly."

But when I went to Mary Lee's dim house in 1972, years after Ida's death, she was waiting alone, old and retired with a weak heart but with young skin still and a cloudless mind. She sat me by her blazing oil stove under huge framed photographs of the dead black side of her family, whom I'd never heard or thought of. And after we'd worked through our years of good memory, Mary Lee bent forward and fixed me with eyes as bright as the flash off the angelic swords that may yet hack my family down at Judgment, "Why do white people hate the black people, Reynolds? Answer me that." I tried to put it in terms of history and ignorant fear; but she wouldn't let me off that easy—"Scared of me, a sick old woman that can't hardly walk; that never yet tried to hurt one *soul?*"

Ida lived into the opening days of the civil rights movement, the march on Washington and other televised sights that reached my mortally ill mother and turned her mind decisively. But in fear maybe, I never probed to see if Ida changed, though I knew that two of her sons thought the whole movement a Communist plot. I'm not by nature a public missionary. I thought that my tacit refusal to join the family males in their hot fears and threats was sufficient (Will was dead by then; he might well have balked too, but later I'll speak of his unpredictable feelings in the matter).

I also thought that, if I took to the platform at home, I'd achieve nothing more than the silence of older entrenched kinsmen who'd trusted me with their private convictions—that deep mine of knowledge that's still my main source of thought and feeling. From its riches I worked to make the stories that are my real voice. But now when I see films of the flocking brave faces, black and white, of the early rights movement in Greensboro, Durham, Selma and elsewhere, I'm more than sorry that my face is missing.

There's no denying that, at this tangled crux, a white Southerner born before 1970 encounters his most painful challenge. He's at least lived on into an open-eyed world, one in which he has frequent chances to amend his old complicity. But what's he to think of the older kin and friends who reared and loved him but who also, however passively, supported a vicious racism? The upper South, and Ida Drake's home, were by no means Nazi Germany; it's a travesty of moral distinction to say so. But the evil committed, sustained and concealed in calm lovely towns and farming hamlets was slow and enormous; and the mystery is insoluble like all the mysteries of evil—forget the ignorant or vicious; they're always available for dirty work. Answer the larger, harder question—how were so many otherwise intelligent, morally sensitive, watchful and generous people trapped in the running of a brute and tragic machine? The only hope for a sane unraveling of those blood-crusted knots of devotion and cruelty lies in a case-by-case weighing of the evidence.

Macon had been a Confederate training camp, and there were live veterans in the county on into my teens. Marvin Drake's father was a Confederate major and lost an arm in battle. Ida and Elizabeth's father Jack was four at the end of the Civil War; their uncle W. P. "Brother" Rodwell was ten. Stone-deaf, Uncle Brother lived with Ida in the last twenty years of his life, and I remember him vividly (he died when I was seven). Both Ida and Marvin were well into middle age before living memories of the War had died off around them. At least two of their black help were almost certainly freed slaves and I knew them. And though, by the time of my childhood, neither of my families preserved actual memories of their own slaveholding past, the stench of de facto slavery paralyzed their moral imagination and that of all the rural white South till toward the end of the Second World War.

So the origins of Ida's moral thought are plain to see. She lived her life in close daily work with black men and women. She honored their skills and arts, their loyalty and the strength of their faith. She could talk and laugh with them easily; she was incapable of verbal abuse, even of a raised voice; and by her standards, unkindness was unthinkable. She would go to self-denying lengths to help a particular black friend, and the insults and jokes of racist hate were as foreign to her as all other ignorant and inhumane labels. She was not highly educated or wealthy; her home was solid and adequate but far from luxurious; her tastes were simple and economical. She'd suffered great pain in her own small body, so she can't be accused of deliberate cruelty or of gazing down from stratospheric heights of money and ease.

But the appalling local chasms of racial difference in housing, nu-

Bill my brother and Ida on the porch in Macon, the summer of 1959. She is seventy-two and Marvin has been dead for three years. She laughs a good deal in her better days, but photographs seldom catch her at it. And this same swing, of dark green oak, was the moving vehicle of so many hours in the thirty-two-year-long conversation that she and I shared.

trition, health, education, private and public rights and all else were literally invisible to her. They were invisible because, like most human beings, Ida never thought to question the bases of her rearing; and no credible teacher (not one: white or black, at home, in school or in church) had ever questioned them for her. The unschooled black people with whom she worked were immemorially hardened to deprivation, grateful to her for a limited genial mercy, showing her mostly the case-hardened cheer they'd won from disaster and fearful of losing their jobs. So they never described their pain, not in words.

Ida could sit in the car by Marvin (she never learned to drive), pass the houses of Mary Lee and her neighbor's cook and wave in good faith. She saw no quandary in the difference between their houses and her own. Admitted, she too had no reliable heat, no indoor plumbing till she herself was fifty; but her roof turned rain and her walls stopped wind. Recall as well that even the sacred texts of her faith—the Jewish law, the words of Christ, the teachings of Paul—far from condemning slavery, explicitly condone its existence, though counseling kindness in the treatment of individual slaves.

If you say that any two eyes should have seen the tragic cruelty of her kin and her race and that Ida Drake was willfully self-blinded, I'd make the elementary point that every American is sealed, at any moment of his or her life, in multiple forms of conscious or unconscious blindness. When did I last offer usable help to the Indians from whom this country was torn by my ancestors or to the homeless on our streets today, the swarming wretched millions of the Earth—not to speak of wrongs beneath my own roof? Like many, I make my yearly donations; but my daily life barely alters course. And with the vast majority of Christians, the speech of Christ that I most ignore is the hardest to hear, *When you have done it to the least of these, you have done it to me.* And by *these* he means all the poor, the sick, every soul in prison, every suffering child.

Even the famous saints pace the moral cells that their cultures provide, give or take a few inches. They differ from us in only one dimension—their cells lack ceilings; they're open to height. If Ida had turned against the roots of her time, place, class and religion, she'd have turned in a vacuum and—worse—she'd have quickly been silenced, if not driven irretrievably mad, before she could do the good work that was open to her (one big piece of which, her care for black Grant Terry, I'll speak of later). Instead she lived in a straitly bound world through which unseen forces guided her to walk with all the mercy at her disposal.

I've paid slim notice to Marvin her husband. His work was the management of two farms and occasional deals in timber, and those seasonal jobs left him at home a good part of the time. So his tall deep-voiced body was another steady presence in the house and a real part of its calm. After Ida's breakdown the sadness of his life from middle-age onward was his inherited and untreatable deafness. From here I can wish I'd known Marvin better and gone with him some days to estimate timber or visit his farm. But he never asked me, and I never pressed. The deafness likely made him feel a poor guardian, and I silently joined the family's gradual withdrawal from the effort to communicate. It seemed only polite not to force his dead ears.

Yet he continued to preside at the crowded table, over food he paid for. He took every chance to rock on the porch with my parents and his own descendants (who were, after all, at their winning hilarious best more often than not). He followed the war and farm news obsessively, with a cupped ear to the radio speaker; and he managed to laugh at eighty percent of all he heard, not in bitterness but ready amusement. Though I was born too late to watch the change, that final Marvin was greatly changed. Years earlier apparently he'd done his own share of drinking and indulged a destructive temper. Once he blinded a black employee who challenged him to fight. But the silence of his world—joined to Ida's long years of anguish against him, which surely devastated any physical bond, not to mention his impotence to help his sons—all those managed to tame him at last.

Whatever an unbiased view might have seen, by the time of my memories, Ida and Marvin moved round each other with unbroken tolerance and the barely acknowledged affection of old work-animals. Many times my mother granted Marvin's patience in the years of Ida's ordeal, "When Ida was not herself, nobody God ever made tried harder than Marvin to bring her back. He'd say something gentle; she'd strike out at him like a cornered snake. Many's the time I've seen him turn to hide a tear, but never once did he raise his voice or show one sign of hurt or anger. If

God hasn't got a golden crown reserved for Marvin, then count me out."
My own sense is that, whether or not his own past harshness or some
aspect of his sexual need contributed to the triggering of Ida's collapse,
his hard-won patience and a grateful love that was plain to see made it
possible for Ida to recover in the safety of her birthplace, not in one of
the brutal asylums of the day.

The evidence of my eyes was all on the side of unbroken thanks and
loyalty between them. I stumbled more than once into rooms where they
stood apart but in genuine laughter, their eyes locked warmly; and Marvin
never showed me a sign of jealousy for what his wife invested in me,
even if my birth brought her a calm beyond his power. The deafness
might well have embittered him; instead he chose to accept its inevitability, a condition of the fate of being a Drake and collaterally descended
from the pirate-explorer Sir Francis Drake. Yet from whatever desert his
lone mind wandered, Marvin always roused and met my visits with out-
stretched arms long as pony legs.

Though I lived beside him and Ida many days when they seemed to
pass only eight or ten syllables—*yes, no, what?* or *never mind*—I always
knew they came as a pair. To have Ida Drake, you also had Marvin close
there behind her, nearly twice her height and waiting intent in his own
silent head to catch her fall, if she fell again. She didn't, not even in 1956
when he succumbed to cancer; and she stayed upright in strong health
and clear mind for ten years longer.

Eight months after Elizabeth's death in the spring of 1965, one of Ida's
daughters-in-law phoned me from Duke Hospital to say they'd just
brought Mrs. Drake in with a heart attack; could I come? It was nine at
night; the hospital was twenty minutes away. But I had a guest and I
stayed home waiting for further word.

I was in a dark room when the call came at ten and Ida was dead. She
was two months short of seventy-nine; I wasn't surprised, and I felt no
trace of the incompletion I'd felt in my parents' early deaths. I went to
her funeral and saw her buried in the Rodwell-Drake plot beside Marvin
and her oldest son, her parents and brothers, with the greater part of her
cousins and friends not twenty yards off. Over them, and taller than anything else in Macon but the Methodist church and Egerton's Store,

stands a thirty-foot cedar, planted as a switch by my mother in her girl-hood. Still shocked from Mother's sudden early death, I left Ida's grave with the sense that one life anyhow had ended in its own time, at home among kin.

But for days I felt a sounding desolation. I might have emptied my house that night and gone to wait with her sons and their wives in one more hospital corridor where the light itself is lethal to hope. But I hadn't believed she was dying. Maybe the nurse would have let me see her and repeat the thanks she already knew, most likely not.

Anyhow in her last three years, she'd seen my first novel, my first book of stories and said she was proud, though I wonder how many naps it took her to finish two consecutive pages. If she read ten pages of either book, she saw how the roots of solitude that she planted in me were free-standing trees now, living on daylight and springs in the Earth. She might also have caught, in the close and utterly vital exchanges of blacks and whites, mirror-flashes of what I'd learned in her crowded kitchen, watching her and Mary Lee at work—struggling blindly to make from courtesy and small attentions a usable bridge over that deep gulf which neither had dug.

If Ida failed to see all I wrote, or again to hear the questions I asked, she can't have failed to know what I told her in words and acts since the day she took me from the doctor's hands, squalling and spent in a night-long labor. She knew she stood at the head of my heart, beside my father and mother, not below them.

3

BLACK HELP

GRANT TERRY, FLORA RUSHING, MARIAN ANDERSON, MANY MORE

FROM NEAR THE FIRST, I remember thinking that their skin was beautiful, especially the smooth two-toned hands. I remember their clean but different odor, as if they were made of a powerful metal— something finer-grained than our fragile skin. I remember their gentle voices and the rub of their stiff starched clothes. The first black face I remember came later and belonged to Doretha Bumpass. I was three, we were living in Roxboro in the first house we had to ourselves, and Doretha was our cook. But she wasn't the first black person whose care I received. A black midwife helped the doctor at my birth; the house I was born in had a fine black cook, and a black man worked outside in the garden. In one of the first pictures of me, at three weeks, I'm held by a black woman. And in other early pictures, I'm standing at a well or walking through flowers with a young black woman named Millie Mae Bobbitt and her brother John Arthur, my playmates.

None of that was unusual for a middle-class white child in eastern North Carolina from the early 1930s down into the early sixties. It didn't mean that my parental families were wealthy; they were well-spoken people of comfortable standing, but numerous children had left them no surplus. The Depression was lowering more heavily each month above them. But Warren County was more than sixty percent black; there was an abundance of able candidates for any domestic job, whatever the conditions and however low the pay. I can't be far wrong in recalling that any number of skilled women would come into your house, cook three hearty

In the garden with John Arthur Bobbitt, my first playmate, Macon in the summer of 1934. Will and Elizabeth are renting rooms from Marvin Drake's widowed sister, Winnie Reeks; John Arthur and his sister Millie Mae live a few yards away.

meals, do a little light cleaning and help with the children six days a week for maybe five dollars and edible leftovers—twenty dollars a month, the equivalent maybe of two hundred dollars now, with another thirty dollars in her own meals and the leftovers.

Even so, my young parents were too strapped for money to hire anyone; but they benefited from the presence of black men and women in their two nearby family homes and in the widows' houses where they rented rooms. Their troubles were individual and marital (Will's drinking, Elizabeth's fear); and later in calmer years, they often spoke of the friendship they felt for the black men and women who helped them through the bad times.

They never called them *black* of course. At the time, members of the Negro race in North Carolina would have heard *black* as a harsh insult. The acceptable word was *colored* or *Negro*. And the latter word was pronounced *Nigra*, not at all to suggest *nigger*, as so many ignorant reporters have tried to suggest, but because in Southern dialects the vowel *e* is frequently pronounced as a short *i*—as in *tin* for *ten*, *min* for *men*, *intrance* for *entrance*. Listen for the word *Negro* in recordings of Martin Luther King, and you'll hear the same vowel shift. And though my parents were at constant pains to be civil to every black they met, and though they chided me fiercely when I once said *nigger*, my parents held to the racial assumptions of their culture.

Their version of the assumption was the least vicious possible in their class, region and time. It held that the white and black races were profoundly different from one another, physically and mentally, and that the differences were probably innate. Whites were generally held to be more intelligent and resourceful, though many whites were acknowledged to have sunk below their racial standard and some blacks surmounted theirs. The Jim Crow laws and customs that followed in the wake of the Civil War, Abolition and Reconstruction decreed a near-total separation of races in matters of domestic life, public accommodation, education and all else. But Christian ethics and human decency demanded a stylized courtesy to all black people and charity to those nearby.

In adolescence when I began to ask awkward questions about the justice and consistency of the code, Will and Elizabeth would acknowledge

a few absurdities—that it was permissible, say, to eat in close proximity
to blacks when all the eaters stood up or were outdoors; but indoors the
races must eat in separate rooms or separate corners if rooms are scarce.
And they quickly recoiled from any news of racial violence. When Will
took me to see *The Birth of a Nation* in 1940, he explained that the
origins of the Ku Klux Klan in the lawless days of Reconstruction were
understandable, though he regretted its present sporadic activities.

Will also told me that his own father, my wryly comic grandfather,
had once prevented a lynching. That same Edward Price was born and
raised only a few miles south of Southampton County, Virginia—the
scene of Nat Turner's slave rebellion, and only forty years after its quick
but appalling thrust. And though my grandfather lived his adult life in
a largely becalmed time and place, Will told me more than once that his
father died in the 1920s, tormented by deathbed visions of a bloody race-
war. For my young parents then, despite the excesses of whites or blacks,
truth was truth—blacks were not whites, could not be expected to be, and
no good could come of pretending otherwise.

Despite Edward Price's visions of a black Armageddon, my family's
allegiance to the code did not proceed from conscious personal evil or
present fear. With a single exception in the two generations before me,
none of the Prices or Rodwells was directly involved in farming; so they'd
had no need for large numbers of black field-hands. And since Warren
County in their time was as peaceful as a day-old glass of water, they
had no apparent cause for fear. They were the modestly educated children of their time and place, a time with hard living memories of a desperate civil war fought visibly among them—a war in which 180,000
Confederate soldiers died, mostly on a devastated homeground. So their
racial convictions were socketed in an unthinking acceptance of tradition.
*Our beloved forebears and the Bible teach us this—we live as we live;
blacks live as they do. We mutually amuse, love or hate and serve each
other. It has always been thus and always will be.*

Unlike many terrified whites in the early days of the civil rights movement, Will and Elizabeth were not concerned with defending their
tradition by resort to the Bible or to fascist anthropology (there was a
large Southern literature dedicated to proving the anatomical and mental
inferiority of blacks, but my parents were uninterested). Though they'd

begun to register the first small changes in their world toward the end of the Second World War, when thousands of black men returned from overseas with their mustering-out pay and their eyes more open than ever, Will died too soon to see the unimaginable results.

When Elizabeth survived to watch Dr. King's march on Washington and to hear him revealed as the most pointed and eloquent orator since Lincoln, she was ambushed by the readiness of her mind and heart to be changed—or not so much changed as repaired. A strange black man had phoned and asked her to join a protest march. She said to me proudly "I told him if I wasn't blind and lame, I'd be there beside him." I knew she meant it, though most of her friends would have thought she'd also lost her mind. By the time of her death in the spring of 1965, she'd told me fully of her sympathy with the movement. But if you'd confronted either of my parents at a much earlier time, each might have taken refuge in the common defense, heard often then—if colored people have been this miserable all these years, why haven't they told us sooner?

As far as it went, their defense had a point. Like the majority of Southern whites of any class, my parents were not highly educated nor were they deep readers. They both graduated from high school in a system that ended with the eleventh grade. They never traveled outside the South before middle age. The state's best newspapers, the radio and—most shamefully—the Christian pulpit made no effort to persuade them otherwise. And what was overwhelmingly the important thing with them as with Ida—they'd never heard a word of black complaint. Again the only audible contrary word from blacks of their acquaintance was an apparent reluctance to work on weekends and a feckless attitude toward Monday mornings. But those were looked on as labor problems or a racial failing—certainly not as a trickle of smoke from a vast covered fire of resentment or worse, a fire that had smoldered since Dutch traders sold the first abducted black Africans into Jamestown, Virginia (some eighty miles northeast of our home) in 1619. Almost incredibly, they never considered that black complaint was generally balked by the certainty of white retaliation.

If a non-Southern American had told my parents and their kin, in simple justice, that they were utterly deaf and blind to an enormous evil in their midst—in their own houses and hands—they'd have told their judge that they spent far more time in the intimate and mutually caring society of blacks than anyone north of Washington or west of Missouri; and they'd keep to what they knew, thank you kindly. What my kin might have been expected to guess, but didn't, was that many of the blacks they worked with were anciently inured to their plight. Like the practiced existentialists they were forced to be, these captive people had taken their plight—moment by moment for more than three centuries—as the cruel but bearable shape of their fate, like August sun or a February night: agonized, tragic, calamitous but *there* forever.

Martin Luther King was only four years older than I; our exact contemporaries were the pivotal generation in the seismic racial changes of the 1960s. And anyone hoping to understand the background of our crucial generation must make a broad imaginative leap and, above all, suspend condemnation for now. We suspend it after all when speaking of cooler, more distant figures like Moses and Isaiah, Socrates and Aeschylus, Cicero and Vergil, Jesus and Paul—all of whom lived in and achieved their work in dense webs of slavery, though none of them appears to have attacked its inevitability.

From the time Will got his first decent job, door-to-door appliance sales, he and Elizabeth were reliably funded for the first time in their nine years of marriage. With Elizabeth's strong dislike for housework and her restless love of movement, we soon had the cook I've mentioned—Doretha Bumpass, whom I called "Duck" (a *Duck* and a *Ducker*: my naming faculty was clearly limited). In our photographs Doretha looks younger than twenty. Youth would explain my few quick memories of her lightness and laughter. Mostly I recall the sound of her high long whoop of delight and the pleasure I took in holding and studying her mysteriously two-toned hands—matt ebony on one side, polished beige in the palms. And I have one fragmentary image from the family's most often repeated and affectionate memory of Duck.

We'd left home for the hour's drive to Macon; Duck was going to wax the kitchen floor after us and then lock up. A few miles out of town, Will remembered he'd left his pills (a night without laxatives was unthinkable, though everyone in Macon was equally well-stocked and could have sup-

Mary Green in Macon, 1959. I've driven up in my black Volkswagen to see her. She tells me she used to cook for my young grandparents, "Mr. Jack and Miss Liz, for a dollar a week and all I could eat. Used to walk to work from way up yonder by the river every day. Started way before light." She's unsure of her age; but since my grandparents married in 1884 when Mary was grown, she may be more than ninety-five here. In that case, she was born a slave. But all the final times I see her, I can never ask (maybe in those days before the civil rights movement came to Warren County, I think the question would be harsh or demeaning). Today in the first three pictures I take, Mary laughs or smiles. Only then does she settle into this admission of the time she's had. Yet when I ask what the safety pins are for, she gives me her best laugh, "In case I need a *pin*." Then she calmly announces she's picked cotton all day long, all week.

plied him). We turned round and, back at the house, I ran in with Will to get an extra toy. Then a strangeness—the bathroom door was shut, and behind it there were noises. It was a time when you didn't automatically expect the worst, murderous burglars. So unafraid, Will turned the bathroom doorknob, strode in and triggered a girl's high voice "Lord *Jesus!*"

Duck was naked in the tub, in mountains of suds—which is all I can see, her wet skin in snowy bubbles. Will begged her pardon, got his pills; and we raced to the car to tell Elizabeth. What I didn't catch for years was the point of their laughter. They liked Duck's nerve; who'd have guessed she'd do it? (The big majority of white families then would have been a lot less than amused to find a cook in the tub. In a time when infectious diseases were largely untreatable, the persistent white anxiety was that a cook might bring disease to the house—TB, typhoid or, the terror, syphilis on a toilet seat. Hence the frequent insistence that cooks get "health certificates" from the County Health Office.)

My substantial memories begin with our next town—Asheboro, a hosiery-mill center and a real promotion for Will in the Power and Light. We lived at first in small apartments and went through fast relays of short-term cooks (few black women had cars, there was no city transport, so your cook either walked or you fetched her). I recall only two names, Mildred and Tossie Mae. And I recall once going with Mother to find Tossie at her house, an unpainted hut jacked up on rock stilts at the crest of a steep incline. I thought it could blow downhill in the night with Tossie in it, but I knew not to say so. It was my introduction to the differences in white and black housing, though the memory comes with no moral strings attached.

Those strings begin to proliferate with my first prolonged experience of a black man. While we were living in a five-room apartment on Cranford Street, Will sent for his black friend Grant Terry. With Grant's arrival I began storing sustained memories of the most important black presence in my life. His first name, presumably for the Union general, and his age indicate that he was born into slavery or shortly after Emancipation. He didn't know his age; but when Will put him on the welfare rolls in 1939, a doctor had to swear that Grant was past sixty-five. After a thorough examination, the doctor said he was well past seventy.

He told us little about the six decades of his life before we knew him. His home town was Chatham, Virginia where he had a wife and a son named Felix. At some early point, he heard of paying jobs in North Carolina. He made his farewells, telling his family he'd "see them in Heaven if not before." Somehow—by train or on foot—he got to Raleigh, where he worked for a Mr. Lassiter who was "paving the streets in all that part of the country." Soon Grant's uncanny manual skills and his loyalty raised him to the rank of foreman. And in the 1920s the Lassiter Company brought him to Halifax County, where he met a young woman whom he loved at once. She was from Macon in the neighboring Warren County; Grant followed her there and they settled down. In that village of vegetable and flower gardens, his carpentry and his botanical sorcery were soon in demand.

One of the women for whom he worked was Winnie Reeks, a sister of Marvin Drake and a widow with whom my parents took rooms shortly after my birth. That was when Will began to form his intricate lifelong attachment to Grant, a trust and an affection that was mutual and that lasted the rest of their lives. At the time of my parents' meeting Grant, he was already known by white people as Uncle Grant, a clear acknowledgement both of his age and their admiration for him. Despite the fact that babysitters from outside the family were unheard of then, and that Ida was only a mile away, Will and Elizabeth told stories of Grant's staying with me when they took social excursions.

One such time they returned later than usual, stopped the car in the yard and looked through the lighted window to see me wide awake so late, standing in my high-sided crib and dancing to the tune of Grant's harmonica. Mother described it more than once, "He'd play it awhile and you'd dance. Then he'd knock the spit out on his thigh, hand it to you and you'd play for him to hop around. Poor Mrs. Reeks thought the house was falling down. A week or so later, you caught gingivitis—your gums swelled so bad they covered your few little teeth—and somebody said Uncle Grant's harp caused it, but Will and I knew he was way too clean."

The bond between Will and Grant was firm, long before my birth. Once I was there, at rare moments the bond might loosen to let me between them or at least to let me watch. But to the end Grant and Will were the magnetic poles; the central current ran between them. When I was four, soon after we got to Asheboro, Grant came for what was literally a visit. I say *literally* because it's the only occasion I recall, in my own family or elsewhere near us, when a black person paid a purely social visit to a white family. We had no yard or garden; beyond washing dishes, Grant didn't do house work or car repair and he couldn't cook. He and Will simply missed each other and arranged to remedy the problem.

Will and I met him at the bus station, his tallish body (no ounce of fat) coming out last with the unhurried grace and self-possession of age and its necessary care. His bright tan face would have been taut with worry till he saw Will Price; then both men grinned and slowly walked to meet, me close by Will. I'm all but sure there was no touch, not even a handshake but not because the code forbade it. Will, all his life, sought friendly touch; so the choice was Grant's, a delicate self-imposed restraint. He'll have marked his greeting with two slow signs—the excellent grin and a sweep of his hat, which he chiefly wore to hide his shaved head (though he shaved in the first place to hide his white hair, "Can't show my ladies this old-man wool").

I can't see his clothes; but I know he'll have worn his perpetual uniform for work or ease—a narrow-brimmed brown felt pork-pie hat, khaki trousers and shirt, both starched and pressed like new cardboard; no tie but the collar button fastened and the collar wings pinned through neatly with a silver bar; suspenders, no belt and spotless hightop leather workshoes.

If he kept to form, he'll have paused to pull out his pocket watch and study it slowly to judge the bus—an exact precision in time-telling was urgent to him. Then he'll have held the watch toward Will and tapped the crystal, "Twenty-two minutes of seven o'clock; supposed to been here eight minutes ago. Beg pardon, Mr. Will. Reynolds, you looking spry." I probably gave a wiggle-dance of deep delight to be among them. His only luggage will have been a neat grocery-bag with changes of clothes.

We took him straight home; he'll have greeted Mother with what he thought a compliment, "Miss Lizbeth, your hair is nice and *long*," which can only have meant a trim was overdue. We stood to watch him eat a hot supper at the kitchen counter, and then we drove him to his sleeping place. Since our apartment had only one bedroom, Will had rented Grant a bed in a black neighborhood called simply "The Hill." But for however long he stayed on that first trip, he spent his days and evenings with us. I've said that we had no real work for him, so what can he have done with the time? (There was only one story. One evening my parents went to a movie, leaving me with Grant. Afterward they stopped by to see Bill and Sarah Headen, and Elizabeth phoned home to check on Grant and me. I was already in bed and couldn't respond. And it hadn't occurred to Mother that Grant had never used a phone, might never have seen one till this visit; so it rang a disturbingly long time. Then at last he answered with three loud words—"They ain't here"—and hung up.)

My memory says he sat all day in the kitchen or, when Will called him, in the breakfast nook and talked in his grave way with whoever passed, of whatever age, station or color (he always called black women "Miss" So-and-So). That's not to say he was incapable of glee. Glee was an emotion he generally announced by a slap of his leg and a cry of "*Great* God A-mighty!" It was on this trip that Elizabeth told Will to ask Grant to go lighter on the use of God's name; Reynolds was beginning to shout "God A-mighty!" in awkward places.

At night after we'd finished our separate meals—we in the breakfast nook, he in the kitchen—Grant and Will would sit and listen to the kitchen radio deep on toward midnight. Often they'd sit for long minutes listening to a program as abstract to them as calculus—say, the news in Spanish on Cuban shortwave. They'd let the announcer machine-gun awhile; then they'd break up laughing to the point where Elizabeth might show quiet jealousy by toning them down. (Oddly Grant's visits were the only times I remember a sense of rivalry on her part; Will often showed how bad he felt about her charm over men. And later Will's sisters insinuated their bemused puzzlement at a friendship extending to unprecedented social visits over so much space. Otherwise Grant would almost surely have lived with us wherever we went.)

My own fascination with him began a few years later; till then I'd enjoyed him as a babysitter. He strained to find ways to amuse me; but the truth was, he wasn't much interested in children, white or black.

Though he often called me "darling" and treasured a fine pocket knife, he never whittled a thing I could play with. His own view of the world was animistic, not childlike; so his patience with childish talk was limited. He apparently had no store of folk- or autobiographical tales that he felt compelled to share with a boy. And since his clothes were so immaculate, even after a day in the yard, he refused any suggestion of roughhouse.

But when I was six and ready for school, we moved into the only house my parents ever built. It was three miles outside Asheboro, among rocky hills that in Europe or the Mideast would be called mountains. The realtor's name for the neighborhood was Dogwood Acres, and it's now a crowded suburb but we were pioneers. In 1939 there were few other houses, and on every side there were deep stretches of hardwood and pine and clear small streams.

Our white-brick house was small. Bill's arrival was two years off; and I had the only extra room, my first private space. But there was a small clean furnace-room off the kitchen; there were large yards and a vacant field on one side and woods on the other three. Will had precise and immediate plans for landscaping; and since wartime food shortages would soon be serious, the government was urging every patriotic family to plant a Victory Garden. So I'd barely unpacked my shelf of Big-Little books before Will sent for Uncle Grant.

In memory Grant seems to have lived with us for all of our three years there, but the likely truth is that he paid us several long visits. He had the red-clay lawn in golf-green state in short order, and he kept it as carefully. In that time of manual lawnmowers, he respected ours like a Damascene sword—tuning it numerous times a day, honing the blades with the various files he required for proper upkeep. Once he'd pushed the balky mower, he'd stow it like a live baby, then squat; and duck-walking for hours, he'd fine-trim the stray grass with his pocket knife. He'd gently rake the hay into piles and wheel it to the garden to mulch his prize vegetables. All his other work was performed with a similar deliberation that amounted to majesty and that seldom permitted playfulness. (Elizabeth once saw him pause in raking fall leaves; he was watching a particular limb. In a moment the single leaf he was watching detached from its limb and sailed down slowly. Grant watched it come, made a graceful leap and caught it.)

Grant Terry on a visit to us in our apartment on Cranford Street in Asheboro, 1938. A year later our doctor will estimate his age at well over seventy, setting his birth also on the cusp between slavery and freedom. This is almost certainly his only picture; and though Will begs Grant to pose, he hides the face that later I'll see is a twin to the face of Akhnaton, the monotheistic pharaoh of Egypt—the same unearthly fearless calm and all-seeing eyes.

So I avoided him during the work-day—not considering that, since he was already over seventy, his lock-jawed focus might have been a way of forcing old joints through painful hours. I was also years away from understanding that benign work performed with his degree of fierce pride is its own art, unimaginably different from the vacant choring of millions of workers far better paid than he (he was fearlessly vocal in his scorn of careless white repairmen, even of the cavalier way our white neighbors used our tools and implements). That his proud work on our land was meant as an image of his love for Will is inescapable, an image as transient as grass and flowers but perfectible and renewable.

Only when he'd finished supper, washed all our dishes at his own insistence and was back in his room would he unbend enough to talk a little with me. I was too young to have the sense to ask about his fabled past; instead I'd show him my drawings and ask him to hear my tales of grade-school joy and grief. They must have seemed as extraterrestrial and encoded as any transmission from Arcturus. He would seem to listen though, his brown eyes hazed almost to blue with age; and occasionally the great pharaonic skull would nod, his dry lips thinning down in lieu— I guessed—of a smile. But he almost never questioned me, he seldom laughed; and while he never seemed bored with my presence, I've said he was no obliging Uncle Remus. With a slow politeness, he generally managed to let me and Elizabeth know that we got in the way.

If Will joined us though, then he and Grant would share stories of their own times together before my birth—often the long and mishap-laden nocturnal rides in Will's Model A. I never heard them say why they'd taken the rides, and it was some time before I understood that Will was out hunting a bootlegger and that Grant was along for company and protection in case of trouble (Will was convinced that he shared his mother's weak heart).

Then we'd listen to the war news on the radio Will had bought for Grant; or Grant would tell stories of his foreman days with Mr. Lassiter— how they all but paved the state and how much he was trusted, how he bossed fifty men and paid them out every Saturday night in silver dollars. He never once mentioned Rhew, the woman he'd followed to Macon; she'd got a good piece of his money and vanished north. Elizabeth told me years later that, for a few years, Rhew would write him letters to say she was tired of cold weather and that, if Grant sent her the fare, she'd pack up finally and move back home. He couldn't read or write, but he'd think it over and bring Elizabeth the fare-money. She'd say "Grant, Rhew didn't come last time, you know." But he'd always ask her to send the money anyhow—it was nothing but money; he could make more of that. Strong and self-possessed as he proved to be, he made young Rhew his entire vision of why to live for more than ten years in his early old age.

We never knew when Grant quit hoping. But the letters stopped around the time I was born; and I've always assumed that, without much planning, his love of Will Price flowered then. Grant was some thirty-five years older than Will; for that reason and more, there was plainly no question of a physical expression between them. But their magnetized eyes, and their inability not to laugh when together, proved that a lot of what they sought in one another was the mutual shapes they made in a room, the prints of their faces and bodies on the air. It was no private delusion either. Recalling them from here, I can see that Grant had the stronger, better-tended face. But for me then—far apart as they were in age, color, bone-type, history and education—they were both as good to watch as any two dignified wild animals, hunting their diet and consuming it whole.

It should be clear by now that they also shared pain—Grant's unmet longing for Rhew, Will's blighting thirst to drink. By the time Grant joined us in the new house, both issues were moot; but I strongly suspect that the reason I sat beside them long nights, watching nothing more lively than two grown men at the radio, was my unconscious sense of watching two creatures heal one another or honor themselves for a healing accomplished.

The radio, incidentally, was one of the few external goads to Grant's imagination. In the kind of thinking with which I still sympathize, he was never able to grasp the idea of invisible waves of broadcast sound. The only explanation had to be that tiny people lived inside the talking box and were responsible for its sounds. He would not, for instance, undress in the same room with a playing radio; and in the face of Will's explanations to the contrary, Grant continued to ask "When do them little peoples sleep?"

With her occasional unease at the smiling exclusion from Will and Grant's bond, Elizabeth granted their intimacy long after they were dead, "Your dad knew Uncle Grant had helped him through, and one thing Will did was never forget a soul that helped him. It wore him out but that was his choice." For me, the sight of the two there in the narrow cinderblock room—a yard apart, hearing the news in Spanish when neither of them understood a word of Spanish—seemed a lesson urgent to learn, a skill I'd need more than once in life. What provided the adhesion in their bond, I couldn't have told you then; but as a boy bound for manhood, I knew to respect it.

They were two human beings who seemed not to notice, certainly not to mind, the ludicrous and tragic limitations which racial custom tried to set on their friendship. Each had an overriding need for the other; and far from blocking their intimacy, racial bars may well have fostered it. They were just foreign enough to one another, sufficiently exotic to provide the polar gap which strong voltage leaps. They might not eat at the same table, especially if a white woman was present; they might not sit in the living room. But they could share bone-deep delight and pain the way two different creatures can, in those odd dependencies that sometimes grow between unlikely, even hostile tribes.

Grant was shut out—by his nature, fate or chance—from the dream of solace in a fruitful marriage. After he resigned himself to Rhew's departure, he loved at least one other young woman in Macon. She would come to his house at night and sit with him for hours. We never knew the extent of their intimacy, but they never kept house. And as loneliness descended, the walls of Grant's nighttime solitude were blanker for his lack of education. He could turn the pages of *Life* magazine or the Sears catalog, with its all-white models, for hours on end; but the words were as useless as logarithms. He might listen endlessly to the radio news, the story shows and comedy hours; but circumscribed as his world had been, what can those visits from Hollywood have meant? How he survived those thousands of solitary dark hours without the aid of reading, television, sex or any other known diversion is another secret he left unexplained.

Will had a wife and two sons in reach. He read the newspaper and, on rare occasions, a page of the Bible; yet now that he'd permanently weaned himself from drink, he still sought this old black man's affection. He got it, full-tide; and as best he could, he returned the force. All his years after, though they lived apart, Will kept a close ear on news from

Grant; and any need of Grant's that Will could provide was quickly delivered—a pair of new work-shoes, a dollar watch, a battery radio for his unelectrified house (when such a thing was a serious purchase and ate dry-cells like buttered popcorn).

When we returned to Warrenton for three years in the forties, Grant was living alone in a one-room house on the east edge of Macon. We'd visit him there—he in one straight chair, Will in the other and Bill and I on the neatly-made cot. I was aging past the point of curiosity about my elders; and I'd concentrate on the more bearable artifacts—an honest pine table made by Grant (and now mine), his watch and change on the bureau; the few magazines, soft as gauze from his careful poring, his spotless oil lamp.

And after we moved to Raleigh, and a finally-aging and lonelier Grant moved at Ida's invitation to another one-room house in her and Marvin's back yard, we saw him every trip. He could still do light chores and garden work; he nearly succeeded in growing grass in that dense oak shade and sandy soil. The rest of the day, despite Mary Lee's profound disapproval, he sat in a kitchen chair and responded to the household traffic with his own thoughtlessly majestic solemnity. He seldom ruffled the tenor of his way except to laugh with Will or, at rare intervals, to resent Mary Lee's envy.

Once Ida was sewing in the kitchen, heard a knock at the door and quickly stuck her needle into a cardboard cereal box and forgot it. Next morning at breakfast, when Mary Lee handed Grant the box and he discovered the needle, he leapt to his feet and shouted for Ida, "Miss Mary here trying to *kill* me, look!" The storm, like others, passed; and Grant stayed there some years, till he needed steady nursing. But by the time he was at Ida's, I was in high school, with all its searing demands; and even the human reminders of my too-recent childhood were hard to face. So once I'd made a courtesy stop on the aging relic, I was ready to leave Grant alone with Will.

There are taller-standing figures from my childhood whose faces are all but gone from my mind. In the absence of photographs, they may be no more than a chin, large ears or a glint of eye. There is only one known photograph of Grant, taken by Will; and his head is almost obscured.

But I can still see his final face as clearly as then, in Ida's kitchen—a perfect twin to the face of the pharaoh Akhnaton, the transparent skin like darkening varnish on his visible skull—and Will near fifty, a stout and satisfied boy in the opposite chair, leaning toward him.

I wondered *why* but held back from asking. And now I can guess no better than this. Will's father had died years before my birth. Will had a near-oriental respect for age, in people and things. Aside from Grant, he had no other older male friend except the Baptist preacher Robert Brickhouse, who'd helped him quit drinking. But Mr. Brickhouse had his own son. So Grant, who'd left his son Felix in Virginia, may have got the unexpended share of Will's great fund of filial care. Still no combination of feasible needs explains their unmarred length of devotion—two men on opposite banks of a canyon with arms that tried, every way they knew, to bridge the gap.

The night before Will's fatal surgery, he told me to sit by his hospital bed; then he made me write down the minimal facts—where he kept his insurance and how far it would go (not nearly far enough, as it grieved him to think; this man who'd labored to provide for his dependents died knowing he'd failed and that soon they'd be in need). When he got to the funeral plans, I said "Now wait. That's premature." But he said "Keep writing" and told me the rest—the undertaker, the type of coffin, a gravestone as much like FDR's as the budget allowed and the names of who should bear him to the grave: kin and in-laws and his one white friend Ray Jackson. Then he said "I wish it could just be Grant." Grant was alive, in an old folks' home, pushing ninety at least; but I knew Will meant it.

I also knew that their time together was as useful to them, and to me its witness, and as inexplicable to the rest of the world as any marriage in its fifth decade. Grant died shortly after; I went off to England and my first real mutual love. Then I began to understand their meaning for my future—*Life is short and often stingy; feast the heart with what it craves, short of cruelty, and let the world wonder.*

A friendship as powerful as Will and Grant's affected us all and went a long way toward changing my mind on racial division. Elizabeth's instincts were as kind as Will's; and her laughing ease with all the world let her move among black people easier than her sisters or any other white woman I've known. But her vast need for warmth was met by her family, so she had no enduring friendship that probed the racial line. And while some of my friends tell of intimate bonds between their mothers and black female companions, my memory contains many more examples of black-and-white friendship between males than females.

Mother and I would be in Macon in Edwin Russell's store; an old black man would turn from the counter with his next dark plug of chewing tobacco. He'd see Elizabeth, study her slowly till he found her old nickname and a smile broke loose, "Jimmy, Lord God, didn't know you at first—you stoutening up so good I didn't *know* you!"

She'd been called Jimmy or James throughout her childhood, presumably because of a tomboy nature; and for local black people, human fat was a beauty aid. But she ran a losing battle with weight and would lob him as good a shot as he gave, "Hey Ben, I see you been nibbling too. Those overalls would fit a damn bull." Then joint laughter.

Through the rest of our lives as a family together, we had a succession of black men and women in the yard and kitchen. Almost all were competent and pleasant, but only one lodged a place in our minds as Grant Terry had. We moved back to Warren County in 1944; and in short order, we had a new cook. She was Flora Rushing—young, again maybe not more than twenty, beautiful and stylish to the tips of her long red nails. An unusually light-handed cook and a willing housekeeper, Flora nonetheless showed us fast that she came from new stock. She did things her way, like it or not, which meant that she and Elizabeth knocked heads fairly often. It was not that they raised their voices in anger, only that they'd go rock-silent at unpredictable moments; and the local air would darken.

At one such point early in her tenure, when Flora was an hour late several days running, Elizabeth fired her. But after a two-month dismal search for Flora's equal, Mother had the courage to admit defeat, then drive out deep in the country to find Flora at her mother's and beg her pardon. (Bill and I rode with her; and as we were leaving, Elizabeth mired her new Studebaker so deep in the mud that we had to wait while a mule was fetched from up the road, harnessed and persuaded to haul us out, as Flora's young nieces and nephews watched with delight—a symbol of something enormous, no doubt, in human folly.) Flora was on time a good many days after that; and when we moved to Raleigh three years later, she came along for a week to help us unpack. And she came back seven years later to help with the work of Will's funeral.

Though Flora wasn't married, she had a young daughter. The father was in the Army in Europe, and Flora said she'd marry him if he got home alive "to give Ammabel a name." But another man, mysteriously exempt from the service, waited out front every night to drive her home. One freezing night when Flora was working late, she asked Elizabeth if Till could come in and wait in the kitchen. Elizabeth said yes and Flora went to call him. I'd always wanted to see Till's face; and when he walked through the side door, he nodded to me. He was shorter than I planned and maybe thirty; but his tight tar-skin was much darker than Flora's, which was golden tan; and a knife scar almost circled his neck. That made him even more compelling to my mind, and I wanted to go to the kitchen and study him, but Mother frowned me off toward my homework.

After that night, when Flora and I were at home alone, she'd sometimes crack the door of her life. I was thirteen by then and galvanized at any chink of light from the world of adult love. Oddly I don't recall a single confidence; but they mostly came in the form of deprecations or jokes with a sting, like "That fool Till thinks he runs my life; he can't even run that pitiful *car* without it miring way up to the axle every time we get on a country road; and country roads are all he's thinking, time I shut that door and sit beside him. Last night, damn if he didn't leave me in this thin dress with"—and here she'd shoot a glance to confirm that my parents were beyond earshot—"my titties freezing in a car cold as snow while he beat the bushes for some poor sucker with a tractor that could haul us out. What Till got to show me, ain't worth *that*; I told him he seen the last of Flora."

I'd nod and picture that scar on his throat and think what I'd never quite known before—this was where grown love could land you. Two nights later Till would be back again in the same car, waiting silent at the curb.

Once when I was even further on in my solitary introduction to sex, Flora asked us to watch her dance at the Hall. The Hall was a big un-painted child's drawing of a building perched on a steep hill, on dan-gerous stilts; and most weekends blacks would congregate to dance there. Will and Elizabeth said sure, we'd come gladly; and Flora spent the slack afternoon hours for the next few days, cutting and sewing a dress for the contest (she made all her own clothes). She even painted her glasses-frames with a matching color of nail polish—dime-store low-power magnifying glasses that she wore some evenings for the hell and the flair of it.

And on Saturday night we drove to the Hall, parked in a huddle of teenaged black men who seemed surprised but glad to see us. It hadn't yet occurred to me that they couldn't come to our Hall, if we had one; so I joined my parents and Bill in returning their greeting and threading through their dressed-up, close-packed bodies to the door. We knew that the Hall was the scene of frequent romantic blood-lettings; but there in the late forties, we entered with fearless ease—safe in our sense of a firm social order and drawn by smiling faces.

We found there was no charge for white spectators, so we climbed to the balcony above the dance floor. Again I didn't notice but now I see that the Hall was nothing but the rawest unpainted pine walls, ceiling and floor—no trace of a stage, no toilets: tinder-dry space. A single match would have sent it and all three hundred occupants up in resinous smoke. (To general amazement it's standing now, more than forty years later.)

I spied Flora right off, upright at the far side, whispering to Till. She was wearing her favorite color, lemon yellow—a scooped-out neck with some brand of ruffles. It made her look like the sun in childhood. Beside her Till looked ten shades blacker, but he had on a baby-blue semi-conservative zoot suit—a droop-shoulder jacket and sway-kneed pants pegged down at the ankle. Something about him kept me from calling out to Flora, though Bill made the attempt. It drowned in the din as the next round started, no band but a record player.

Only when dancers took to the floor did I notice the obvious. Till was one of the few grown men in sight; most of the males were barely my age, with a sprinkling of elders. The real young men were under fire in

Germany tonight or the South Pacific (the moment Germany surrendered, Flora's future husband—Ammabel's father—was shipped from Europe straight through the Panama Canal to fight in the planned invasion of Japan).

Why after all was Till around? Will whispered that he might have a penitentiary record, and about then Till and Flora moved. She'd never looked our way, and I was getting anxious—I wanted full credit for attendance. At first the music was slow; and all the dancers stood more or less in place and did the Shag, a slow and elegant warm-up. Flora had taught it to me months back, and she and I would dance a quick turn in the kitchen when Mother was gone; but this was the first time I'd seen it done right, with both of the partners (even scarred-up Till) cool and graceful as two tall waterfowl courting on a lake.

Then the music got faster; and in two more minutes, Flora and Till were left alone in the midst of the space for their own purpose. I could try a prose poem here, straining to copy the figures they made on a gapped pine floor and in three hundred sets of other eyes; but that would be an old routine. Enough to say they didn't go wild or dirty or mean; but somewhere after midpoint in the record, they signaled each other invisibly and spent the next minute changing into creatures till then unknown, in my mind at least. For all my high-stoked sexual guessing—and the drawings I'd made, in the absence of commercial pornography—something new and urgent as a gasoline fire was going *down* here before my eyes.

I'd seen a lot of musical-comedy movies since the thirties, the best of Fred Astaire and Gene Kelly; and I'd been to two black church revivals, with howling raptures when more than one sister got the Spirit and spasmed out on the floor at our feet, with flailing arms and purple tongue, or climbed upright over pews toward the preacher: "*Coming,* Jesus! Hold the train!" But I'd never seen bodies do what these did—Flora who'd be back with us on Monday, frying up breakfast, and Till with his ruined and rescued throat. Will nearly hit it when he leaned to say "Flora hasn't got a bone left in her body." She'd gone that fluid and yielding all over.

Down at the end though, she suddenly stiffened. The last twenty seconds she stalked at Till on tin-woman joints. He let her come on; then right at the end, he turned table on her and regained ground in long low strides. By the final blast she was bent over backward with her hair to the floor, and Till's nose slowly rubbed on hers like the Eskimo kisses we learned as children.

Everybody clapped, including us. If that was the contest, no question they'd won. But they didn't even bow; they loped to the sidelines and then out of sight. Flora had still never looked our way. We sat on through another half-hour of other good dancers but none like ours. We figured Flora and Till would be back or would climb to see us or beckon us down. But they never showed and when we left, the boy selling tickets said "Flora said hey."

Will said "When?"

"When they left out of here."

Will said "Going where?"

The boy laughed outright on a rank of fine teeth, "Flora carve my gizzard if I *look* at her, much less ask her plans." Some unseen boy said "Going to church, I heard em say"; and everybody fell out laughing, Will first.

In my pubescent wisdom I figured I knew why they'd left so fast, and Will and Elizabeth treated themselves to amused allusions. But on Monday morning, there was Flora on time—clear-faced, smiling, thanking us all for being at the dance and asking how we liked it. Will finally said "You sure-God streaked off somewhere when you finished."

Flora said "Mr. Price, I am *ashamed*. I wanted to climb up and see you all, but Till had to run get him a sandwich before the place shut. Y'all were gone when he finished."

Will said "That's all right, Flora. We had all the fun we could stand for one night."

Maybe all of us were wrong, black and white—spinning our spider-dreams around Flora; maybe Till really wanted a sandwich. She was that fine to watch though, that grand a prey to bundle tight in your mind's harmless silk.

In my mind at least, it seems about then that Flora began her signals to me. They were light and quick, never obscene but couched in wit; and it's possible they weren't real signals, just the unavoidable flares and flashes of a natural fire, over-read by a hot adolescent. But if my parents were gone, say, and Flora caught me unconsciously scratching my crotch, she might whisper "Sporty, leave that thing alone; *it'll* grow." Or when I began spending longer and longer times locked in the bathroom, "Some of the kidneys around this place are taking serious damage from you; it better be worth it when the great day comes."

The "great day" became our secret theme. It appeared to mean my sexual initiation. I honestly doubt that Flora imagined I might take the bait, if there was any bait. She'd joined us when I was still a safe child, there was no whit of evidence she felt drawn to me, and nothing but jokes even hinted she might have thought of obliging. God knows, I placed her in my crowded gallery of fantasy flesh; and we had the house to ourselves more than one hot slow afternoon. But only another American boy of that time will understand when I admit that at age thirteen— with Flora or any other woman nearby—the possibility of actual union never crossed my mind. Like all my known contemporaries, however I yearned for beautiful-others on the screen of my mind, for now I was glad to yearn alone, safe in the airless cave of my head.

Whatever I missed, I owe Flora thanks for another gift. My parents and both their families were far from prudish. They belonged to churches and took their faith seriously, but most of them saw no conflict between the open-hearted worship of a God who made their bodies and their own rich delight in such lovely facilities. So I grew up in a healthily sensual, ribald but never indecent world. To be sure, I'd heard of the terrors of the flesh—Will's sisters' sad choices, Ida's deluded but agonized pregnancy, Mother's bleeding labors, Till's scar and the razor fights at the Hall or the whole Young family. They'd rented our Warrenton house before us; and on our eventual premises—in drunken jealousy—Mr. Young killed his wife, then his adult son, then wounded his daughter and killed himself (a year later, our guest bedroom still showed neat bullet holes).

But a good deal stronger in the air around me was the general sense that grown people were drawn together by unseen magnets under their skin that gave them pleasure and fuel for life and that hurt no worse than the rest of the world. Years later, discovering the comic novels of Fielding and Smollett, I often felt that the atmosphere of both my families resembled that world of frolicsome ease more than the harsh prevailing wind from other parts of America—an ease poised knowingly on the lip of disaster and death.

When a large group of kin was gathered, sometimes Will would say "Children, run on outside and play awhile." We knew he was cranking up for the jokes he told so brilliantly; and if I left the other dumb kids after fifteen minutes and slipped back to hear the shank end of his tale, he never expelled me. I was often in total dark as to the point of everyone's laughter. (Instead of revealing my presence by asking though, I'd memorize the punchline and test it Monday, on the mill boys at school; they could usually help me.) But parents are parents; they still half-own you. As you hack your path toward the great day, the last thing you want from your parents is notice, a knowing look or word—"We're in this together." God in Heaven forbid; you want to enter this largest of all human rooms on your own vast head of live gorgeous steam.

Flora then was my bridge, my vivid guide—she and several friendly black children my age. She was pretty and kind; she was no more than six years older than me; she knew the whole secret of what was simmering in my body and mind, and she knew that I knew or was ready to know. If I didn't press on her to hand me the answer, she all the same showed me that a new young man, with no big pain or guilt at stake, could step on forward and find the answer, at a Saturday dance or in a dark car on a cold country road—even if, for Flora, the answer came with a face like Till's and his cut-through neck. Her unspoiled face and body further witnessed to the goodness waiting in sexual ease, and none of her exploits marred the voice for which she was also locally famous. To have Flora Rushing sing at your funeral was a high reward, for the living at least.

The matter goes much further and takes more explaining than anyone's managed, but here are a few preliminary sketches and questions. So far as we know, there is no native American strain of *Homo sapiens*; every known group appears to have migrated here from other continents. The one ethnic group in this nation who came here entirely against their will are blacks. Indians, Anglo-Saxons, Hispanics, Jews, Asians, Slavs and all others came with varying degrees of choice. Blacks were stolen and brought here in chains; even their sexual faculties were suborned to their masters, for the breeding of more slaves or for the enactment of a master's private dreams. Yet the most paradoxical of all their gifts to the South was sexual health.

Despite a narrow torrent of fundamentalist Protestantism from the late eighteenth century to now, and barring the odd sexual psychotic, the South remains the single large region of the United States which has fought off the sexual dreads of a decadent Puritanism that blighted, and continues to blight, many other regional cultures. To be sure, the white South has known its own erotic dreads and repressions; but set by the frozen sexual blast of New England or, say, American Irish Catholicism, the air of the South seems a mild caress and a robust laugh.

Our escape from the lethal hand of Puritan flesh-hatred owes much thanks to the black men and women who worked among us, who fed and bathed our bodies and—shamefully often—bore the lust of white men. Torn from the customs and codes of their own tribes and regions, subjected to foreign and evil laws and the sexual tyranny of their masters, black men and women nonetheless continued to show white Southerners that the flesh itself, when honorably used, is a healing power.

The Elizabethan Book of Common Prayer contains a clause in the wedding service whose frank audacity strikes me still. The bride and groom say to one another *"With my body, I thee worship."* At first it sounds breathtakingly blasphemous, a mutual human idolatry. But on slow study, the phrase seems to hope that the ideal marriage will grow from or toward a fleshly tenderness that in time becomes a guiding clue to the deepest mysteries of the Christian faith. How in this fragile dying flesh are we made in God's "likeness"? And why do the gospels and the letters of Paul insist that Jesus rose from death in his palpable, though transformed, flesh—in that same "resurrection of the body" which Christians assert in their creeds?

It was not from immigrant seventeenth-century English cavaliers, or indentured white servants, that the white South learned its wisdom of the flesh. It came to us slowly in the constant presence of a powerfully sane African people whom white Americans bought and used. Yet through every outrage they rose again strong; they warned us in their own sexual candor of the secret kinship in both our bodies' need and of the havoc which that need could wreak, if ignored or carelessly managed.

Plainly such candor was never intended as a lesson for the improvement of repressed white masters. It was an intricate compound of human need, African traditions and, above all, the endless resource with which black people invented their adamant freedom in the midst of bondage and the long hail of white sexual extortion. But since the masters and their families lived for more than three centuries in daily companionship with such a freedom, they could not escape hearing a magnanimous truth. *A human body, in the bounds of reason, is worthy of worship.*

I'm aware of awful dangers in the claim. At no other point are a white Southerner's unconscious racial assumptions more likely to surface. But since I've never encountered the point in any discussion of black-white relations; and since it's long past time for the white South to acknowledge one more huge debt it owes to its nearly four centuries of black companions, I'll take the risk.

One crucial reason for the white South's present wide lead in racial integration lies in the fact of a hidden and often monstrous sexual exchange between the two races. In every human sense—good and evil, sane and diseased—American slaveholders, with all their fear, were sexually drawn to black people from the absolute start. With whatever threadbare scriptural license my ancestors propped their claim to mastery, they saw in their hearts that they could not kill the radiant kernel of freedom that blacks had seized—even in the hardest throes of their bondage, even as they were helpless not to make more slaves for the fields.

To say as much is not to lapse into yet another vision of the noble savage or the lawless innocent. It is crucial however to grant that, in the absence of so many other freedoms and pleasures—and often obeying their own old codes—many black people made for themselves a broader view of the human body and the use of its splendors than any white Christian church could grant. There were, to be sure, black abstainers and ascetics; but the generally visible sanity won by slaves, and maintained at great cost, lent them a splendor and a secret force that transformed the merciless body-hatred that blighted so much of the white republic.

Is that secret a further hint to another mystery—how, despite the all-male Klans and lynch mobs, white Southern women were the chief conveyors of the racist code? They certainly were in my families and in the majority of those I watched. As white women were the group most fearful of the mental freedom of black men and women, so those women were inevitably—and with the immense tragic power to affect children—the custodians of fear and repression. Whatever the weight of any guess, and far more than Grant Terry could ever have dreamed—or Flora Rushing flinging her beauty to the ringing night—that bitterly paradoxical love of white and black is finally at work in the hope of justice.

One other black woman changed my life, the great contralto Marian Anderson. By 1946 or '47, the year I first heard her sing on stage, I'd studied piano for three or four years. I was already forming the enthusiasm for individual pieces and performers which is often an early symptom of a lifelong taste for music itself. Short of violence, it would have been difficult to be outlandish about Marian Anderson's gift. Her voice was one of the physical phenomena in the history of singing; and the instrument was deployed with a fervent intelligence, a linguistic mastery and a nobility of presence that bathed her in almost mystical light, an effect that might have been ludicrous if the audible result had not fulfilled the visible promise.

I must have heard her first on the radio; she was a regular on the Monday-night "Bell Telephone Hour." Then my father would have told me of the national incident that occurred in 1939 when the Daughters of the American Revolution denied her the use of their Constitution Hall in Washington. By then her European and American artistic reputation was established, and she'd won the special admiration of Eleanor and Franklin Roosevelt. So immediately after the Daughters issued their ban, Anderson was invited by Harold Ickes, Secretary of the Interior, to sing on the steps of the Lincoln Memorial. That recital was broadcast widely; and though it consisted entirely of music sung to a large outdoor audience, no placards or speeches, it quickly swelled in public imagination to become the first modern mass-demonstration for racial justice in America. And surviving recordings prove it to be without later parallel for unanswerable eloquence. With no word of comment Anderson peals out her first song,

> *My country, 'tis of thee—*
> *Sweet land of liberty—*
> *Of thee I sing.*

When I was thirteen or fourteen then and saw the announcement of an Anderson recital in Raleigh, I determined to be there. Neither of my parents was fond of classical music, but they never scorned it or failed to back my interests. And Elizabeth and I (with Ida and Cousin Joyce) were there when Anderson strode majestically to center-stage in Memorial Auditorium. As ever she folded her hands, shut her eyes and once again poured her phenomenal igneous voice through Schubert, Schumann, Brahms and Negro spirituals. Records and photographs of this tall beautiful woman had prepared me for admiration. But there in Raleigh near the thing itself, I was ambushed as never before. Life in small towns had limited my musical and dramatic experience to the movies, but I'd seen some bone-rattlers. Nothing in the past though, literally nothing I'd seen or heard, had moved me as much.

If I'd absorbed any of the racial convictions of my world—and how could I not?—I was changed down deep, in that one night. A woman had done it and mostly without words. I couldn't speak German, Italian or French; but I understood the spirituals,

> *They crucified my Lord*
> *And he never said a mumbling word—*
> *Not a word, not a word, not a word.*

In those two hours Marian Anderson led me through an immeasurably complex equation to an answer as simple and irrefutable as sunlight— God endowed this dark woman with this immense gift, the grandest I'd faced; the racial laws of the place I lived in, the people I loved, were wrong and evil. I would not obey and would find ways to change them.

Within two weeks I had a handcrank Victrola; and my father had bought me two of Anderson's Schubert songs, "Ave Maria" and "Aufenthalt." Within another two years I owned every in-print record she'd made (and forty years later, I have them all, clean and uncracked). Once a physically gifted singer has mastered the requisite technical and stylistic skills, the final indispensable quality that makes a splendid voice into a great singer is an unmistakable personal sound. A lover of voices can identify a past great singer at the sound of a single phrase, often a single note.

Even in her earliest recordings, Anderson's contralto can never be mistaken for another voice. She avoided the prime danger for large dark female voices—she never sounds mannish—and the molten richness of her lower notes was seamlessly bound to a girlish but never coy top. Yet through a long international career, almost unfortunately for her as an artist, she was as much a racial icon as a singer. But no other human proved a more impeccable image of surpassing excellence (I recall an interview in which Anderson was asked if she'd join a protest march against Alabama's white-supremacist governor. She said she would gladly sing for him). After my conversion in her presence, that racial aspect vanished for me; and I prized her as, first and last, a supreme artist— something I meant to be.

In 1948 or '49 she sang again in Raleigh. By then we were living there; and this time I met her, in a strange and doubly significant way. I attended the recital, had my earlier satisfactions deepened and went backstage afterward to stand in line for a word of thanks and a quick autograph. That seemed enough but two days later Will and I were dining alone at the downtown S & W cafeteria. I spotted Anderson's long-time accompanist Franz Rupp, eating alone at a single table. I'd never have had the courage; but Will, who hadn't attended the recital and was no enthusiast for vocal music, was dauntless. He approached Rupp politely and asked if Anderson was still in town. Yes, she was staying just two blocks away in the Episcopal rectory-home of her brother-in-law, Reverend Fisher.

Again there was no stopping Will, and his impetus won me. In ten minutes we were on the Fishers' doorstep on South Wilmington Street, only a block from Will's office. Mrs. Fisher answered and I politely asked to see Miss Anderson (recall what I've said about the informal rules of social visitation in those days; no one would have thought our unannounced appearance rude, inconvenient maybe but normal). We were warmly met. Miss Anderson was still in the back of the house at supper; would we wait in the living room? As we sat quietly in the small space, I realized what a startling experience this must be for my father, yet it was he who'd arranged it. He'd entered humbler black homes dozens of times on errands of friendship, charity or business; but he'd never called on any black man or woman who was so unquestionably his superior in all visible ways—this world-famed woman whom his son (and his idol Franklin Roosevelt) esteemed. Being adolescent still, I froze at the prospect of his committing an innocent rudeness. Surely he wouldn't call her "Marian"?

Suddenly she was with us; and we stood to greet her—a serene woman, then in her late forties, in a suit and blouse. Seen at eye-level and in a suit, not a velvet gown, she was shorter than I'd guessed, though her eyes were as strong. As with most such early meetings, I was too elated to preserve details. We all sat again; she asked about my love of music. Will said little but was thoroughly pleasant and passed every test. After a quarter-hour she said simply, and her speaking voice was unexpectedly light, that she must now go back to the family's guests but that I might come back tomorrow morning at ten, if I liked.

Liked? I was back at the stroke of ten. Again I waited in the living room; again she was suddenly and briskly with me. We sat and talked for twenty minutes. I'd read accounts of her life and work. I knew of the praise that had come to her from Sibelius, Stanislavsky, Toscanini and Bruno Walter. So I could have asked informed questions, but again my excitement blanked clear memory. I do remember wishing I could step to the upright piano, three feet beyond me, and lead her through the full scale of her range; but of course I didn't ask. She thanked me, wished me luck in my music and all my life. She had the further gift of speaking *at* you. She was nowhere else; her eyes were yours, for the time you were with her. Then I was back outside in the sun, with my signed album of her Brahms *Alto Rhapsody*, as happy as I could remember being.

She'd paid me the highest compliment you can pay a stranger, patient courtesy. What she couldn't have begun to sense was how far the respect with which she received a young white Southerner went toward validating my own ambitions to make—like her, with only the strengths of my body and the Spirit's inspiration—works of art. By then, for all that the South around me had decades of racial pain still to suffer, the fact of Marian Anderson's racial origin was important to me only in the credible radiance it lent to the sense of possibility she'd given me—credible because of my unbroken experience with black men and women before her.

At fifteen or sixteen my artistic hopes centered on painting. Within a year though, through fate or the luck of the game, I entered a junior English class taught by Phyllis Peacock. The first paper I wrote for her was a description of the voice and presence of Marian Anderson. She encouraged me at once. And under her steady discriminating goad, I began to write more prose and then poems. Before the school year ended, my artistic hopes had settled for good on language—stories, poems, plays and essays.

Through the few more years in which I lived with my parents, I proceeded with pleasure, much profit and little social doubt through an all-white high school and college; but with increasing awareness of offense, I attended white churches. And though I often aired my rebellious feelings at home and unsettled my parents, I never protested in public. Maybe my own conversion by uncomplaining helpers, and by a woman who sang both German *lieder* and the sacred songs of Grant and Flora, had left me too passive. My first defense now is that there were literally no visible means of public protest in the South in the 1940s and early fifties. Until black people made their own stand, a white Southerner who protested the divisions of his society had two options—to leave the region or to stay on, powerless, and hope for change.

In my last semester of high school, I made one of my first public gestures. I'd recently encountered a striking photograph of an old black man; and in response I wrote a poem that was one of my first to be published (my first published short story, written a few weeks before the poem, concerns a young white boy's awakening to racial injustice). The dated manuscript of the poem shows that I was a week short of my eighteenth birthday when I wrote it; and while its faults are apparent now, it throws light back to where I stood.

To a Negro

This is the dusty head of time
And all its beauty that is gone.
This is the face that first was made on a dark remembered day.
These are the hands that built the ships
Which vivid Helen's face sent forth.
And the dark, Babylonian slave beside
The waters where we wept when we remembered Zion,
Who hanged our harps without our hearts
In willows weeping by.
It is all the death of ages. Graveyard of a sacred race.

January 22, 1951

Admitted, the boy was working from a picture, not a live model; and he saw the old man as something of an aesthetic object. But the boy had living models in his mind; he showed that he already felt an obscure, maybe redemptive tragedy at work in black servitude; and he'd never heard remotely similar thoughts from anyone at home, from the local liberal daily or from church, Congress or the White House.

In Raleigh in the late forties, though the black neighborhoods were miles across town from us, we continued to have occasional black help in the kitchen and yard. One of the cleaning-and-laundry help was Margaret Banks, a light-skinned woman in her late thirties. She suffered badly with diabetes and would die early, but the suffering may well have contributed to the heat and brightness of her skewed wit and the pith of phrase in which she conveyed it. I was driving her home from work one afternoon; and as we proceeded up Glenwood Avenue, we passed several spots where the street department was, as usual, repairing wide holes in the road. I complained about their inability to work at some time other than peak-traffic hours, and Margaret said "Raleigh might be a nice town if they'd *finish* it." In general though, in moving to a city we'd lost direct contact with the rural world in which such pointed interchange was inevitable and welcome daily. From then on, the meetings would come otherwise.

In 1950 after a New York performance of *The Member of the Wedding*, I had a warm and funny meeting with Ethel Waters, whose portrait I'd drawn in her role as Carson McCullers' Bernice Sadie Brown. And in my third year of segregated college, November 1953—back in New York with friends for a Duke-Army football game at the Polo Grounds—I heard a performance of *Porgy and Bess* at the Ziegfeld Theatre on Sixth Avenue. Into the teeming midst of that particular Catfish Row strode a young black woman who shared my family name. She was Leontyne Price, in her first big role; and from the first, she sang with a voice like a shaft of unmitigated light that could nonetheless be watched, even tasted.

In that one evening she left me hoping—despite my fledgling moral sense—that the Warren County Price who took his family and his race horses to Mississippi in the nineteenth century might somehow have linked me genetically to such a stunning creature—"hanky-panky on the old plantation," as she later called the chance. Her sound and the figure she cut were entirely different from Anderson's but were instantly as unmistakable, unforgettable, troubling and consoling. (What if, hearing

Grant's one-room house in Ida and Marvin's garden. As age began to hamper Grant in his house in the woods to the west of Macon, Marvin bought this house and moved it here, fifty yards from the kitchen. Grant works an acre of flowers and vegetables with the creaky push plow; he chops firewood and warms himself by the kitchen stove. He'll stay here the last eight years of his life, then die in a nearby nursing home.

her there, far beyond me at the start of her unparalleled career, I could have known that—more than thirty years later—her rock-firm solicitude would help as much as any other friend's in a long tunnel of illness?)

A year later the Supreme Court struck down the old sham of separate-but-equal racial schooling and, by implication, the whole legal super-structure of segregation. I was in my third year of college; and the news amazed and excited me. I hadn't followed the progress of Brown vs. Board of Education; so the news struck me, as it did most of the nation, as incredible. I remember the stunned wrangles in my fraternity and my concealed delight at the rueful confiding tone of a vice president of Duke University as he said of the decision, "Now they've *got* us—all the Federal money we take, we'll have to obey."

The receptive ground on which a young white Southerner could aban-don one of the central convictions of his home and culture had been prepared since the day of my birth by a linked succession of courtly and generous men and women, some of whom I've described. (Should I add, for anyone who thinks I'm offering mass beatification, that I've known proportionately as many flawed black people as white?) And there were dozens of others—at home, on the street, on the sit-up-all-night Silver Meteor from Raleigh to Penn Station when kind old ladies would give me chicken from boxes they were taking to Nathan or Emily Ann in Harlem—and I tried to thank them all on the spot. God knows, they thanked me for the smallest good deed or word. And since my first sight of Marian Anderson, I'd known that the same skin could cover hopes as high as my own and achievements far higher. If those conclusions thud for you like whimpered but offensive cliches, then you weren't alive with eyes and ears in the United States in 1954.

Except for four years in England, I've never lived outside North Caro-lina, the state which sent more men to the Confederate Army than any other. Unlike a number of Southern writers in my generation, I never felt driven out of my region, whatever its wrongs. Despite the heat of close-up witness, I'm more than glad that chances and temperament let me stay. I monitored the civil rights movement with passionate sympathy from the first sit-in, which occurred just down the highway from here, at the Greensboro Woolworth's from which I bought my boyhood tin-soldiers. And I sat through hours of the impotent rant of kin, even loved ones—sad but useful hours in which I learned a lot about ignorance and all its links with fear and hope. I've said that I also had the great reward of watching my mother's changed understanding.

My commitment to the role of observer came mainly from my own nature and my close family-ties; but it was strengthened by a knowledge of James Joyce's prescription for himself—*silence, exile and cunning.* I'd be a resident exile, but the silence and cunning required that I partici- pate in no marches. I discussed my feelings freely with my colleagues, and I observed local boycotts. And with no attempt to evangelize my unreconstructed kin, when pressed I never denied my convictions. Maybe in the fear of my defection, or maybe because to their older eyes I was still a child, they almost never pressed.

Twenty years later though, I accept the charge that I might have found ways to be more actively involved in the heat of the struggle. I might but then I could never have moved with watchful freedom through the heart of the enemy, the homes and minds of those otherwise decent white men and women who had, with such mutilation to themselves, continued to dig and maintain the gulf for three centuries. No one who knew my published work doubted my allegiance with the demand for justice. It had been on display in much of what I published since 1949, but few of the old guard read the fiction written about them. I knew it and knew I was free to listen and learn.

Long after I left my family home and lost that easy but compromised daily contact with black people, I continue to have rewarding and far more equably grounded friendships with black men and women, espe- cially among my fellows in writing and music. With many of them, I feel a bond as complete as with any other kind of human being. I can go further—in my adult relations with black people, I find that we often communicate a good deal more easily and economically because we share a lifelong fluency in the ancient and mutually forged black-white South- ern dialects of speech and caring-mocking gesture, a speech that far sur- passes all other American dialects in its visual attentiveness, capacity for hardcore truth-telling and constant metaphoric delight.

Yet even in those benign friendships, there come moments when I see my friends' faces lock for an instant, and I know that I've scraped again on recalcitrant scars older than either of us. I remind myself I didn't invent, or consciously man, the old wrong. And I take an odd comfort in acknowledging similar failures in all relations—mine with others, theirs with me: instants when friends relax their care and treat one another as less than the explosive compounds we are, of past and present, with our own secret and still-fresh lesions. But because of the history of my native country, the willing involvement of my family and my own childhood in a blind and slow-paced evil and because of the huge debt that my life owes to black people—in a real sense to the race itself, its endlessly complex American strain—none of my failures give me longer pause than those I make on any heir of the people my own kin brought here in chains.

Macon Thornton near twenty-five years old, in Durham about 1911. Though he sat for the picture some twenty-five years before I knew him, it's the only good full-face likeness I've found. And even this early, the black eyes are steady and fixed in solitude.

4

AN ABSOLUTE HUNTER

MACON THORNTON

A CHILD WHO GOES ON into his thirties, unmarried and living at home with his parents is now thought strange. If he or she persists on the course thereafter, we begin to think we smell mental or emotional trouble, even danger. That's a new feeling in America, almost unheard of before the 1950s; and it says a sad lot about the rootless mentality that overtook us toward the end of the Second War. It says even more about the constricted set of sexual choices we agreed to accept in the wake of the dilute quack Freudianism that made its first wide advance in those same years of upheaval. And after the free-love revolution of the sixties, we were tyrannized by a code which prescribed that any unwed man or woman over thirty was tragic at best, psychotic at worst.

Before the soldiers returned from Europe and Asia in 1945, restless for movement, it was considered normal if one or more children in a litter chose to stay at home, tending the parents as they aged and in time assuming the farm or other family business. If the parents died and the children continued unmarried, only then were they referred to as old maids or confirmed bachelors. Unless the old maid was misanthropic to the point of poisoning the neighborhood dogs, she was looked on with affectionate condescension—"Missed the boat, poor thing; but she makes the loveliest quilts." And the pity was replaced by a certain awed thanks when the old maid worked usefully at the business of teaching school or running the county library. The bachelor, with his stamp (or money) collection, was almost invariably considered eccentric but harmless, unless he'd openly violated trust by stroking too young a girl or boy.

Otherwise until the late 1940s, a celibate life was considered a little to the right of normal but still an acceptable choice or condition (old maids were assumed to have no choice in the matter, even if they shared rooms with other old maids who wore neckties). Far from reflecting a puritanical Victorian constriction, such a view was broader than the "healthier" one which replaced it. The old view acknowledged celibacy not as an enforced and sterile fate but as a peculiar skill or calling (the French phrase that approximates "confirmed bachelor" is *célibataire de vocation*, a "celibate by vocation"); and it saw no necessary ill-health implicit in even more complicated arrangements.

There was nothing suspect, for instance, in brothers and sisters living together after their parents' deaths. Nor in two brothers or sisters keeping house. The combinations were multiple and each one assumed, realistically and admirably, that a brother might have found no one in the world whom he cherished or needed more than his sister; and if so and she agreed, well and good—it was nobody else's damned business, especially what happened when the shades were down, if anything but sleep. The richly functional combinations served as healthy models for a child whose experience of the great procreative family might well have prepared him or her for some fate other than marriage and children.

Southern fiction and drama have contributed to the current sense that celibate households were bizarre, even cursed. But there were several such real households in the midst of my childhood, and some of them burned with an oddly bright health. Five of my first seven school teachers were never-married women, and one of those married had obvious and alarming sadistic tendencies. My seventh-grade never-married teacher Jane Alston—"Miss Jennie"—was a mythic figure in our county, famed for kind sternness, didactic excellence and her height (in a time of small women, she stood a proud six feet tall; and I heard a bold boy ask her once, "Miss Jennie, how's the weather up there?"). I visited her rural home several times. She lived in Cherry Hill, a handsome antebellum country house that also sheltered her widowed near-hundred-year-old mother, a never-married brother and sister, a never-married aunt and a cousin with a speech impairment. Considering my already extensive experience of family love and strife, the six celibate Alstons were one of the happiest households I'd seen; and they remain so in hindsight.

But the home, other than my parents' and my birthplace, that affected me most powerfully was in my birthplace, Macon. It sheltered three Thorntons—two never-married brothers and a long-widowed sister. Their mother, who died before my time, was an Egerton; and through her connection with John Egerton Rodwell, Elizabeth's father, we were close cousins to the Thorntons.

One of the bachelor brothers, Frank, had served a thirty-year stint in the Army and returned home in my childhood. He was locally thought to be slow-witted. My own experience was that, whatever Frank's intelligence, he kept his own counsel so successfully that it was impossible to judge. In any case his only visible activity was alternate shifts of sitting on the front porch or walking the five hundred yards to Edwin Russell's grocery store and watching the eternal checker game in equally endless but apparently well-intended silence. He was seldom spoken to except by strangers or a recently returned native who'd forgot his nature.

At such awkward moments Frank would rise, offer a boneless hand for a one-pump shake; and his face would painfully arrange its extraplanetary guess at a smile. I was present once when someone asked what he did all those years in the Army; he eventually managed two words, "Messenger boy." Someone else, I trust, wrote the messages; for Frank's single message was silent, "Just watch." Because of my own family's bemusement and Frank's avoidance of us all, I made no attempt to enter his world. Yet from here I can guess, with more than surprise, that he was one of the models for the road I was laying one step ahead of my life (Frank also lent a trait or two to a similarly peripheral but wise character in three of my novels, the enigmatic but self-possessed and apparently contented Rato Mustian).

The widowed sister, Emma Thornton Nowell, was considered an exceptionally smart woman. She'd attended the Littleton Female Academy a few miles east and was plainly an authority on poetry, music, genealogy and history—framed in the hall was the original land grant, signed by the English Earl Granville, to our Egerton forebears. Yet she was badly afflicted with seasonal depression. From late fall till early spring, she hid herself at home. Her condition was unique in Macon and was called "the kinks."

Only the gravest errand could compel anyone to attempt to visit her from Thanksgiving till early spring, though she seems to have been under-

foot in her home. Anyone calling with business for her farmer-brother
was likely to glimpse Emma's narrow back, escaping to safety. But when
we looked out one morning in late March and saw her walking up the
road to church, someone could be counted on to say "Miss Emma's out
of the kinks." And so she would be—a fountain of intense, intelligent
and witty discourse till the next gray December. I know of no Indian
strains in her lines or ours; but she had Indian hair, jet black till her
death and with no help from chemicals. Her prominent facial bones
were equally unyielding. And that combination of a Sioux-squaw skull
with such a fund of genealogical information was magnetic for me. She
was the first, for instance, to tell me of our likely connection with John
Milton's Egertons, though she didn't know that the family's literary con-
nections went even further—Milton's Egerton, John, was the son of old
Sir Thomas, who was Keeper of the Seal under Elizabeth and Lord High
Chancellor under James I. Among his other acts he'd imprisoned the
young John Donne for eloping with Sir Thomas's ward Anne; hence
Donne's famed,

> John Donne,
> Anne Donne,
> Undone.

Two other Thornton sisters lived away; and one was hampered by a
paralyzed arm, the result of a stroke in childbirth. The never-mentioned
and never-married sister Lucy died before my time. But Elizabeth and
Ida often told me of her final torments of delusion. Lucy could see germs
crawling on everyone and everything; she'd order people to stay away—
germs were visibly swarming on their faces. Eventually she wore white
gloves for protection, but the germs won at last. Of another brother who
died young, my aunt Louise said "Doc may not have been afflicted, but
he was certainly backward in coming forward." And yet another brother
died in profound depression; so the old Thornton line—not the Thorntons today—seems to have had a genetic flaw that amounted to a curse
and rivaled any in Greek tragedy or modern Southern fiction and drama.

But the member who pertained directly to me was a healthy man, who
managed a long successful life. His name was Macon Thornton, after

his kinsman, Nathaniel Macon—"the last of the Romans," as Jefferson called him—who had lived in extreme simplicity a few miles east (I've said he was Speaker of the House under Jefferson). My friend Macon was always called by the first syllable of his name, pronounced *Make* but spelled by him as *Mac*. I'll spell it *Mac* hereafter; but the proper sound is worth recalling, *Make*. He was born in 1886; and by the time our friendship started, he was fifty. In his youth he'd worked in the two-story brick department store owned by his uncle Will Egerton, a driven collector of farms and forests (he was the first man I heard described as "land poor"). When Uncle Will died, his notoriously erratic widow closed the store. But Mac had inherited a part of his uncle's land, and the management of his in-law aunt's even larger portion; so he moved with ease from clerking to the management of thousands of acres of farms and woodlands.

Those were the boom days of bright-leaf tobacco; and even with the Roosevelt administration's quotas on acreage, by the time I knew him, Mac Thornton was a wealthy man. He was clean; he was a neat, if not stylish, country-gentleman dresser. He mostly wore ironed wash trousers, big-waisted for his moderate belly, with a shirt and tie. If he left off the tie, he always buttoned his collar. In the winter he wore a sport coat, never a hunting jacket or lumberjack shirt. I never saw him in brogans; year round he wore comfortably scuffed street shoes. He traded pickup trucks a little more often than most. But despite his being one of the largest landowners in the county, you'd never have guessed the extent of his holdings. And he'd never have told you. He gave no signs of miserliness; but like any self-respecting country squire, Mac's taste forbade the mention of personal finances.

The house in which the Thorntons lived was in sight of the Rodwell-Drake family home, three hundred yards west, across the tracks and the highway. Surrounded on three sides by rolling pasture, the Thornton house was nondescript but solid, two-story wood; and the little I ever saw of the inside was dim and gloomy. In all the years I knew them, I never spent more than a half-hour, all told, indoors; and that was to hear Miss Emma at the piano or to gaze again at the land grant (I never ate a meal or even a snack there; I doubt I drank a glass of water—eating was something the Thorntons seemed to low-rate). Once I glanced into Mac's bedroom, and I remember a *Life* magazine picture of FDR

on the wall and a single old hairbrush. Otherwise I either sat on the
front porch talking or wandering through the yard and pasture with
Mac. Or because of Emma's winter kinks, I avoided the place and met
Mac elsewhere.

The place to see Mac was in his truck and wherever else the truck took
us. In my early childhood visits to Macon, I'd see him on trips downtown
with Elizabeth, whom Mac also called "Jimmy." From the start I'd had
the true impression that the whole village, white and black, was more or
less in love with Jimmy or was at least in league to deck her with praise,
gifts and laughter. But Jimmy and Mac were special favorites of one another. When he'd been head-clerk at Egerton's Store, Mac let her in-
dulge in a fair amount of petty larceny—the soft drinks and pocket
knives that were beyond the reach of an orphan's budget. So apart from
our actual blood-kinship, my universally adored mother set me at birth
on an inner track with Mac. And by the time I began paying independent
summer visits to Ida, at age five or six, Mac and I were already friends.

At first he'd stop at Ida's on random mornings and ask if I'd like to
take a ride. Few Americans of that sedentary time refused the offer of a
ride—and on a hot summer morning with white clouds stacking, the
asphalt beneath us already bubbling, the acres of tobacco we aimed to
see were sucked from the ground by the visible moment.

Mac's man Joe would be driving. "Joe" was the nickname of Forrest
Harris, a strong young black man in his early twenties when I first knew
him. Joe had his own family and slept with them; but from dawn till
dark six days a week, he was at Mac's side, driving him to his scattered
farms and timber stands, tending the livestock at the homeplace and
cooking for the brothers when Emma was indisposed. The fact that Joe
looked more than half white may explain why Ida and a few other wom-
en, not Elizabeth, were almost resentful of him. In a day before most
black men sported mustaches, Joe wore one; and it probably contributed
to the look that got him called "insolent" more than once in my hearing.
But I liked him from the start. Joe laughed with me, never at me; and he
seemed all the better once I'd seen *Gone with the Wind* and discovered
that he was a dead ringer for the scalawag who nearly rapes Scarlett in
her carriage, outside postwar Atlanta.

Not only did Joe take me seriously; he possessed that prime virtue in a child's eyes, *readiness*. Joe would do anything I dreamed up. He'd saddle two horses and ride with me; or he'd let me practice with Mac's .22 against the barn door—anything my heart desired so long as he looked to Mac and said "Can we, Mr. Thornton?" and Mac said "Yes but use your damned head." (Only now do I recall that Joe never said the usual intimate "Mr. Mac" but the more formal "Mr. Thornton," as if they didn't spend twelve hours a day together all year.) I also liked the fact that Joe's skin had a wild copper glint, more like an Indian than anything else; and Indians, in their tragic decline, were one of my early fascinations. I took nothing but pleasure in the fact that both Joe and Miss Emma looked Indian and that Mac's black eyes would have sat with ease in the skull of Crazy Horse.

The question never occurred to me till recently, but could Joe have been Mac's son? Given the time and place, he could but was he? Did a mutually understood paternity explain the devotion, and the peculiar unbreached formality, between Joe and Mac? I know nothing about Joe's origins except that he was native to the village, and I never heard a whisper of the possibility of any blood relation to Mac or any other white man. Interracial sex was high on the minuscule list of taboo subjects in my family, especially when women were present. Yet in lone male company, I overheard whispers of blending among the men; and I've mentioned knowing early that Mary Lee, in Ida's kitchen, claimed to be a white man's daughter.

The truth about Mac and Joe is more than likely to be a firm no. What I saw of their relation suggested no more than a rough guarded respect and a strong dependency on both sides. And I never saw the trace of a hint that Mac was an actively sexual man. His manner was courteously masculine with no trace of the eunuchoid or effeminate; but in our hundreds of private hours together, Mac never hinted at a sexual propensity of his own, in any direction. He never expressed a word of such curiosity or warning to me as I advanced into manhood, and I never caught so much as a hint of speculation about Mac from my sexually inquisitive family.

Whatever, if I'd thought to ask Mac about a possible relation with

Joe, he wouldn't have taken the least offense. If the true answer was no, he'd have said it in a high fit of laughter (his voice was deep but his laugh was high). Then he'd have said "What gave you that damned fool idea—Joe being ugly as me?" The longest laugher would have been Joe, whose sense of the ludicrous was keen, as any sane black man's had to be. Far stranger conjunctions occurred in all slaveholding societies. But both men are long dead; no documents appear to survive, and the hope of an answer died with them.

Modern studies of slavery and its enduring aftermath have made it common knowledge that such bonds were frequent in the deceptively quiet century between Emancipation and the beginnings of forced integration. Any middle-class white Southerner with a memory that runs as far back as the 1940s can give you examples. The present tendency is to deny the validity of such relations because they were founded on morally corrupt bases; that reductive view however not only ignores a multitude of complex loves and loyalties of ancient and modern history, it also denies two of the common denominators of human life. Almost no men or women are prepared to live without the warmth and approval of at least one fellow human, whatever degrees of self-regard must vanish in the process. And only in the past few decades, since the imprisonment and defection of American soldiers in Korea, have we begun to explore the subtle but mutually nourishing, even redemptive, collusions that may form between master and man, jailer and prisoner.

Despite the contorted paradox, many of those old black-white relations built lasting measures of devotion, whether between two men or two women. I've suggested that such relations were seldom built across gender lines. Any such crossings were profoundly secret and generally quick. And sexual relations between black men and white women were sworn, by the white race, never to occur. Deeper than anyone noticed, and far below their power to foresee, the seeds of mutual understanding were planted in that dark covered passage from slavery to freedom.

Joe, Mac and I—all three of us crowded into the one seat, and our rides would take us to more than one farm. Joe would stop the truck, we'd swarm out, the tenant's yard dogs would lope down to meet us, then the tenant's wife with the baby at her skirt-tails. All of Mac's tenants that I saw were white. He'd pass a polite few words with the wife, chuck the baby's chin or, if it was old enough, give it a dime. Then he'd say "Where's Delbert?" The wife would try to hide her mouth—missing teeth or a lipload of snuff—then point us in the vague direction; and Joe would lead us through sandy furrows of chest-high tobacco (chest-high to the men but over my head).

When we found Delbert, he might be pausing at the end of a row in a patch of shade with his oldest boy Spencer, maybe twelve, tanned the color of antique walnut and with no more fat than a well-planed board. I'd watch Spencer closely and soon he'd seem the goal of my striving, not his actual body but his lofty state—that tall and strong, with water-blue eyes as sure and unblinking. If his father said "Fetch this or that," he'd leap to get it with the swift intention of an eight-pointed buck.

Delbert would be in bib overalls and a short-sleeved shirt—a short man with a look of being pounded-in by a stake, driven into dirt by a broad wood mallet; and all his limbs were stronger for it. He and Mac would talk in short sentences, the hopes of the crop and last year's disappointment. Delbert would talk the lion's share (so many country people were chatterboxes, wild to talk after days of silence). Mac would just say "Yes, yes" or "I understand." Joe would head on deeper into pines to take a leak, or he'd stand in the sunlight and throw rocks at the white trunk of a dead sycamore. When all Mac's business was done, there'd come a long moment when silence would spread. I'd begin to be bored by then; but after a while I realized that these transactions were somehow related to being in church, some awesome invisible cards were being laid out for an urgent game. Then Mac would cast one more look around, feel a tobacco leaf and say "Delbert, I'll see you next week unless it hails" (summer hail storms are common in east Carolina and can ruin green tobacco).

Though the slowness of those visits often bored me—the times when Mac would step away from me and do nothing but watch a field or a line of woods—I never complained or refused the trip. And by the time I was six or seven, I'd had parallel experiences of my own, of which I'll speak later. So I'd come to believe Mac was not wasting time. He was doing a silent thing in his mind that meant a lot to him and the world. He was watching the bigness of what was his for a few short years or sorrowing quietly for its failure to yield, through no human fault of his or Delbert's but the hand of God's inscrutable will. (I heard of a similar farmer who lost his barn and cow to a spring tornado, though his neighbors were spared. When asked if such selective devastation might not be God's judgment against him for sin, the victim said "Well, *God*—you take Him up one side and down the other, He does about as much harm as good.")

In my hearing Mac never delivered so much as a line of agrarian thought or primitive poetry; but the way his lively face would halt, then go serene for maybe ten seconds said more than any bucolic of Vergil's or any hundred seminars at the State Ag. and Normal; and even a townboy, bookish as I, could watch it and wonder how many more people found that much peace in a lifetime's work.

Even to a half-bored watchful child, Mac's days plainly said that something could speak, through dirt and leaves and human sweat, and give a sane man this much return. I knew that money was partly involved, though I was still too young to care much for money. I couldn't speak for Delbert or Spencer, but I knew from far back that Macon Thornton was not in this for anything as solemn and joyless as money. I've already said that Mac never flaunted wealth nor was he a skinflint. For all their faults, none of my grown kin were in love with money. Though again, I was born in the pit of the Great Depression, I never heard within my family a whole conversation on the subject of money. There'd be little snatches of worry about a bill, little dry quick laughs at the specter of loss; but money was neither their goal nor theme.

I also knew what I couldn't have said, that Mac lived as pure a life of contemplation as any cloistered monk. I never saw him engaged in harder work than saddling a horse or stepping off the dimensions of a field, but that's not to say he was lazy. He kept the standard farmer's day, sunup to past dark and then early sleep. On an average day he'd visit two farms, overseeing and guiding, encouraging and curbing. To one he'd haul a load of fertilizer; to another, lime and chicken-feed and maybe a case of Carnation milk for the bottle-fed baby that seemed to be failing. He'd listen and watch, laugh and console. It was all the business he'd made for himself but also a steady brand of meditation.

The only visits that gave him obvious worry were the ones to Uncle

Will Egerton's widow, who was prone to wildness and was also named Emma. Even in youth and in a tolerant village, she'd been known as *mean*. Ida told me that one freezing morning a black man knocked on Uncle Will's door with a message. Mrs. Egerton had just come from the well with a five-gallon bucket of water. When she saw the man standing there, she suddenly dashed all the water in his face (her explanation was "He looked like a fool just standing there grinning"). By the time I was riding with Mac, she was well into a clearly deranged old age. She wouldn't live with the Thorntons, or maybe they couldn't have stood her; so Mac had the duty of finding decent white families in the county to give her room and board and the necessary curbing.

I recall a particular day in the late forties when Mac and Joe came to get me, and we headed out for the Snipes place where Mrs. Egerton had been staying with apparent satisfaction. A straw had finally broken the Snipeses' back; and they'd sent a postcard for Mac to come get her—the previous Sunday in church, she'd noticed that her dress was wrong-side-out; and when most heads were bowed in prayer, she'd simply stood up, stripped off the dress and put it on the right way. When we got there, Mrs. Egerton was waiting on the porch with her Gladstone bag—tall for her age, with wild white hair from under her black hat, dying gardenias pinned to the brim. I can't recall where we took her next. But as always she and I rode in the bed of the pickup on straight chairs; and she ate from her inexhaustible bag of dried Smyrna figs, "Good for your bowels, boy; here eat you one."

On the way back to Ida's in late afternoon, Joe would stop us downtown for the mail and a drink; mine was always Nu-Grape that left a purple arc on your upper lip. Mac and I would stay in the store, by the checker game, and drink ours slowly beneath the fan—Mac watched but never played. Once Joe got his drink, he'd go outside where black men sat on the window ledge with cold drinks and cakes (no signs were posted, no word was said; but everybody knew blacks sat outside).

So I'd have Mac alone for the first time today, and that was my chance for a swift operation. I'd beckon him down and whisper fast. I'd seen an ad for a microscope in one of my funny books, $2.98; it would help me in school.

Mac would nod "Yes, yes" but make no move. So I'd be left to wonder if he heard or had just said no. In fact through the years, my least request, if it sounded "educational," was sure to be met. Mac seemed to read nothing but the Raleigh paper and maybe a few farm publications; and I seem to recall him telling stories of a year or so at Trinity College down in Durham, later Duke University. So his own education was hardly extensive, but he firmly backed my interest in school. His last word to me as I left each summer was "Be smart, Ren. Any damned fool can fail. Look at me, dumb as dirt. You be some count, hear?"

And there in the store, among six or eight white men watching a game, he'd palm me a wadded five-dollar bill with one long hushing finger to his lips, "Don't tell Emma, hear?"

At the end of my visit the summer I was ten, Mac came by to see me on my last afternoon. The pickup stopped out front in the road, Ida called me and I ran out to find Mac alone at the wheel. He said "Let me show you a pretty sight." I was more than ready, but he made me run back for Ida's permission. Then we turned and headed for the fields by the Baptist Church, the ones more or less face-to-face with his house. More tall tobacco, all he had to show; I could hardly act thrilled. Still I climbed out with him and walked down a row till we came to the end by the curing barns, the scene of catfish fries and Brunswick stews in hundred-gallon iron pots. From there Mac faced the road and said "Can you see Mrs. Nowell?" He always referred to his sister Emma by her married name, and it was time for Emma's late afternoon pause on the front porch.

Short as I was, I told him I couldn't see anything but green.

Mac said "Which one of these rows you like the best?"

He'd tried to teach me to judge tobacco, so I eyed it slowly and finally said "This one." The row stretched in a clear line right on to the dirt road, a hundred yards.

Mac said "Then it's yours. In late September you watch the mail."

I barely understood.

Then he led the way out and drove me back. We exchanged the usual farewell—his admonitions to "be some damned *count*," my thanks for good times and the microscope. Then we'd part for long months, no hug or handshake. I've said his eyes were blacker than any brave's; he'd set them on you and watch you go for as long as you took. But you could

wave your arm off, he'd never look back and wave again. That was the
limit his mind allowed.

I almost forgot the row of tobacco. Then in early October I biked
home for lunch and found a letter addressed in Mac's hand, which was
always more like printing than script. Mother was curious and stood
close in as I opened the envelope. It held one sheet of lined tablet-paper
with a penciled note, "Dear Ren, Here is what your tobacco brought.
Be smart. Love, Mac." The note was folded around a fifty-dollar bill. I'd
never seen one before—neither had Mother—with its picture of Ulysses
Grant, looking as sour as if he hadn't won the War. Our household
finances were nearer stability than they'd ever been; but fifty dollars was
still a serious sum in 1943, the equivalent of maybe five hundred now.
First we were speechless; then we must have danced. I know we were both
so elated that I took the letter and the bill back to school and, with my
teacher's permission, showed it to the thunderstruck class (those were
days when you didn't fear an after-school mugging).

I've long since forgot my purchases. I was already an obsessive collector of totemic objects—palpable things, mostly hand-size, that hummed
for me with mysterious energy: a statuette of Superman, my own copy
of a favorite library book (*Tales from Shakespeare* by Charles and Mary
Lamb), a set of flint arrowheads from a mail-order company in Montana,
the stamps I collected, the model airplanes I made, a bronze coin of the
Emperor Hadrian. I sent Mac more than one short letter, notifying him
of major acquisitions, explaining their relevance to my education and
thanking him again. His replies came promptly on penny postcards,
seldom more than two sentences—he was glad to hear my news, he hoped
to see me soon, be smart.

It didn't occur to me for some years that he was always secretive about
his gifts. Whenever he gave me the ritual "Don't tell Emma," I'd nod
and comply—accustomed, like any child, to family conspiracies. He'd
told me to tell Ida and Elizabeth (he always said "your mammy"), so
I rushed to tell and then was sorry. A child that young has too few
secrets; I should have kept mine. I also never wondered why Emma might
have minded. In her good months Miss Emma seemed as generous as
Mac, with her time and intelligence. Like any busy child I filed such
questions as insoluble adult mysteries and went downtown to open my

first checking account at the First National Bank. The manager was a friend of Will's and came to the teller's window to thank me—"Reynolds, I bet you're our youngest depositor. Welcome to the family." And with Mac's continued help, I never looked back in my life as a junior financier.

From then on, Mac cut an even larger figure in my mind. He was not just the cousin who gave me outings from Ida's house and exposed me to the useful mysteries of farming, tenant-owner relations, the horrific skills of hog killing and butchering, saddling and riding a horse and the deep satisfactions of generosity. He was the only friend, except my parents, who confirmed his love for me with tangible gifts on any occasion but Christmas and my birthday. He was the one reliable financial benefactor of my childhood. Various aunts and cousins would strike unexpectedly with birthday checks or the odd dollar-bill; but Mac not only endowed me each fall, and in the most enjoyable way (secretly), he also responded to every interim hint. And since he never asked for thanks or bargained for any return from me, the dignified silence of his giving taught me volumes about the difficulties and duties of receiving. Simone Weil states the dilemma precisely, "Our friends owe us what we think they will give us. We must forgive them this debt."

Once Mac began his harvest gift—and as long as his tobacco thrived— he knew I expected the money and that I might even hope for occasional increases. And I knew that he knew that I knew. Will and Elizabeth's only concern in the matter was that I thank Mac appropriately and that I write him from time to time. Neither of them, in their own childhood, had faced so early a training in gratitude, so I was on my own to steer a true course. By the time of the second year's harvest, I'd begun to see at least some of the ways in which generosity can be, not a burden but a real enhancement of mutual care. Mac seemed all the grander, less old and secret, much funnier and all the more trustworthy as a friend. In his eyes I hope I seemed to get smarter, though Mother had warned me not to show off or to correct my elders unless they were doing something actively dangerous.

By the time of that second gift, we'd moved back to Warrenton, five miles from Mac; and the long summer visits to Ida stopped. But since

Mac came to town most Saturdays, he'd drop me a card every few weeks
and ask me to meet him on the courthouse square or at his truck, which
was always parked by the Farm Agent's office. He mostly came to town
without Joe; so we'd have twenty minutes to talk alone, the same old
exchanges—school work, my family's health ("Be good to your mammy;
she's a mighty fine woman") and a word or two about Emma and Frank—
how Frank had seen the first snake of spring, the signal for taking off his
long underwear. If it was spring or summer, Mac would give a short crop
report, "Tobacco's looking right good, yes, yes. Maybe a little better than
last year." At Christmas and birthday-time, he'd pass me a tight green
wad, ten or fifteen dollars.

My feelings then were something like this. Mac Thornton was one of
the five people who loved me most; the rest were Mother, Father, Bill
and Ida. Since his love involved no leaning, no pressure, no chance of
tears, Mac stood in my mind with Ida as a model of perfect friendship or
charity. All my family liked him as much as I (in later years Bill was also
his friend and beneficiary). And since I had few contemporary town-
friends, I was not tempted then by one of the dumbest revulsions of adolescence—the fear that a school friend might see me with a plump old
farmer and taunt me with the sight.

So Mac and I navigated three more years safely. I recall his taking me
to Ringling Brothers Circus in Rocky Mount in about 1945, and his
amazed delight at their world-famed gorilla, the enormous Gargantua
the Great. His coal-black hulk lived in the corners of a glassed-in cage,
and Mac knew his tragic story and could tell me—a vicious keeper had
thrown acid in Gargantua's face years ago and fueled his unsleeping
enmity to the human race. Later I recall Mac's asking me to join him at
the Warren Theater one Saturday night for a hillbilly stage-show with
the famous team of Mustard and Gravy; well-launched on a love of Bach
and Chopin, I passed up Mustard and Gravy for good. So after Ringling
Brothers, the one addition to our shared pleasures in those later years
was fox hunting.

A fox hunt then in the upper South bore no resemblance to the red-
coated pastime of people too rich to know better. Mac's method was
typical of real country hunters with a purpose for killing, men for whom
the fox is a costly enemy of domestic fowl. I'd go to Macon on a Friday

night, sleep at Ida's, eat a quick breakfast and be ready when Mac came to get me at dawn. He was always alone; for whatever reason, Joe never hunted with us. We'd ride deeper into the country to another white tenant's house—call him Woodrow Stegall—where Mac kept his dogs.

Woody would be out by the dog pen, a good many yards on past the chickens. We'd join him there, in a wide globe of the rank clean odor of working dogs. Mac would count the dozen or fifteen smart-faced, wigglesome and ever-ready hounds; and he'd name them over with no hesitation (to my valuable instruction—that so many of any one thing deserved proper and characteristic names and got them, even from these busy men). The dogs had risen to the mere sight of Mac's truck; the sound of his voice was almost more than they could bear. So Woody would either lay down the ramp, and they'd run into the bed of the pick-up; or if Mac were short of time and wanted a quick taste of dog voices, Woody would just wave them off toward the nearest woods.

If we had a few hours, we'd shut the tailgate and ride up the road to whatever spot Woody chose that day; Mac always let him run the show. Once the dogs were unloaded, they'd moil at our ankles, frantic for per-mission. Woody might stand stock-still for a minute, letting their hope and dread boil higher. Then he might dig into his back pocket, find a worn old foxtail and give the smartest bitch a sniff, but that was merely a teasing delay—they all knew the point so truly that their hearts nearly burst with forethought till Woody raised his stubby horn and blew a high bellow. They'd pound out of sight like a small herd of footstools, that stiff and fast. And for the next hour or more, we'd stand near the truck or go to a cluster of rocks and sit to hear the dogs. There'd be a good deal of spitting, whittling and a lot of farm and weather talk but very little else. The son for instance seldom came with us; and when he did, he was far too grandly gone at sixteen to spare a look or word my way, least of all a secret from his side of puberty that I longed to know.

And I doubt that my youth or innocence suppressed a natural bawdry in Mac—other cousins and uncles were freely ribald in my presence—but for his private reason, I never heard Mac say an obscene word or tell a blue joke. And none of his men did either in his presence, though all would say *nigger* at least once a day; and ever so often we'd meet one of those compelled poor-whites who had to say it every two or three min-utes, like a wrenching tic that ruined his face. I'd wince inside, knowing how my parents hated the word. Mac never flinched and would sometimes say it himself but always lightly, with a built-in grin as if he meant it as the joke it was when black people said it to one another, though I knew it was different and tried not to hear.

The hounds would be conducting the hunt. At first their cries were as foreign as Finnish; but soon I came to know the random early solos and then the business-like full-cry fugue. That wild polyphony could run for whole long minutes of chase, then crumble in an instant if the fox escaped, as it generally did every four or five minutes. Then lastly the hectic screams of the catch, the young dogs' cries of incredulous triumph. I never attained Mac's or Woody's powers of detection; they could name individual hounds by their voices—"That's old Rowlet," "Big Molly's hurting" (with senile arthritis) or "They've lost poor Stitch. I knew he was too young. Hope to God he can find his way back"—but at least I could share their vicarious pleasure. They'd give the dogs ten minutes with the corpse; then Mac would say "Woody, hail em on in."

Woody would walk to the edge of the pines and blow long wails in several directions, notes so native to our Celtic bones that even Mac would laugh and say "Ren, don't that make your damned beard stand up?"

I'd have to remind him I still wasn't shaving.

And he'd say "Thank your damned blessings then" and heist up his trousers with the sides of his arms. We'd wait awhile longer till the hounds limped one by one from the woods. Tired as they were, they came right to us and sought our eyes. Before they could rest though, they wanted our report.

Mac was manly with them; he'd never squat and scratch their ears, but he would call their names and give them short reviews of their work, "Tim, you done all right. Lucy, where *were* you? Never heard your voice. Don't expect no extra cornbread tonight."

And that satisfied them. They were far too self-respecting to cringe or to run through a round of house-pet stunts to beg an embrace from any idle human. Once they were judged, they'd haul their tails back up the ramp or, if we'd stayed at Woodrow's, on down past the chickens (whose blood arch-enemy they'd just now killed) to their own pen and a day-long nap. They knew they'd paid their room and board.

Since no masculine code of courage-near-death had ever been conveyed to me, I was never the classic spooked lad so common in fiction, trembling on the verge of manly blood-knowledge. No fox was likely to turn on me, though rabid foxes were not unknown. In the company of certified men like Mac and Woody, I could stand through hunts with no big worries about my performance. So the hyper-male obsessions that threaten so many boyhoods passed me luckily by. The exact-right killing equipment, the precise body-stance for deadly blows, the approved cast of eye, the mystic goal of oneness through death with nature and beast and a few other men—any such concerns would have thrown Mac and Woody, or any man I knew, to the ground in laughter.

If Mac and Woody could have told you why they hunted, near a village with three cheap grocery-stores, they might have said "Oh to pass a little time and not hurt anything anybody cares about more than a fox. It's good for the dogs too, lets them feel useful." And Mac might have added "It pays Woody back for feeding them good." If you'd said "Fine but it's hard on foxes," they'd have looked you over, grinned and said "How many chickens you raising, sport?"

Even so I tried to look as nearly grown as I could, to be as calm and intent as the men (I was already spitting through my front teeth so often that Mother had warned me of dehydration). And when Mac and I were alone again, and he didn't correct me on anything, I knew I'd passed with no demerit through one more almost invisible gate. I'd watched a squealing bloody pig-slaughter in Mac's yard, but I was never present at the actual death of any wild creature larger than a rabbit, so I had the luck to miss the temptation to deface with sentiment the killing of things as grand in their beastliness as deer or bear. What Mac spared me, in our strange detached hunts, was the poisonous narcissism that fuels bloodsports in well-fed societies. What he taught me was one more use of male companionship—a friend will stand with you, still and easy, while you run your dogs, whatever dogs you need to run at the time.

The summer I was fourteen, we moved to Raleigh. This time the neighbor children and my classmates welcomed me; so within a few weeks, I felt no pressing need for trips back to Macon or the safe-harbor friendship of Mac and Ida. Still a buried lobe of my brain knew not to cut all ties with my past, however quaint they might now feel. Early in high school somebody told me one of those facts that brand your mind, flares that light your particular darkness and show some truth that will only grow. I learned that, among the Greek gods, the mother of the muses was Mnemosyne or *Memory*; and Zeus was their father. Even that young, I knew I had a past. And since I'd meant to be an artist from age six onward, I somehow knew not to cut a deep taproot—any ready tie to the memory of my short past or my family's long reach.

So I kept writing notes to Mac, not just to thank him at harvest time. And the winter I was nearly sixteen, here came a postcard asking us all to the circus. Ringling Brothers pitched their annual tent at the State Fairgrounds in Raleigh; and all four of us kept the rendezvous, to meet Mac Thornton at the ticket wagon. Despite the mob I saw Mac well before he saw me, so I had a long moment to frisk him over. I'd never yet seen him in a sizable town. I had to know how countrified he looked, in case I saw any of my now-numerous friends from school and needed to hide.

He still wore an old gray-felt fedora, when even Will had given up hats; but Mac's khaki pants were clean and pressed, though they clung in some danger to the under-edge of the growing belly. The black eyes were still as strong as Geronimo's in old photographs. He saw me then and stepped forward to me with just a hand to shake. I knew I could relax; he'd passed the test.

All afternoon he absorbed the circus like a large sober child, well-behaved and grateful. In the midst of some acts, and always at the end, he'd tap my side with a gentle elbow, "Don't believe it, Ren. *Bound* to be a damned trick." It seemed important to him still to keep me posted, moment by moment, on what was illusion and what was fact. Yet he plainly believed each instant of the hours, so I joined with him and conducted myself as if I thought it was splendid too. By then I was at the point of thinking Laurence Olivier's filmed *Hamlet* the finest thing on land or sea, a fact I couldn't even mention to Mac. He'd have said "Yes, yes"; but another gap would have yawned between us. Never mind; we had my entire childhood behind us, a country we'd shared. And though I didn't know it then, we had whatever hope Mac had seen in me and tried to feed. That proved bond enough for the few years to come.

Only at the distant end—after sunset, with the spring air chilly and all of us worn to nubbins by the annual discovery that Ringling Brothers gives twice as much as you paid for—did trouble surface. Elizabeth had laid in steaks at home, and now she invited Mac to join us; he'd never seen our house. But no, he said, he'd better head home—Emma and Frank were there alone.

He'd always been a giver not a taker, but I was too young to smell a rat. Anybody past thirty looked the same age to me; and I saw no reason to wonder why he'd pass up a chance to visit the only real home we'd had, the only real quarters of ours he might have entered. Mac was just over sixty; I thought it was time old people got tired and their eyes couldn't see the road at night.

But once we were safe in the family car and moving, Elizabeth asked Will how he thought Mac looked.

Will said "A little ashy."

She said "He's yellow as a gourd. And he smells a little strange, like burning paper. That mostly means cancer."

We never knew for sure. Some months later I heard from Ida that Mac had suffered a curious spell and was in the Roanoke Rapids hospital. I wrote him at once; and by the time school was out in June, he was back at home. I drove up to Macon to see him. He met me at the front door, and that was a fact disturbing in itself—farmers are never home in summer daylight. He said Joe would be coming for him shortly. So we sat on the porch, with Emma coming to the screen now and then to say something trivial or ask a question. That was also a new arrangement—to see her plainly checking on Mac when she'd barely noticed his presence before—and it made me think he was still sick, whatever he said.

He said he was fine, "Yes, yes, just thin." The chief sign of that was, the black eyes blaring in his shrunken face; but he showed no trace of invalid neglect. He was dressed as neatly as always, with a starched white shirt buttoned at the neck and no tie. He even wore his black street shoes, and they looked as if Joe might have halfway shined them. To my now-suspicious eye, Mac's face looked healthy all the same. He'd never been fat—the belly was the product of weak abdominal muscles—but the longer I watched and heard his new voice, a note too high, a fresh unnerving boy began to materialize in my old friend's place. Death had begun another in its broad array of tricks; it was moving Mac's body backward through time.

Our conversation followed the old pattern, me and my schooling. By then I was aimed toward college—Duke University, if they'd have me: the successor to his old Trinity. As a Methodist steward and a long enthusiast for education, Mac was hot for me to go. I told him I'd need to win a big scholarship.

He pointed toward the house, and Emma inside, and shook his head, then lowered his voice, "I'll help you out."

I wasn't about to press for details, but at least I thanked him; and then we went silent, staring across the road to the young tobacco that embraced the Baptist Church, where he'd given me the first row six years before. When I faced him again, I could see his eyes were full. I'd never seen Mac show a trace of sorrow, but tears were in danger of spilling now, and he wouldn't move to wipe them.

Then still not facing me, he told me what had happened. "Ren, I woke up in my bed, way in the night; and my pillow was sopping wet. Everything was dark and I couldn't see my hand before me, but then I felt around, and damned if the whole sheet down to my waist wasn't soaked. I said 'Well, Macon, you're in your second childhood'—I thought I'd started back pissing in the bed. Nothing to do but change my damned pajamas and stretch out on the floor till day. I stood up to turn on the light, but I never found the switch. Next thing I knew, I was waking up in a pitch-black world—not one chink of light—with something big pressing down on my face. I thought 'Oh Lord, I'm in my grave. They've buried me and damned if I ain't still alive.' But then I found out my arms could move, far as they could reach—I knew Emma hadn't bought me no coffin with that much room. I had to be dead though, wherever I was; and let me tell you, Ren, I knew it wasn't Heaven. But I went on to sleep or passed out again, and it wasn't till daylight hit my window that I came to. I was *under* my bed in cobwebs and dust—God only knows how. Joe thinks I passed out, then halfway woke up, started to crawling and wound up way in under the bed. Anyhow now I could see my way clear. I crawled on out and got to my feet and—oh Lord Jesus— my bed was all bloody, my face, my chest. Before I could wake anybody else up, Joe came in to find me. Time to cook breakfast and I hadn't showed up, so Joe was worried but nothing compared to what he was the minute he saw me."

*   *   *

The Thorntons were famous, in a village of confessors, for keeping their counsel; they kept their own bad news at home. Maybe the curse of insanity had made them wary of confirming or checking their neighbors' curiosity. In my presence anyhow Mac never mentioned his sister Lucy's mad death, Emma's winter depression or Frank's eccentricity. He spoke of his family only to praise them or in an occasional affectionate joke. (One of his sisters had married a man of reputed thrift; so Mac once told me "Yes, he's very economical—takes Mamie's false teeth downtown every morning in the pocket of his vest; can't have her at home there, eating between meals.")

Like us all, Mac well understood that the point of such stories had no necessary bearing on the facts of the case. They were instant, and instantly welcome, attempts to augment the ongoing myth of the family—everyone's hope for outlasting the grave. And now having pictured his harrowing night, he gave me no further clue to what struck him—a lung hemorrhage from TB or cancer, an abdominal ulcer, a ruptured aneurysm or a stroke?

Rumors about him proliferated but my memory is that Mac puttered along for a year or so, running his farms and strengthening a little but not regaining the weight. And in my first semester at Duke, I got another postcard—he would check into Duke Hospital soon for tests. He stayed about two weeks, and every day I'd walk the few hundred yards off main campus to see him.

Mac had a private room and mostly stayed in bed, though he could sit up on the edge for meals. I was in his room several times when his supper tray arrived—always a big bowl of unadorned white rice, with a tablespoon of honey for optional seasoning. Then as now the hospital offered a famous rice diet. Originally a therapy for hypertension, it had soon become a regimen for weight loss. Mac no longer seemed overweight, so maybe blood pressure was the concern. But again he never said and I didn't ask. We'd talk the old talk; I'd stay half an hour, telling him most of my tranquil news. All my life, in the presence of reluctant talkers, I tend to rattle on—any foolishness to fill the holes. But always with Mac I could tolerate silence as a natural state, a function of our ease and trust. So in the hospital we'd often sit through long mute stretches. By then though, I was finally old enough to wonder what he thought at such times.

Did his mind turn into the kind of blank screen we assume in, say, a grazing animal; or was he poring on dreadful visions of what lay ahead? I never asked. Sometimes he'd end the silence between us with a sudden assertion, old as our closeness, "You've got a fine mammy. Always treat her right—but I know you do." Can all his thoughts have been about others? And what had he thought, those thousands of evenings at home with only Emma, Frank, the radio and *Life* magazine? All my evidence, from the years I knew him, says he thought of nothing but others. How and in what terms, though? In any case, once he described that first nightmare, he never said one more word on the subject of age and death. And when he'd catch the hint that I was restless, he'd thank me and say "Yes, yes—do your lessons." And I'd be back the next day.

Once with his hairless ankles dangling at the edge of the bed, I suddenly realized what young people seldom know, especially in America now where children hardly know anyone over fifty. I saw that this old man was once young as me. Neither Ida, who was his old grammar-schoolmate, nor Elizabeth had photographs of him in youth; and with all the compulsive snapping I'd done since age thirteen, I'd never taken one picture of Mac and now I couldn't. So I tried to imagine him as a boy—the one who figured so mischievously in Ida's school memories—or as Mother's memory of him as a fond openhanded store-clerk. All I could ever be sure of was the eyes; surely they'd never changed. They were threatening to outlast his shrinking body; and in my mind till now, so they have.

Without me, in the hospital he'd have been almost entirely alone. Emma couldn't travel the seventy miles, Frank wouldn't and Joe was so busy with the extra chores that he only came at rare intervals. But I got to the room one afternoon and found Joe with Mac. It was one of the few times I'd seen Joe indoors; he looked as uneasy as a buffalo in the parlor and was already on his feet, anxious to leave—in those days, any country person's first aim was to get home by dark. When we'd shaken hands Joe clapped his felt hat back on.

Mac said "Joe, take your damned hat off. Ain't raining in here." But he laughed and told Joe to get on back and cook Emma and Frank's supper.

Joe said "Mr. Frank ain't been eating a whole lot since you come up here. I keep making him boiled custard; he'll drink a glass of that every hour or so. Miss Emma now, she's *bolting* her feed." Of course we laughed; Emma's appetite was legendary—she'd eat a dry saltine every week or so. Her blue-flame focus came from something less earthy than food.

Once Joe was gone Mac paid him the ritual compliment, "Joe's all right. Been mighty good to me." But that day he supplemented it, "People in general have."

I told him he'd earned everything he got and more.

Mac said "I loved my fellow man." This time his eyes stayed dry; but I remember noticing he used the past tense, though I saw no signs of imminent death.

The doctors still hadn't scheduled his departure; so when I stood to go, I said I'd see him tomorrow.

Mac said "Please sir. But here, put this in your inside pocket." He handed me a sealed white dime-store envelope, no sign of writing. "Don't lose it now."

I assumed it was this year's tobacco profit—my number of rows had risen; by then the yield had climbed to two hundred. Mac hadn't said "Don't tell Emma," so I wondered if I misunderstood. Still I said "Whatever it is, I thank you."

He looked out his window on the university gardens, stripping now for winter. Then he said "How damned old are you, Ren?"

"Eighteen, nineteen in February."

He faced me. "Then I'm thanking you for eighteen years."

The walk to my room was the equivalent of two city blocks; but since my arms were heavy with books, I didn't stop to open the envelope. I just knew that two hundred dollars would come in handy for my Christmas trip to New York; I already had tickets to see Laurence Olivier and Vivien Leigh in *Caesar and Cleopatra* and *Antony and Cleopatra*, and they hadn't come cheap.

Jack my roommate was in from band practice, already working at the broad desk we shared. The light through our single window was the same bluish haze of so many school memories—late walks home from senior-play practice or touch football when the actual players become near-ghosts, the light of late childhood longing and sorrow mingled in an unendurable sadness that we mostly endure. Jack asked if I'd seen my cousin; was he better?

It struck me as polite but odd that he asked every day but had never joined me on a visit, though Mac had asked more than one question about him; still I was glad of a well-meaning partner my age. I had to say "He's dying." Only then did I see that, of people I'd loved, Mac would be the first to die. I took out the envelope and cut it open—the usual lined tablet-paper wrapper, but with no written message, and three crisp thousand-dollar bills.

In student eyes today that would be a princely gift. In 1951 and in the circles I moved in, it was almost unimaginable. Mac had said years before that he meant to help me through college. Then in my last year of high school, I'd won a full scholarship. At that point he apparently decided to lie back. Now this. The customs of our friendship said I shouldn't run back to Mac now and pour out thanks. It would rile us both, in unknown ways; and one of us might do something uncontrollable like weep. But the next afternoon I went straight to him.

And then more than ever, I could hear his death. When I'd said my thanks and renewed my promise to "be some count," Mac said, not just the old "Don't tell Emma" but then "I can't leave you anything in my damned will."

I told him I meant to put it aside for graduate school.

He said the old "Yes, yes" of any country preacher and then "Ren, don't never stop studying."

Only now do I wonder what he hoped I'd learn.

A quick year passed—quick for me—and I have no memory of Mac's whereabouts. He was surely at home and partly active or I'd recall. But in my sophomore year at Duke, when I was home for Christmas, I got another postcard from Mac. He was back in the hospital, again in Roanoke Rapids; and he wished he could see me. It was eighty miles from home; but when we went up to Ida's after Christmas, Will, Elizabeth, Bill and I all drove the further fifteen miles and climbed to Mac's room.

Again he was lying alone in a single; the walls were that hue of milky green with which otherwise merciful institutions punish their charges. He was slightly thinner than the last time at Duke, and oxygen tubes ran into his nostrils, but the black eyes caught us with no surprise. He'd never been a jovial greeter; and even this near an end, he kept up a courtly self-possession.

Despite the hissing tubes, talk was much the same as always, though manners required him to share his attention among the four of us. I know he never mentioned his health, and none of us asked. I know he never joked, even with Bill. He also never spoke of going back home; but he managed, as we did, with no gulp or tear. It was all just questions, short pointless questions—was it cold outdoors, did we have a new car, had we got good grades? ("Don't think I doubt you; I know you have.")

After fifteen minutes Elizabeth saw that we tired him. When she leaned to kiss him and say goodbye, he didn't protest. He held her hand an extra moment and said "Old James" (*James* for *Jimmy*). She was one of the hemisphere's tenderest hearts; tears sprang up in her ten times a day, but now she restrained them.

So when he extended his hand to me, I followed Mother's lead and kissed him once on the bare domed head, the first time ever. At the door I paused for one look back. For another first time, he was watching for that. The eyes were untouched by his enemy, and the further leanness made his scimitar nose as much a prow as Abraham's when he bent to slay Isaac. But the cool restraint of all our past forbade me even to make a farewell, though common sense and animal need told me to say "I'll remember you every day of my life."

Mac said "You know what I say to that."

I trusted he meant he'd return the service. I know he believed in on-going life; and like all our kin, and the large majority of human beings always, he thought his soul would recall those he left and could go on doing them further good deeds. His body anyhow died in that room.

So late in January, Bill and I drove to Macon to sit through his funeral at the church he shared with all Mother's family, the tall white room where he'd spent so many hot Sunday mornings over on the left in the Amen Corner. Will and Elizabeth had gone to Portsmouth for the simultaneous funeral of her brother Stooks, whose lovely daughter died in agony at nine years old, of a bone infection, just before I was born. But though Mac's nephews bore his coffin, for once I knew my place and was there. If I'd been asked to say a few words, I hope I'd have said that he moved unpropped through sixty-five years with wit, generosity and un-dimmed eyes.

It took two pastors to lay him away. The Methodist minister mainly presided; but Will's old helper Robert Brickhouse delivered a short fine eulogy. At the end he said that he'd been asked by Miss Emma Nowell—Mrs. John Nowell, Macon Thornton's sister—to read a poem that had been Macon's favorite.

I thought "Mac Thornton never read a whole poem."

But Robert Brickhouse forged ahead; and when he got to the final line of Leigh Hunt's swaying "Abou Ben Adhem," I heard a startling echo of Mac's own voice—

Write me as one that loved his fellow-man.

It's not a line you could read these days, for a dead old bachelor, with-out suppressed laughter. But even as late as the 1950s, you could say what you meant and not be foolish. Mac had said his version of the line to me some months before, and I hadn't recognized it. He'd always said "Mrs. Nowell's a most remarkable woman," and again she'd proved it. She also saw that the words were cut on his tall white gravestone.

It stands no more than fifty feet from the graves of my Rodwell grand-parents, Ida and Marvin, all three of their sons, other Rodwells and Drakes and the high dark cedar my own mother planted in her child-hood. Now that I'm only ten years short of Mac's last age, I can say that no one buried there gave me more of a single crucial gift than Mac Thornton gave—not the years of money but a deep-cut picture to study and learn: a single figure, no visible props, consuming life gladly and giving it back.

His visible love was always for children. I saw him show his nieces and nephews and my brother Bill the brisk watchful courtesy that chil-dren rarely get. (In the years of my childhood, it mostly came from un-married kin or from married men and women who'd failed to thrive in

The Thornton tombstone in the Macon cemetery. It stands over Mac and several more Thorntons but was put up only after his death. And it bears the line he adapted for me from "Abou Ben Adhem."

tandem and had turned aside to hunt elsewhere for the loyal devotion that children can pledge, if they trust your eyes.) But with Mac Thornton dead more than half of my life now, I still don't know of another child he watched and guarded as closely as me. Our tastes could hardly have been more different, the satisfactions we took in the world—he loved baseball, hillbilly music in its raw old country-fiddle days, loud Protestant sermons, possum and tripe and a good deal else I live without. So what could have bound us, early and late?

Maybe quite early he saw in me another lone rider, a renegade who seldom leaves home and is thought by his friends to be safe as a spaniel when, in his heart, he's a trapped wolverine. Whatever the cause of Mac's solitude—and it seemed as different from Ida Drake's as a room of children differs from space—he silently made long efforts to palm me his secret code through dozens of hours on back dirt-roads, studying fields of green tobacco as raptly as if they could guarantee bliss, though he never smoked or chewed a leaf and barely used the money they made.

Or maybe I saw the core of his knowledge in one quick moment of an August day, near 1940. We'd stopped in the country at a strange crossroads. Mac opened the icebox, pulled out the Nu-Grape he knew I wanted and a tall brown Orange Crush for himself. Then he saw a dusty black child staring at us, a boy about five. Serious as if he was offering handcuffs, Mac held out the Orange. The child was so startled, he crouched to run; but thirst and curiosity turned him. *Who in the world was this big white man and what did he mean?* He edged on forward though toward Mac's loaded hand, took the cold bottle and pulled a swallow so long it seemed his throat lacked a stop.

When he finally paused, Mac said "Is it good?"

The boy said "Yes sir." He still hadn't smiled.

But Mac grinned wide. "Tell me *how* damned good."

In the years I knew him, he made the same plea to me many times. How good was something, how strong, smart, true? In his unpretending, unlettered way, Mac Thornton's hunt was for absolute answers to the mysteries he watched—pleasure, pain, madness and horse sense: the outer limits of human reach in a world he must have known was tragic but never accused.

The four of us in the yard of our last Asheboro house, 625 Sunset Avenue, on Easter Sunday 1944. None of us knows we'll be leaving in the summer for three hard years in Warren County. If I look wary, Bill and his curls are poised for levitation. Elizabeth is hale and, as always, eager for the next deal of cards in the game. Will is trim again and, though he has never done manual labor, his left hand is huge. The wedding ring, which I have now, swallows my adult finger.

5

A NORMAL, ALL BUT FATAL, CHILDHOOD

WILL PRICE, THE GERMAN, THE MYOPIC

A CLOSE WATCH on any normal infant is likely to see that its prime emotions are hunger and fear—fear of hunger, pain and whatever nameless dreads prowl the sleep behind those jittering eyelids. It's later, after six months generally, that children develop the private gallery of frights which are as personal as our genetic codes and are likely to remain constant, though augmented, through a lifetime.

None of my own earliest memories is of fear. I've described my first quick memory—the delight I took, sunbathing in the yard while Topsy attacked my diaper. I'd sat on her back several times already and was happy in her attention. All the other flash memories, to the age of three, are of pleasant or at least peaceful occasions—Christmas morning and a loaded tree, my ancient grandmother sick in bed, me swimming in the creek, the close attentions of my parents and kin.

As for the possibly buried bad memories from those years, it took me as long as last week to learn that Bill my brother didn't learn of Will's drinking until after Will's death. Bill was fourteen and riding in a car with Ida's three sons, who were swapping stories of their own drinking days. Time after time, they topped one another in reckless memory till one of them said (the one who'd cured himself by then), "Nothing we ever did though was as bad as Will Price."

So more than ever, I go on wondering if I may not have witnessed actual skirmishes in those dim bedrooms. My hypnotist's suggestion that I might have seen a sexual act and stored it as violent is a real possibility.

At age eleven, when we'd moved back to Warrenton and were all temporarily in a one-bedroom hotel-apartment, I did wake early once to see my parents making love. But by then I was old enough to know what was happening. It seemed both gentle, awesome, instructive and amusing, not at all violent.

From infancy I understood their tempestuous natures—sudden wild storms, then calm glad repairs—and I recall at least two confrontations of high megatonnage, in 1940 and '44. Yet those two struggles used nothing but words, loud terrible words but no slap or touch. And with all her readiness to share old secrets with Bill and me, Elizabeth never once claimed that Will had struck her. Her temper was as volatile as his; maybe I saw her rush against him, maybe nothing but tears.

My continuing sense is of something darker, but I'm not yet ready to fish in that gulf. At moments I feel I'm on the verge of piercing a final opaque screen. The sense is of noise; I'm about to hear strong voices, blaming and pleading. But till now I've lived with no words or pictures, only the partial hope to know what's stored in the cellars, avoiding light. So I have no present way of knowing what later fears may have been hooked into the deepest quick of my mind, almost at the start—the fear of active present harm or every child's dread of abandonment.

I've said that I was three and a half, in the spring of 1936, before I began to store narrative memories more than a few seconds long. The first is of that laden evening when Will, Elizabeth and I went for an aimless ride—a placid and unremarkable evening except that, at its end in our driveway, I experienced a revelation: the three of us were bound forever. Our lives, our chance of moving on, were truly at one another's mercy. Though I knew the intricate fact so suddenly, I couldn't foresee what work it would cause me and with what long consequences, still fresh today.

Recall that, at the end of the evening, Will powdered his hair and came to sing me his dying song, "When I Grow Too Old to Dream." My heartbreak then precluded tears, and even Elizabeth's intervention with the damp washcloth that restored his youth only partly consoled me. The sight had branded itself as my first warning that love is doomed, in this body at least. The human body is a fragile medium of loves that often outlast the flesh. Most of our loved ones eventually leave us, against their will, as they yield to death.

And when I think through the rest of my childhood, to the age of eleven, my fears continued to center in my parents. The fears were *for* them as much as for me. At my birth they were older than usual for the time—Will was thirty-three, Elizabeth twenty-eight. Again, he was the fifth child of six; she the youngest of eight. So like most veterans of clan society, before they had their own threatened infant, they'd witnessed at close range a wide assortment of the dangers of life, especially of infancy and age.

The early deaths of Elizabeth's parents and an infant brother might well have made her see the world as hostile. Awhile before her death at sixty, she told me that she'd always been "more scared than I let on." She bore her final oncoming blindness with stoic composure; but when the cause was found after months of searching—cerebral aneurysms beyond repair—I went in to tell her. She listened dry-eyed and then said, calmly as if she were an oak tree putting out leaves, "All my life I've been the Jonah." Veterans of the Jewish Bible will understand. Jonah was a Hebrew prophet who fled God's command and took to the sea. When a storm struck the ship on which he was fleeing, the sailors threw Jonah overboard in hope of surviving. So in her own mind toward the end of her life, Elizabeth saw herself as a sacrifice—orphaned at eleven and fourteen, married for the first nine years to a drunk, torn in three labors, widowed at forty-nine, blind at fifty-seven and soon to be dead at sixty.

Through childhood though, I mistook my mother—not in love; her love was a high steady flame. My error lay in thinking she trusted the world, its goodness, the sweetness of its outcomes. From here looking back, I'm glad I misunderstood. For Will, despite his comic gift and his taste for beauty, was openly fearful. Brave enough to give up drinking and to work at his amends, still he knew that the world was sewn with traps. He was never a shaking coward; he'd have fought barehanded any visible threat to his family. But all his fears were unseen. His size alone, the big gray eyes and firm voice, gave his dread an unanswerable force. And sporadic laughter thrust him on through most ordeals. But where had he got his Roman sense of the world as a gorgeous lethal funhouse?

I've stressed his mother's powerful presence. She had been thirty-seven at his birth; and whether because of a hard ensuing menopause or a born-anxious mind (the wit came from her), she taught Will early that the world has plots to maim and kill. His sisters told me how Muddy would send Will off to school each morning with a farewell kiss and the warning that her weak heart might fail before he returned. They said he would pound up the steps each afternoon, always half-expecting to find her coffin inside.

Whatever the cause, and after all he was right in the end, Will endowed me with his suspicions. Even in grade school, I was troubled when my friends announced plans. Maybe I was further conditioned by the black people who worked for us. Obedient to an injunction in the fourth chapter of the New Testament book of James, blacks would never express a hope without acknowledging the prerogative of fate, which is to say No. If you told the cook you'd see her tomorrow, she'd have set you right, "You'll see me *if* the Lord be willing and we don't die." So when I was faced with a playmate's heedless certainty, I'd flinch invisibly and think "You *hope*. We *want* to but can we?" I knew enough to hide that caution, and thus I'm not remembered as gloomy.

But all the while, the force of Will's deep sense of doom and my early encounters with the deaths of kin, young and old, gave me a low-grade permanent case of the tragic sense of earthly life. I knew that the unexpected—reward and disaster—hangs just above our heads; and our daily actions have sure but unpredictable effects on the stay or fall of those dangers. It's no easy sight-line for a child to maintain, though millions do. I was well into manhood before I learned of the necessary compensations—how to move with economy of noise and gesture so as not to lure a malevolent fate; how to compose your damaged face if axes fall, as someday they will. But as fate turned ironic on me in adolescence, my caution proved true and oddly consoling. Trouble, when it came, was at least no surprise; and however I howled, I mostly knew better than to blame the sky or the nearest human being.

The strongest remembered fear of my childhood was of Will's drinking, and at times the fear amounted to terror. I've said that before I can now recall, he'd managed to quit and he never relapsed. From 1936 on, he

could watch his friends drink and not feel tempted. So in conscious memory I never see him as even mildly tight; but from age five, when Skinny
Rodwell spilled the history, I quickly became a sleepless home-detective.
Elizabeth had tried to explain the past, Will's promise to God, and to
assure me of the future. But with my old sense of our working triad, I
agonized. Among my uncles and male cousins, I'd already seen an array
of the effects of those quick snorts of brown liquid (in the small-town
South, liquor was always drunk in the kitchen or outdoors and in one
hard swallow, followed by a frown). Then would come the loud laughing, then wrangles and shouts at my contemporary cousins, then weeping wives and heartbroken parents. Any possibility that my father
might renege on his promise became the worst fear, and none since has
eclipsed it.

The early fear was stoked even higher by Will's very ease around his
friendly drinkers. Through any such gathering, especially after baseball
games or horseshoe matches, I'd prowl as a plainclothes spy. I'd laugh
at even the jokes that missed me; I'd answer questions brightly; but I'd
avoid the lurches and grabs of the drinkers and keep an unblinking eye
on Will. The worst moment was bedtime when I had to go off duty and
leave my excited father on his own recognizance in the midst of friends
already glazed and raucous. I believed Will meant to keep his promise,
but I also knew that one of his life's aims was pleasing his friends (no one
who drank in sight of my father was a friend of mine, even now in hindsight). Because a child knows so little of the possible strength of human
will, I doubted Will's power to keep his vow. I'd lie in the dark as long as
I could, my favorite toys all near at hand but powerless to help; and I'd
listen through the door till the final weight of my diligence drowned me.

What did I think would happen if my guard failed and Will drank
again? I've said that I saw numerous examples of the bad effects of drink
on grown men (I can't remember seeing a woman take a drink till I was
in college). I knew how my favorite cousins, two girls near my age, had
suffered from a drinking father—no physical abuse but a lot of mental
cruelty and gypsy living as he hauled them from town to town, from
houses to apartments to freezing rooms in a hectic search for one more
job. There were tales of their mother's gathering coal off the railroad

Will and I in our apartment on Cranford Street in Asheboro, 1938. Like other great comedians, he seldom smiles in pictures. And he never removes his tie till bedtime; but we sit at a natural ease with one another, despite the fact that some of our friends are drinking in the kitchen.

tracks near one of their basement apartments, of pawning and losing her wedding silver. Luckily it was years before they and I knew that— strong as she was, with her Indian bones (Pocahontas was her eighth-great-grandmother)—their mother was eventually driven to turn on the gas and wait till a last-minute knock at the door changed her mind.

So destitution was what I feared, that and the shame of my self-respecting parents. Few adults grow up to recall the entirety with which even healthy children lean on the notion of their parents' strength and reliability. Even in our darkest days of the thirties, we in the triad had our solid families behind us. We'd never have ended in a squatters' camp. Yet surrounded by the sights of the late Depression years—Will's worried brow as he contemplated his weekly stack of bills—and conditioned by Elizabeth's orphan-past, I took no comfort from the safety net. I feared exactly the danger they'd have spared us: homelessness, one or both of my parents gone.

Family lore had already taught me what students of drug addiction now confirm. If Will had taken a single drink, it might well have triggered the slide. Our balanced triad would smash in an instant; the house would silently vanish around us (my toys and food), and I'd be surely left alone in a desolate field. No child in Dickens eyed the workhouse more shakily than I, perched on the ledges of the white middle class before the Second War began to slow the drain. By then Will's abstinence was credible at last.

If my recollection sounds neurotically extreme, believe that I hear the same remembered fears from recent and affluent college students. Especially now when divorce is common, millions of children live in chilled anticipation of the moment when Mother or Father sits them down and recites the news—the family is dead; your world has ended. A further component of their dread is the guilt they're more than ready to accept—*When they fail, and they will, I'll have caused it.* In light of the present divorce rate and the fact that roughly half those fears are realized, how many million young minds are we permanently freezing in the lobes of love and calm? And how many of them will later muster the courage to trust another soul?

When I was seven, after a Saturday-night party at our house, I woke next morning before Will and Elizabeth and went straight to the kitchen

in search of evidence. There on the counter among dirty dishes, as un-
concealed as if it were tame as a butter knife, was a half-drunk fifth of
bourbon. Instant desolation. Like all children, I knew that I'd caused
it—some obscure fault of mine, some skill I'd failed to learn and provide.
For now though there was nothing to do but wake my parents, a thing
I was told not to do on Sundays, and confront Will with his treachery.
Luckily I was grown before I glimpsed the underside of his deal with
God; till then I'd never thought that, if Will broke his bargain, God
might well repossess me. But I still taste that Sunday morning's cold
heartbreak.

When I managed to voice my accusation at their bedside, both of
them tried to silence the fears. The bottle belonged to Gale Hightower,
a high-voltage lineman who worked with Will at the Power and Light;
Gale just forgot to take it. Neither Will nor Elizabeth had touched a
drop. I was partly relieved—Will was sober now—but something in the
air plainly troubled him. He threw back the covers and walked as straight
to the kitchen as I'd just done. He opened the bottle, looked down at
me and said "Preacher, here's how much this means to me." Then he
poured the remaining whisky down the drain. I was perfectly relieved
and that one fear was gone for good, from my consciousness at least.

Organizations now exist for the mates and children of alcoholics. One
of their principal contentions is that a fear of relapse is the steady
weather hanging above a drunk's kin, even the families of recovered
drunks. I don't deny the claim, but I can say that I never recall another
conscious doubt in my relations with Will. Few real anxieties vanish.
At best, they leave a vacant rail on which other fears can speed. But none
of my later fears was knowingly concerned with Will.

Before I entered adolescence, he was spending the better part of every
week on the road as a salesman of electrical appliances—stoves, refrigerators, freezers, irons. Fired by my own growing desires but powerless to
enact them, I imagined a succession of adventures for him, who was
likely the truest of husbands. As secret home-theatrics, they pleased me.
I'd tell myself stories of the women he'd meet in salesman's hotels, the
gifts he'd bring them and how they'd thank him. I even imagined a
second bigamous family for him, with a half-brother or -sister for me,
when the worries of our small legal household were almost more than

Will could bear. But I never thought he was laid out drunk on a whore's stale bed or even alone with the radio and a ceiling fan above in the dark.

The story of the poured-out bottle reveals another of Will's two nicknames for me. Nobody but Will used his two favorites, but I liked each one a good deal more than the "Rennie" that I mostly refused and eventually stamped out. At times for him I was "Ed" from my first name, after his father Edward; but more often I was "Preacher Jones" or "Preacher." Will was dead before I thought to wonder why "Preacher," and no one else could explain. The poured-out bottle might suggest that he thought of me as a pocket-sized prohibitionist minister, a vocation he respected; but the nickname may precede my fears. It seems more likely that "Preacher" was a warning to himself—*This child is both the emblem and hostage of my pledge.* Again I hope the name doesn't suggest that I struck him or anyone else in the family as grim. My memories preserve more laughter than fear; and in most of their early pictures, I'm smiling.

Except for one other large fear, the remaining worries of my childhood were normal, certainly in middle-class families of my time and place. To catalog them here, and demonstrate their commonness, would demean the fact that all griefs are suffered individually and alone. No children and few adults are consoled to hear that a present trouble is ordinary and is shared by many. The local version of that strategy, when I contended with it, employed the children of China who were then the victims of brutality in the Japanese invasion of Manchuria. Their stricken faces were visible everywhere on Red Cross posters and in newsreels— "You think you're unhappy? Then think of the pitiful Chinese children." To a six-year-old in North Carolina, grumbling over spinach, that meant less than nothing. I and my contemporaries—and all the children I know today—were left, alone and helpless, to assume that life would be what it is this minute, from here till death.

Why does no one attempt to find ways of convincing children that the nature of time is forward motion, not paralyzed suffering? Maybe any such try would have been as lost on me as the plight of the Asians. But whenever I look back at early fear and sadness, I find myself still wishing that one of the credible adults in my family—Ida, Mac or Grant, say—

Bill and I in Asheboro, 1943. If the photographer is behind the camera, then who are we smiling at?—Elizabeth surely. I've recently got my full-sized front teeth and flash them. Bill, already a winning laugher, is momentarily still. Clearly no Cain and Abel here.

had told me a simple version, with illustrations from his or her own child-life, of something like this: "This bad afternoon, and your feeling about it, is painful but it's already ending—look, the sun's going down; soon you'll be asleep. Time keeps moving. Nothing stays the same and you'll be better soon."

My parents and other kin were kind; I had fine teachers, with the one cruel exception; but no one told me a thing I needed to hear—*You're not trapped forever.* I'd grow up eventually and run my own life, more than now at least. I believed most other urgent things they told me—I took Will's advice and was never run-over, shot, drowned or lost for more than a few minutes. However much I doubted their loyalty, at times when they left and were late returning, they never vanished and always begged my pardon for slowness. So at bottom I trusted them; I might have believed them on other threats, like vicious onslaughts on my right to be. But I'm sure that a simple answer is the entire truth—it never occurred to Will or Elizabeth to try to help me. No one had shown them how, in their childhoods. And I've never met another adult who heard one word of such news in childhood, nor can there be one who wouldn't have welcomed it.

So with slow time and the gradual learning of navigation skills, my other fears and pains dissolved at their own pace. A few of them were apparently innate, if not instinctive, and have dogged me always—a certain nervousness, for instance, about trips and partings that I've always suspected might be a result of my difficult birth, that first and hardest parting for us all. But one more fear resulted from another choice of Will's, and it worked in me for three long years.

When I was eleven and had just completed five grades in the same good public school in Asheboro, Will was offered a better job. This time he'd manage the sale of appliances in all of eastern North Carolina for the Farmers Cooperative Exchange, a young but thriving co-op centered in Raleigh. We would finally begin to be solvent. And what was even more attractive for him and Elizabeth, it would let us reel in the hundred miles of navel string between themselves and the family homes we trekked to visit over such long roads—we could live once more in Warren County.

With the big exceptions of Ida and Mac, I liked my country relatives in varying degrees. But I hated the thought of leaving Asheboro, the town where I'd lived for as long as I had substantial memory. I was prospering at school, and I relished the work. I had dozens of friends with whom I played everything from football to King Arthur model-dolls, and I had no enemies. There were three first-run picture shows, and I was midway through a sweep of the possible Cub Scout ranks and eager for the Boy Scouts. No part of town was foreign to me and my friends on our bikes; and far as I could see, I was in firm control of a long clear future. In addition, my body had lately begun to notice itself with sensuous care— my own best irreplaceable, and apparently inexhaustible, toy. It, like all my other contentments, was socketed deeply in this one place—the only home I really remembered. Any move would ruin or scatter it all. No Russian prince ever faced exile with stronger fears.

When Will's offer came, school had just turned out for the summer. So I had long hot days for dread and hope. And I took to my knees in fervent prayer—let him not take the job; let us stay on here. But in early July I met with my first bitter No from the sky. Will took the job, he and Elizabeth went up to scout a likely house, we'd leave in early August. My sadness tainted my parents' relieved delight—prosperity at last, in the bosom of home—but the coming change lay on me with a heaviness that proved prophetic. In the last weeks before moving, I avoided sight of all my friends. Loneliness was better than a frenzied last bout of company. David Sumner, Harry Anderson, Chisholm Story— the names are still a little hard to say, the first of a lifetime's casualty lists. Will and Elizabeth said I could come back and visit anytime, but I knew I'd lost them for good and I had. This was America; no look back. I've never seen one of them, that day to this.

It was more than a year before Will and Elizabeth realized their error. "Home" was no longer home but a set of changed houses full of edgy kin. Most of their old school friends were gone or sunk in their own domestic bogs, and their other contemporaries had already woven complex social webs that had no room for one new couple. But oblivious at first, they swam and dived in a crowded bath of familiarity. Bill, at age three, rolled easily with the change; he'd left only one playmate behind. And in a matter of weeks, even I was considering eating my tears. My age-mates in town, all dozen of them, welcomed me in. I was biking, swimming and—as summer ended—playing touch football. Though I didn't feel weaned enough from Asheboro to accompany Mother and Bill back for a first fall visit, I'd begun signaling to the family that this new place might not be the disaster I'd foretold. And by the time school opened, Will and Elizabeth's guilt at uprooting me was almost allayed.

I had a good sixth-grade teacher; and to the roll of my new town friends, I added a number of children bused in from farms in the country. By the start of cool weather in mid-October, I seemed rooted in a life as rewarding as the one I'd left. The only hitch was a temporary annoyance. Stable and old-line as it was, Warrenton had almost no rental property; so while we waited for a vacant house, we packed into a four-room second-floor hot apartment at the Hotel Warren.

Then came a crucial afternoon, two weeks before Halloween, one of those days on which a whole life is rudely bent but which starts with nothing more special than sunlight. Late October but the late afternoon was still so warm I'd pulled off my sweater and tied it around my waist in a manner that always felt jaunty. Three of my new town friends and I had biked away from school together and were aimlessly cruising the back streets of town. One of them was my first friend here, a distant cousin small enough to be called Midget. One was the myopic but powerfully magnetic, mouth-breathing son of my father's second-best boyhood friend.

The other had no close connection with my family, though Will had known his mother forever. Aryan blond and blue-eyed, the boy was a third-generation son of wealthy English stock and poor German immigrant farmers. His father had made good, moved to town and married. The Second War had six months to run; so of course we called our friend "the German," which he seemed not to mind. I still suspect the German caused what happened next. All my life I'd had my instinct for slicing a way into tight-sealed bonds—Will and Elizabeth, Ida and Marvin, some Asheboro boys. Now I'd sliced into dangerous ground; I'd got too close to the myopic friend—too close, too fast—and the German wouldn't have it.

By four o'clock we were down near the jail. I thought we'd stopped to hear the prisoner sing. For more than a week, there'd been a black prisoner who stood at his barred window, singing hymns. But that afternoon he didn't appear, and the German said his bike tires were low. Everybody's tires are always low, so we rolled a few yards downhill for air at Shorty Gillam's garage and bus station. The air pump was on the jail side of the building, behind a five-foot pile of coal. It was my turn next. I was off my bike and squatting by the tire; my school books were strapped to the red back-fender. The German said one clear word, "Ready?" I thought he meant me—was I ready to go?—but when I looked up, he was facing the myopic.

With no further sound, they came down on me. First they knocked me back into the coal; my bike fell too and my books hit the coal. Then as I scrambled up, more shoves and kicks—no blood or cuts and still no words. My midget cousin only watched, still as they. Thirty seconds' pummeling spent their purpose on my actual body; but for his climax, the German found a pointed stick and pounded deep holes in the lid of a box of watercolor pencils I prized and had kept in perfect condition. Still silent, they mounted their bikes and left. Midget had watched without protest, and he rode off with them.

From the first grade on, instead of renting my textbooks from the school, Will had bought me new copies at my request (I liked to color the illustrations and have them to keep when the school year ended). But now as I gathered the coal-grimed books and the pierced pencil-box, they seemed the real victims. And at once they shared the victim's curse. They were ruined past my power to forgive; at every glimpse, they'd revive my shame. I'd already copied Will's fastidious respect for useful objects—keep them clean and orderly; they'll serve you all the better. At once I knew I'd throw these away.

A man's voice said "Son, are you all right?" I looked toward a grown man ten yards away. He was a friend of Elizabeth's, named Johnny Adcock; and he worked at the garage. He'd stood there smoking a cigarette and watching the scene.

I said I was fine, but silently I hoped he would die or disappear. I didn't resent his passive witness; I only felt that he knew too much. So I hoped I'd never see him again, alive in this world or dead in the next.

I was only a single long block from our hotel, up a back street where nobody much but blacks ever walked; and they wouldn't know me. Not that I was crying or bleeding. A genuine Rodwell, all my life I've misted over readily for minor emotions, mostly small delights; but at big events, I'm desert dry. And not till I'd turned in at the hotel parking lot, leaned my bike on the wall and thrown the pencils in a garbage can, did I realize that the target was me and would always be till I left this ingrown, sealed and hateful town. If I'd trusted my foresight back in Asheboro, I'd have fought for a way to stay behind.

A moppet melodrama? A standard heartbreak suffered by billions of new children in whatever town and easily mended by vigorous reaction the next day at school? *Hit the bastards back, throw their books down the coal chute (not that they give a damn about their books). In another week you'll have won your spurs and be safe again.* Right?—in Newark maybe or South Philadelphia. This was small-town North Carolina in the forties; the total white population was under a thousand. Those were literally the main white boys of my exact age and class (and class was a power, in my parents' eyes). What was worse, till the moment of that word "Ready," all three boys had convinced me of their friendship. Now they'd not only ruined my books and pencils, they'd revealed me as a whey-faced fool to trust them. I hadn't understood that, while children can generally spot deceit in adults, they're blind to their age-mates.

I was neither a pacifist, a coward nor a bloodless boy-saint; but telling me to hit back was as useful as telling me to vaporize. I understood the purpose and technique of fist-fighting about as well as your dog understands algebra. Aside from mild switchings, I'd never felt an angry hand; and though I enjoyed healthy tussles and pillow fights and had watched playground scuffles, I'd never had the least occasion to strike out at anyone. And cowboy movies, along with family drunks, had shown me enough of the pain of hateful acts to convince me that fighting was a skill I didn't mean to learn. Finally I saw no future in another dust-up. Like my books and watercolor pencils, these friends were ruined. I'd never want them again.

The only treacheries I'd ever suspected lay well behind me and had proved imaginary—the thought that my parents might someday remove

In my Cub Scout uniform, behind our house on Sunset Avenue in Asheboro, late in the winter of 1944. The knickers are not a foppish touch but are fall-to-winter issue for boys between the first grade and puberty. In the South they were always worn without knee socks. The bicycle, red and white with a much-prized speedometer, will be beside me in the coal-pile drubbing that waits in Warrenton, seven months from now.

their masks of love to show other faces or that they might call me in one evening and, far from announcing their own divorce, reveal that they'd adopted me, that I hadn't worked out and was being sent back. So I was unprepared for one of the worst human discoveries—that friends you trusted have plotted your ruin. If that word "Ready" hadn't hung in the air, I might have waded back in the next day. But "Ready" was nailed up in those few yards between Shorty Gillam's and the jailed black singer like a red roadsign. That certain proof stopped me—the German and the myopic planned the attack. I already knew their lock-jawed natures; they'd never relent.

When I got to our apartment, Elizabeth and Bill were out. Will was there; he looked me over for bruises, heard my story and responded kindly but with no understanding of my sense of permanent disaster. Next time, fight back. And Mother agreed. In an hour she served my favorite supper, country-style steak; but with my afternoon and their effortless air of conduct-as-normal, it stuck in my throat.

Given their big-family knockabout childhoods, it probably never occurred to Will and Elizabeth to contact the lead-boys' parents, lifelong friends that they were, and tactfully suggest a pullback. That brand of intervention was so foreign to the parent-child thought of those days that I doubt I even thought of asking for it. I'd like to think my refusal to fight back came from a naturally gentle nature. Of course it didn't. If I could have eliminated the German from the landscape, bloodlessly, with the press of a button, I'd likely have pressed. But lacking such dream technology, I was mired like my parents in an ancient code of meaningless honor. I'd accepted shame; there was no way back.

Two weeks later, despite large misgivings but at Will and Elizabeth's insistence, I dressed and madeup as an Arab and went to Buddy Gibbs's nighttime Halloween party. It was a warm evening, and the children who'd arrived before me were playing under lanterns in the front yard. Buddy's mother Mary offered me a warm welcome, but I'd already sighted my two attackers. They lurked snickering in the shrubbery as long as Mary Gibbs was near. Once she left, they seeped out of hiding like a stain in water and worked over toward me with laughing stops to catch the crowd's attention. But they didn't dawdle; they knew they only had a short space till Mary returned. I don't recall the next two minutes, no one act or sound. It was the first bad event of my life that I'm sure I've concealed from conscious memory. Strangest of all, I don't remember my enemies' disguises, though I know they wore thick makeup, not masks. Their familiar voices and the taste of their purpose blanked all sensation. I suspect I made no self-defense; I know I was thrown to the ground and kicked in the presence of a dozen other masked and madeup witnesses.

I must have known every witness present, boys and girls; but with their disguises and in the dark, I couldn't be sure. I only guessed that their lips were smiling; and plainly none joined, on either side of the mute transaction. When my memory revives I was on the ground, entirely surrounded. It felt like waking on another planet to find yourself tortured by a ring of creatures who seem to want to give you the pleasure they so plainly feel.

My next memory is of running, in my bedspread-burnous, to the nearest sanctuary—Will's home and his sisters, a long block away. No one followed, for good or bad. I told the true story, that still feels incredible to me; and my aunts believed it. Each of them had suffered serious pain, and now they were merciful. But the youngest, Martha Reynolds, was the most understanding. When I'd told my story, she drove me home.

First, she told Will and Elizabeth she couldn't imagine why they forced me to go. They could only look sheepish. She went on to say that, when she was a child, Muddy had made her go places she hated; and she could still taste the pain she'd felt—"And none of it did me a particle of good." Then she had the brave grace to take my hand, not in a pitying way but like an equal in the actual world; she met my eyes and told me that she knew exactly how I felt and that I had no need whatever of friends who were that damned mean (I honored her for it to the end of her life and visited her early deathbed to thank her).

Something in her voice and in the strength of the gray Price eyes showed me the first sign of hope—this sane grown woman knew all I felt and sided with me. She'd lasted till now; then I'd last with her. God knows, what she said was better to hear than my parents' clear, though unstated, worry that my reception was already clouding their homecoming. Elizabeth checked my scrapes and washed off my makeup with muttered vows it would all blow over. I knew she was dead wrong and told her so.

My worst fear was proved; the hatred had lasted more than a week. It was therefore eternal. With the true finality that only Greek dramatists and children manage, I accepted the end of one more world and was miserable for a good part of the thirty more months we stayed in Warrenton. In hopes of seeming less fragile than the narrative suggests, I can add that my prediction came true—the rejection never relented. There were repeated incidents at school, taunting and traps. The intensity of their hatred was pure and hard as diamond, and I still wonder what in me helped fuel a force that I've yet to meet elsewhere.

The only extenuation lay in the accident that, though the tormentors were my age, they were a year ahead of me in school; so I was never in classes with them. Nearly three years later, shortly before we left for good, I was riding my bike in the midst of town; and the myopic managed to sight accurately enough with his air rifle to hit my moving head. A few inches either way, I might have lost an eye. Some days later Will met the boy's father by chance at a restaurant, mentioned the shooting and suggested that a word of caution might be wise—years too late.

Again I'm uneasy. Even this distant rehearsal, after forty-four years with all their compensations, is unpleasant to conduct and shameful to expose. But I've tried to explain in what way my experience differed from the stock-model rejection of the sensitive offense-collecting pre-pubescent child. Maybe my experience differs from the model only in the fact that this boy bided his time long years and only now serves the ghastly feast of his vengeance—vengeance being a dish that's best served cold as the grave. But vengeance is as peripheral to my purpose now as a cry for retroactive pity. What I mean to outline is the moment when one more wry figure began to scribe itself, deep and large, on the still-uncrowded field of my life.

No one could have known, and certainly couldn't have convinced me, that expulsion from that brief Eden would prove a permanent gift—that old ladies' favorite, a "blessing in disguise." Again as far back as I've kept visual memories, solitude or at least silent meditative time is a constant absolute need of my mind. In those last days of innocent childhood, I was treading water in a dangerous contentment. Like so many bright and much-loved children, I'd learned to play the success-keyboard with dazzling speed, at school and after; I could sweep across its octaves, eyes shut. So there's no guessing what would have happened if I'd stayed in the uncontested small world of Asheboro or if Warrenton had proved to be more of the same. Would I now be a "well-liked," modestly prosperous, bottled-in-bond smalltown deed-and-divorce lawyer who reads Confederate history late into the night, owns a Lincoln, has a whisky-bass wife in too much jewelry, grown grandchildren and a family pew in the Episcopal church? So long as I was a popular boy, and did my homework three nights a week, that was the course my world had set for me.

The fact is, when the fire curtain fell that October between me and my town contemporaries, I entered a loneliness that lasted through the crucial first years of adolescence. I've said that, in my eight years of only-childhood, I'd acquired a number of skills for dealing with lone time—drawing, reading, solo games in the woods and a fascination with my role as spy on the lives of my parents and on our teeming larger family.

The same skills served in Warrenton, with an important addition at which I've glanced earlier. By the age of four I'd discovered my body's resources for physical pleasure; but with the opening of the sluice-gates of maturity, I was almost overnight the impresario of a brilliantly successful home-entertainment facility. Furthermore it led to my first extended and steady writing. Blissfully astounded by these new carnal gifts, which (lacking male friends) I could mention to no one in sight, I confessed them to one of those leather-bound five-year diaries with six lines per day and a lock and key. I kept not only a skeleton-log of each day's home and school events but a minutely attentive chart of my maturation, with drawings that were Germanic in the rapt care expended on every follicle, curl and vein, plus measurements (all of which I burned in 1958 on learning that I'd got my first full job, teaching the young).

The onset of sexual need is accompanied, in Americans at least, by an even deeper immersion in the narcissism and self-obsession that come with birth. My sudden ostracism from the children of my class in a small town meant that I spent more time than ever in the company of my ceaselessly narrative adult family. It also meant that my school teachers, almost always demigods in my eyes, were more than ever worth watching for hints (I'll speak of them later). From my adult kin and all the unusually fine teachers of those years, I acquired a time-deep fund of news that ultimately counted for more in my life than a warm bath of adolescent chatter.

My tormentors were focused on Friday night's party while I was the secret sharer of knotted tales of family hatreds, addictions, elopements, abortions and adulteries as cruel as pistol shots in the naked face. The threat of further violence also required that I activate my retired alcohol-detection skills and hone them to service as a 360-degree observational system. Figuratively, and literally when possible, I sat and still sit with my back to the wall—that choice vantage point of the hunted and of all serious writers—eye-frisking the room and above all the door.

Equally valuable, I was forced to seek friendship among the bussed-in farm children who were more than half my school's population and the poorly fed, thin-faced children of production-line workers at the box mill west of town. To a person, they were oblivious to the power politics of the prosperous and idle town children, whom they saw with considerable accuracy as stuck-up rich fops. Unbeknownst, these shut-out but unembittered children were already steeped in agrarian or proletarian fatalism. But the realism of their meager hopes never precluded an outrageous taste for ribald and self-directed fun.

The world of piano lessons, neighborhood team-sports, clothing fads and the rest of that crowded American arcade of children's amusement—which was only just cranking up around us—was as distant from their minds as the chance of careers in law, medicine or investment banking. The openfaced kindness they showed me, without exception but credibly soured with raillery, and the facts they taught me about a life lived close to the ground in merciless weather—it all poured deep into my storage cellars and slept for years.

I vaguely knew they were giving me something better than fun; and I thanked them for it by asking each year, at school-picture time, for copies of their faces. I have them still, with their held-back smiles—Dody Miller, Frederick Williams, Nancy Lee King, Mildred Tharrington, Willie B. Overby, Martha Duke Aycock, Earl Haithcock, Belle Limer. Now I can see how, even that early, their eyes were watching the whole hard future—lives like their parents': dawn-to-dark labor six days a week, early marriage and children in stair-steps. From this far off, their smiles seem all the more earned and hardy.

Eight years later when I was reaching for the start of a story I had to write in a college course, I knew I must try to encompass Will's death, then a year behind me. And I needed a tale-bearer different from me, to watch our pain and try to bend toward it. It had to be somebody I understood but who was better, kinder and braver than me. Prompt to my need, a country girl rose suddenly to mind, tall and strong and lovely as a month-old colt. Her name came with her—Rosacoke Mustian, an adolescent farm girl from Afton, N.C. Afton had been the crossroads home of many of my school friends; and though neither Rosa nor any other person in the story was based on them, the odor of life that hangs in the pages—and all the seen and unseen furniture of her daily existence—came straight from the evidence I unthinkingly gathered in three school years that, while I was in them, seemed a lifetime sentence.

I had two more summers to navigate before we moved to Raleigh and happiness returned. And though Midget repented of his passive betrayal and restored his friendship, and a few younger town children were congenial, the summers were so long and idle that I missed my country friends. I even wrote a few of them letters to which they seldom responded. They might as well have been a continent away, not just five miles. And since they were working members of families bent on making the crop that was food-or-famine, none of them ever asked me to visit. So I never entered one of their houses; and in all the fiction I've set in their midst, unrealistic as it means to be (that first long story and, till now, three novels in twenty-six years), I've used the faces they showed me in school and have guessed the remainder, the nighttime half.

Nearly thirty years after publishing "A Chain of Love," the first story, I've yet to hear from one of them. Has any of them read it? Did they like it or lump it? Did I get it so wrong they can't bear to tell me?—tact was never their longest suit. I've heard from strange Marines in Chu-Lai, cloistered nuns and barking madmen but never a word from Afton, N.C. or any of its voters. When you left their sight, you left for good. They'd wave you off with genuine regret, but they worked too hard to moon over anything that couldn't be used in the house or barn in the next year or so.

*   *   *

In my bad times a few years ago—entranced by the depredations and paradoxical gifts of spinal cancer and paraplegia—I tried to recall other days when life seemed to end just there up ahead in a huge gray wall with no painted slogans and, God knows, no instructions. The rest of my youth after Warrenton and most of my hard-working middle age could hardly be called dashing. There were no actual battlefields, few treks up glorious features of the landscape, few outsized gestures on the visible air. Yet there have been a number of the inner, less visible brands of dare and failure. I've moved through the deaths of loved ones, through steady solitary work with its public rewards, then huge successes and failures in love, and those alkali flats where the spirit seems all but dead for water. So every backward glance reminded me firmly that the first and ultimate property of time, in human life anyhow, is onward motion—however sidling, wandering or crawling belly-down.

Yet none of the fears I met at fifty-one, when my life was broken like a stick across some broad but unseen knee and the fractured pieces were flung back into my numb hands to use as I could—no terror matched the childhood threats I've described. My guess is, a great many people will grant the same as the trials of age fly up in their road like actual demons whose harmless shadows we met and partly tamed in Halloween games. Any soul that endures a normal childhood—not to speak of the all but unthinkable innocents who last through torture at the hands of adults or disease or God—is made of strong stuff, a thing worth trusting thereafter in the dark.

Elizabeth and I in Asheboro, 1938. She is thirty-three and in her best dress, black with a small design in purple sequins. I'm holding the current pick of my totemic elephant collection. Though our eyes don't meet, no other picture shows so openly our delight in one another. And whenever I hope to convey the combination of readiness, open-heartedness, vulnerability and radiance that all her friends agree was hers only, I point to this.

6

REAL COPIES

WILL PRICE, CRICHTON DAVIS,
PHYLLIS PEACOCK AND MORE

WHEREVER WE LIVED, my parents read the daily paper.
Will claimed further that he'd read one novel in his life, *All Quiet on
the Western Front*. He surely never read another while I knew him, even
in all his nights on the road. Since he came near to serving in the trenches
in the First War, his choice was apt. He and Elizabeth lived in the boom
years of American periodicals; and even in our hard times, they bought
and read a lot of magazines—*Life, Liberty, Look, The Reader's Digest,
True Detective, The Saturday Evening Post* only begin the list. Like her
three sisters Elizabeth tended to fall asleep soon after beginning to read,
as if she had a hereditary print-induced narcolepsy. So I'm not sure how
many she finished; but I saw her attempt an occasional best-seller, especially if it was scandalous—"banned in Boston" was the code word then.
I remember on her bedside table, borrowed copies of *Gone with the
Wind, The Grapes of Wrath, Forever Amber* and *The Naked and the
Dead*. I sneaked long, mostly puzzled looks at them all; but what and
where was the scandal? I was too young to find it.

So books were not a big part of the furniture of my early childhood.
But Will's mother and sisters soon began to remedy the lack with excellent baby books and then the Wyeth-illustrated classics like *Robin
Hood* and *Treasure Island*. The first, when I was three, was a book of
Bible stories; and it's the only one of my baby books to survive, inscribed
to me from my grandmother Price. It's well-worn and scribbled with my
drawings in blue crayon—schematic human faces, none smiling.

And since Will would never have knowingly let me scribble on a book his mother gave me, I could strain the point and suggest that the drawings show me working on my own very early—no hovering parents to shepherd me toward the peaceful, mind-improving arts. In our sparsely populated rooms, I had unusual stretches of quiet time, with the only two adults murmuring beyond me. I was quick then to be my own companion.

As they left me mostly alone to play, so Will and Elizabeth seldom read to me. I have no memory whatever of hearing their voices in the words of a book, though I can recall asking them questions from whole rooms away, about a certain illustration—what's happening here where the boy is throwing the rock at the big man? All my books were profusely illustrated; and since I was so often alone, apparently I was content to decipher the pictures and make my own stories till I began learning to read in the first grade.

Visual art was another domestic scarcity. My earliest memories of household decor are also from age three. By then we had a framed color reproduction of an avenue of Lombardy poplars in late afternoon; Elizabeth called it "Harp of the Winds." And there was one long horizontal oil painting, an imaginary and moody night-seascape by Will's sister Mary Eleanor. Before her elopement at sixteen with her old schoolteacher, she studied art with a doctor's wife in Warrenton. The teacher seems to have given her pupils an excellent technical grounding but never to have encouraged their working outdoors or from a live subject, even something as safe as a pear. So Mary Eleanor's surviving oils show a real flair, for the copying of other pictures and for free invention—all are landscapes but none is painted from nature. Yet when she and her young son abandoned the teacher and returned home, she spent the next sixty years in the local Building and Loan and never lifted a brush. In her spare time she assembled fiendishly difficult jigsaw puzzles.

Otherwise there were sprays of family photographs on our walls and table-tops and a framed undecorated announcement of my parents' marriage. But the little we had was interesting and honorable, nothing that would shame conservative good taste even now. And in the absence of playmates or the gorgon-eye of television, I would often watch a picture till my mind broke through it; and its flat surface became what most artists hope their work is—an actual door in the wall of a room onto whatever scene or face is offered.

Will's home in Warrenton had more of Mary Eleanor's landscapes (I particularly liked "The Matterhorn on a Summer Day") and a fine mid-nineteenth-century pastel portrait of his Price grandfather John Meredith Price, artist unknown. Even a child could see how powerfully our ancestor's high forehead and bemused gray eyes had survived to stamp his living grand- and great-grandchildren. Better still, he had a miniature pair of spectacles propped jauntily on his forehead like a strange but enviable anatomical fixture; and they made me long prematurely for glasses.

Elizabeth's home had its two tall paintings, both the work of a friend of Ida's and neither as good as Mary Eleanor's (*good* meant recognizable, lifelike). One was a hefty female angel, the other a buck in snow. On every shelf there were squads of handpainted porcelain miniatures of our kin from the past three generations; and in the front hall, there was a hand-illuminated copy of the state song—

> *Here's to the land of the Long-leaf Pine,*
> *The summer land, where the sun doth shine,*
> *Where the weak grow strong and the strong grow great;*
> *Here's to down home—the old North State!*

Again, in my languorous summer stays with Ida, I spent real time consuming the walls and pictures that, however amateurish, were whole worlds to me, literal icons of sacred facts—an angel, an elk and a pine-tree bough: things different from me, worth knowing. Some human being had sat down, looked and—using only her mind and paints—had brought the fact, through the empty air, onto canvas or paper. I could do the same.

By the age of four I was investing a good deal of energy into drawing on the yellow pads Will brought from the office. Except for the Bible-story scribbles, no sample of my early work survives; but I can still see a few of the obsessive shapes. I'm convinced that I can even draw some of them still, in the original primitive lines. They showed no obvious flair, no cause for adult wonder—though in memory they do bear an odd kinship to James Thurber's big eloquent profiles of dumb animals, which I can't have seen since *The New Yorker* was not one of our magazines.

And since my drawings were normally childish, Will and Elizabeth acknowledged their thanks for my peaceful self-help. But they gave me no fawning encouragement.

In that, they were old-fashioned parents. They loved me round-the-clock, but they saw no reason to flop on the floor and prod a mind that was growing on its own at the general pace. There was a prodigious boy in Asheboro, whose parents taught him to read at four. And I recall Elizabeth's scorn at the forcing, "Let the poor boy be a child. God knows, it ends soon enough." With rapid changes since the 1960s in the teaching of pre-school students, graphic arts are now standard features of contemporary childhood. Most refrigerator doors are papered with the gleeful and mostly dismal results.* In the early thirties though, of all my contemporary kin, I was the only early painter. And for a reason I wish I could discover, my first repeated subject was elephants.

I can't say whether I developed an interest in the species first and asked Will to help me draw them, or whether he began to draw them for me and roused my interest. Whichever, I soon had a passion for the grandest land mammal, a love that continues unabated. Almost the only unanswered prayer of my childhood was the nightly request for a live pet elephant. On one occasion, a wire service ran a photograph of a baby elephant in Tampa, Florida; it was eating its owner out of house and home—any volunteers to take it? Will wrote to the named owner c/o Tampa; but the letter returned, marked "Insufficient address."

In the absence of the thing itself, I stood by Will at the table after supper many nights and watched with unfailing awe as he put down lines of elephants in bare profile. I can see his unshaded representations as clearly as my own. As realistic renderings his weren't a lot better than mine, which of course were copies of his. But they were recognizable—a hunting Bushman would have known them. Anyhow my delight in the transaction lay elsewhere than in the quality of my father's draftsmanship.

* In Paris in the late 1940s, a friend of mine accompanied Picasso to a UNESCO exhibition of children's art. The great man sped round the room, delighted, pointing out the marked resemblances, "Ah! Ça c'est Braque . . . ça c'est Matisse . . . ça c'est moi!" Only at the end did he turn to my friend and say "It's extraordinary. Young as they are, they're drawing like us. When I was their age, I was drawing like Raphael."

Throughout my childhood Elizabeth was quick in response to any show of affection, and all her life she was ready for play. But Will was no easier chum than before. He often talked of his boyhood baseball team, always naming the players—"Pat Hunter at first and Baby Lou at shortstop . . ." (Baby Lou was a girl and black). Still for whatever reason he and I seldom played games. And though he was also quick to accept a hug or touch (he loved to "eat a little souse-meat," which meant a grunting nibble at my ear lobe), he was also a fastidious dresser. That precluded floor-romps or lap-sitting. Gently but firmly he'd say "Darling, I got to wear this shirt tomorrow. Let's don't get it dirty." So our evening drawing is the only early joint pleasure I recall.

If Will had been skilled in line and shading, I might have been daunted. I had an older first cousin who graduated from a Chicago art school; the elephant she drew for me was so fine as to stop me for days. But since my father's thin-line elephants were on the knife-edge of resemblance, I had the joy of seeing a loved thing bloom almost to life on the blank page at the hand of another thing that was loved and needed far more than a pachyderm and that already seemed as unattainable.

I learned a basic love of the visual arts because I loved Will in them. I learned to love music mostly from Elizabeth, who was seldom far from a radio playing any brand of music; and so on through movies, architecture and the other arts. Though my own tastes often veered from those of my guides, I can think of no art that I've loved alone without a kind seducer (maybe my reluctance before all but the grandest ballet results from the lack of an early loved mentor). Conversely my earliest efforts to make works of art—drawings, poems, plays, stories, vocal and piano music—were shamelessly naked valentines, aimed like arrows at the heart of the world. But something even deeper down than love may have been at issue, and here I need to step aside briefly from the line of memory for a wider look.

Most of the visible animals on Earth, from elephants to ants, appear to gain most of their knowledge and pleasure from imitation. We can look low down on the tree of life and see infants of every species engaged in the act of watching, copying and learning. When do human beings start the same kind of witness? Maybe sooner than we now acknowledge. To start at our beginning, an indescribably complex feat of cellular imitation occurs in our nine months of life in our mother's womb. That immense job of copying is done by our parents' genes, our mother's health and energy and our own. And so far as we know, it's done without conscious effort by our mothers or ourselves.

I'm tentative here because I have the lingering conviction of uterine memory which I've mentioned earlier, those uncomplicated but still-consoling pictures of light as it works through Elizabeth's skin to my open embryonic eyes. A pale rose glow, hushed distant sounds, enormous warm peace. Each time I recall them, they seem more likely. If I'd been rewarding myself with invention, surely I'd have gone further.

But most mothers appear to feel that their child's first act of imitation, at three or four months, is its reproduction of a parent's smile. We gratify ourselves by thinking that the baby's smile is a product of its joy in our presence, and smiling babies do often proceed to other signs of near-spastic pleasure before us. But recent experiments have shown that they also respond to large pictures of smiling faces. They see the simplest drawing of an upturned mouth; and if their minds and muscles are old enough, they copy it.

So vast numbers of species are engaged in copying across the generations, copying for the purpose of preserving or enhancing life. It's plain too that some species copy things outside their own family bounds—a chimpanzee mimics human foibles, a mockingbird repeats the backfiring of a car. What good is done them by the copying? It seems undeniable that they enjoy the activity; it's initially at least a kind of play. Chimps dissolve into chuckles at their accurate mimicry, dolphins and killer whales relish the games they're taught in captivity, and talking birds may have a shrewder gift for the embarrassing rejoinder than we'd previously guessed.

But are we the single species that copies the *look* of the external world, in all its profusion of things and live creatures? Bizarre but brilliantly successful powers of camouflage are available to millions of lower species—the ability of an insect to resemble the leaf it sits on, the chameleon's shifting color. They copy the surrounding world in the almost surely unconscious hope of safety, survival and pleasure. There's little question that *Homo sapiens* does the same, with compulsive urgency from earliest childhood. Few well-tended infants fail to pick up a crayon and scribble a proudly offered likeness of Dad or the dog. And a sizable share of the doodles of our lifetimes will consist of efforts at the human face and form.

What brain structures or electrical circuits, what unconscious needs are involved in that kind of literal copying of ourselves and our kind, fair or foul? Again we can start far down on the tree and note that animals a good deal simpler than ourselves appear to sense loneliness. So strong is the need that they'll occasionally seek company from another species (the dog who mothers the orphan squirrel, the lonely man and his dog). Certainly a huge stretch of animal life is engaged in sexual pursuit and in the resulting need to protect the mate and the offspring. It's apparently that drive which in turn arouses one of the first brands of love—fierce care.

I've pointed to an early awareness that I could attract notice, even love, into my empty spaces by means of my various imitations, my disguises and decoys. And I suspect that I'm now far enough along in my life to grant that the making of irresistible decoys was the chief conscious energy in all my work before my mid-forties. The solitude required for serious writing is so unbroken that I wonder if I'd have continued the job if I hadn't been steadily rewarded with the one-by-one arrival of friendship and love that I knew were drawn by the work?

My start may have gone like this. When I was three Will brought me from the local dime store a foot-high plaster elephant, painted in garish orange and yellow and glittered with silver. I was elated; big as it was, the statue became my inseparable companion till I dropped it on a Saturday night. By then I was so attached to the thing that I couldn't contemplate waiting till Monday for a new one. Will had no recourse but to phone the manager on Saturday night and beg him to open the store long enough to supply a new elephant. Those were the days, 1936, and the town was so small that the manager politely complied. Bliss was restored; and I could beam at my father again, however briefly.

Maybe it was his well-meaning failure as a provider of elephants that acted as the first goad in prodding me forward to copies of my own, those eternally doomed tries at summoning a loved thing into the midst of my life. In any case, long before I entered grade school, I was a dedicated artist, a visual mime, a forger of my world—as Will mimed his in disguises and voices. And at about age five, to the elephants I added a new compulsion. I continually built houses, towns, parks and circuses from a grander set of rock-maple building-blocks than any that were then available in the upper South.

The blocks were sent one Christmas from Marshall Field in Chicago by our only rich relative—Will's cousin Mary Judd Clancy, who soon became another spontaneous feeder of my imagination. I stored her blocks in their heavy canvas bags with the fascinating drawstrings. Then I poured them out and detoured my drawing energy into the making of miniature houses, cities and zoos for my growing elephant collection. By then other benefactors had added the odd great cat and an ape or two to my menagerie, and the word itself—*menagerie*—was sweet in my mouth.

I caged and uncaged them all the ways I could imagine, strangely foreseeing the famous and pathetic New Guinea cargo-cult. There in response to the overhead traffic of Japanese and American planes during the Second War, a primitive tribe built mock airfields, even grounded mockplanes to lure the gods who so temptingly flew above them with cargoes of unimagined bounty.

The building blocks substituted for my next unsatisfied craving too— a Noah's Ark set, with all the Noahs, the big lifeboat and a pair of all living creatures. I'd seen such a set in a Victorian children's book, and my kin scoured the stores of America. Arks didn't exist, there toward the shank end of the Depression, even in Chicago and New York. But if my craving for elephants remains a mystery, so does the one for Noah's Ark.

I must have gathered the bare lines of the story from my Bible-story book. Aside from the bonanza of animals an Ark would have brought me, could my mind have dimly seen that Noah was the prime instance of what I soon would hope to be—a man who made, or at least populated, the world in which he lived? Since I worked toward the goal so steadily, I may have told myself such a story. Like most children, I already knew stories stranger than that, which I kept to myself.

Shortly after the block cities, I acquired the five-inch-high figures of a Japanese Christmas crèche. And again I'm unsure where the need arose. At four I was taken to see our friend Sarah Headen play Mary in a Presbyterian Christmas pageant of which I still have ringing memories. And with Mother's love of shopping, I'd have prowled the aisles of the local dime store where I ultimately saw the figures waiting. They were sold individually then, not as a set. You could have the Holy Family with just shepherds and sheep; or you could add an angel or Wise Men, with or without camels. I wanted them all, to be sure, and keep them to this day, having only lost the angel. (Oddly I seem to have bought five Wise Men, all different. When a child-friend named one of them The Manager recently, I said "Manager of what?" And she said "The *inn*.")

Even now they have an enduring power for me, in the right time and place. At the start, once Will and Elizabeth told me of the nativity, it was a story that became important in my early sense of the sacred unseen center of the world, a center which nonetheless attempts to declare itself to us in visible objects—burning bushes, arks and straw cribs. Luckily for my growing hunger to imitate the world, I didn't yet know the commandment that so sternly forbids the making of all such copies.

It's relevant to ask why God set that commandment so high in his list of ten. My guess is that he meant to forestall the temptation faced by any normal human being who makes or encounters a manmade copy of some beautiful or powerful thing. We are tempted to love it, even to worship it, to the exclusion of a God who tells us "I am jealous."

Just such an idolatry has been accorded for centuries to the pictures and images of the Orthodox and Roman Catholic churches. Their statues and icons are intended to remind us of the veneration owed to the unseen reality at which they hint. And in fact, their ancient painters were inspired to stylize their images. They worked to portray with a cool abstraction those faces and figures that, realistically portrayed, might snag our minds on a seductive face and end our meditation. Yet when I enter a sanctuary that harbors such an image, it's plain to see that many of the other visitors are praying *to* the image, not at it or beyond. And I, a lifelong all-but-idolmaker, have endured similar temptations to join my literal-minded fellows in adoring a painted doll or Michelangelo's youthful *Pietà* with its huge young Virgin and languid Christ.

*   *   *

When I was eight and my crèche was complete, my generous parents bought me another of my wants—a Sears-Roebuck dovetailed-wood box of oil paints and brushes, complete with palette, canvases and easel. Though we lived at the time in a pine woods with a clear rocky stream, my first attempt was an imaginary landscape, like those of my aunt Mary Eleanor—a line of distant mountains, the sky and clouds and falling water. I sketched my ground plan on the canvas and, almost at once, discovered that the scene in my head outstripped the skills of my hand.

From the first day, I could imagine and actually see far more intricate and satisfying pictures than I was capable of transcribing with my spanking-new and demanding equipment. So the fine box languished under my bed till the tubes of paint solidified and I retrenched. Since by then I was in the second grade, I'd learned to read; and books could begin to absorb some of the force that had gone into picture-making.

I'd also pretty well digested my discovery at age six, tramping alone through the woods near our house, that a single life-power was present in all creation. I knew that it was a power of which all things—rocks, trees and animals—were aware, as they were also aware of and somehow interested in one another. It would be four or five years before that knowledge began to mature and flow into my Sunday-school notions of God, the bearded man who made me in his likeness and who monitored my behavior. Were all these drawings and paintings, my first artistic ventures, related to that simultaneous awareness of an unseen world of power and witness?

Not consciously, no. That ultimate power may have pressed toward me long before I suspected its presence or intent—I believe it did—but my pencil-and-paint copying felt to me like a human job. It was my work, as Will's work was selling stoves and Elizabeth's work was me, the house and her world of confiding friends. Since painting is almost the only out-of-school work (except lawnmowing) that I remember before puberty, my mind plainly registered the pictures as serious and vital. What was vital actually was the work itself, the perfect vision so bright there before me and my aim to show it. My early results may have pleased my elders; they sadly failed me.

Yet I went on hatching projects that were much too ambitious for my

knowledge or technique. I've mentioned the thunderous mental landscapes. I also planned to paint a portrait of myself each year on my birthday (my cousin Taw Gay had introduced me to the visible passage of
time by marking my height each summer on a tree in the front yard of
the Price family home). I scheduled portraits of my favorite kin and a
long series of my own Bible pictures, meant to surpass all those in books.

But I was no boy-Samuel at service in the tabernacle; I had no sense of
serving or pleasing God in my work. So far as I knew, I was filling up
time; and though few parents recall it, filling time is childhood's biggest
chore. I was securing the love of parents who already loved me almost too
much but of whose continued presence I was still uncertain, even to the
point (as I've said) of suspecting that I was an orphan adopted on pro-
bation. As the only child for all my pre-school years, I'd had a lot of
adult love, however I mistrusted it. And I had two girl-cousins, Marcia
and Pat Drake, who served as my near-sisters. But as I hove in on age six
and the prospect of school, I felt powerful qualms.

It was a time in the South when there were almost no kindergartens,
so I was hardly alone in anticipating the first grade with shaky knees.
Will and Elizabeth predicted I'd love it. And in a summer enrollment
visit to the building, I glimpsed the wonders to come—those tall sturdy
easels and big pots of paint. Here were places where grown women
promised to teach you to paint and to watch you at it. The same women
offered you aquariums and ant farms, pinned-up drawings with your
name emblazoned, model alphabets, mysterious charts of other names on
which a few children had rows of gold stars while many had none. It was
plainly a grand and brave outlook, but nothing could hide the equally
enormous truth—the first grade faced me with an absolutely new world.
As a breech baby I'd done badly enough in my entry to planet Earth.
How would I manage a whole new sphere now, called Park Street
School?

There are photographs of me coming home from the great day—white-
shirted, blazered and bookbagged. I'm smiling a little wanly at Elizabeth,
behind the lens and waving as I head to my room to think it all over,
those crowded hours that forecast the next twelve years of my life. The
last thing I can have considered was World War II. It had started twelve

Home from my first day of school, Asheboro, September 14th 1939. I call this a thoroughly unconvinced smile; the boy knows he's taken the first giant step toward leaving home. The only total success of the day was my new book bag—dark blue canvas with brown leather trim, though it's oversized for the one textbook, a reading primer. The house is the new one we've built in Dogwood Acres, a wooded suburb.

days earlier, with Hitler's invasion of Poland. I was relieved just to have got through so momentous a day in my personal history—much less the world's—with no tears, toilet accidents, paddling from the teacher or worse humiliation.

And I was further relieved to see that, by the end of the first week, Lucy Leigh Lovett the teacher was responding warmly, like most adults I'd known, to my efforts to amuse her and reward her attention. (I'd experienced no home abuse, only the occasional light "switching"; but do lucky middle-class children still share my bone-deep feeling that adults are unpredictable contraptions that may hug you one minute and then vanish into thin air or send you to the principal's office the next?)

The packed roomful of boys and girls was initially as strange as the panther to the fox on the gangplank of Noah's Ark. I don't recall fear exactly; I think I managed to conceal my unease. But since I distrusted the force of my own wild hunger for all that was offered here—children, art, books, cool adult love and fame—I was sure I had a problem on my hands. Like most children I'd come to expect a sudden *challenge* from every new human, old or young. Now here were more children than I'd ever seen, except in an *Our Gang* movie, plus a tall grown woman with power over me. My first thought was, they'd need quick appeasement, then steady continuous charming like snakes in baskets. I also thought I had nothing to give them. I turned out wrong.

On the second day of school, after we learned the way to answer roll call and how to sit through the daily devotional, Miss Lovett started the drawing and coloring; and I knew I was safe. Three years of practice, alone and with Will, had taught me what was called for—a sizable elephant in realistic gray, not the glaring reds and greens of classmates far less loyal to the real world than I. My picture met with immediate endorsement from Miss Lovett and muffled admiration from most of the other children (the dissenters mainly accused me of "tracing," one of the lower forms of cheating in elementary school).

In hindsight I see that my work had no original angle or flair. Memory says that schools were still inculcating order and neatness more than vision and self-expression. Miss Lovett would pass out mimeographed copies of the silhouette of a small duck on a large sheet of paper; we'd color it with wax crayons. She'd select several of the best and tack them above the blackboard till our next bright wave displaced them. *Best* meant that you'd stayed inside the lines and hadn't scribbled, another grave mistake.

I'm not demeaning the methods of the time—far from it. The early grades were a place where Will's lessons in neatness and order got powerfully seconded for me, in ways that are still useful. I'm only admitting that it would have taken a keen eye to detect any talent in my first exercises. An especially merciful talent scout might have grasped at a few straws—I did stay inside the lines (it was years before I began my own guerilla wars); I added small touches, like a bright eye for the duck or a stab at indicating its long and short feathers; and I always chose lifelike colors. Since Miss Lovett had posted wild ducks from *The National Geographic*, I tried to make mine a recognizable copy of a real mallard drake, not a bizarre pink or purple toy like those of my tablemates. But that was about it, for early promise.

If I'd been handed cups of fingerpaint, a swatch of butcher paper, a smock and told to explore my imagination as boldly as possible when I heard the word *duck*, would I be a zillionaire painter now and not a writer? There's no telling. Instead I was given a duck in blank outline and was steadily rewarded for a fastidious use of materials and an increasing realism, in all my forms of copying. The basic skills of a writer—an innate bold grace with language and a fluency in narrative—were encoded in both lines of my inheritance: Prices and Rodwells, those ceaseless tale-makers and tellers. And my home life fed my narrative curiosity from the day I began to hear voices. So maybe writing was fated from the start.

If I'd been meant for a painter, my school training might have led me years later into competent portrayals and transformations of the world's visible skin. With luck and focus I might have worked in the same room at least with the art of Edward Hopper or Andrew Wyeth, those priests at the altar of the world. Or I might have turned and rended my teachers' prescribed neatness with gorgeously ugly swipes and swags of expressionist invention that said "Reynolds Price declines the real world and offers his replacement." But I went neither way.

Whenever the choice was made—whoever made it and why—for the next ten years, I continued drawing and painting with the rapt dedication that marks a need on the order of urgency. I was as dead-earnest in the order-making business as a traffic cop. I was mesmerized by the visible world as deeply as any snake-spied bird. And the first big project I recall was heroes. I would make a collection of the faces of heroes, from Alexander the Great down to the present of 1944 with Roosevelt, Eisenhower and a wide spread of other reliable faces. I copied the ancients from the bold pen and brush drawings in my favorite book, *Minute Biographies*; the moderns were on easy display in every week's *Life* and *Look* or the monthly movie magazines that Elizabeth liked as much as me.

Simultaneously I wrote to several live heroes on my Cub Scout stationery. At the top it bore the Cub insignia and, below, a campfire whose smoke trailed up the whole left side of the paper. And it got surprisingly prompt and generous responses—especially from those generals and admirals who were, at the moment, likewise engaged in running tidy operations on the order of the Normandy Invasion and the Battle of the Coral Sea. I was ten and eleven, and soon I'd collected a thick stack of portraits. Why heroes though?

First, because ten is near the age at which most children begin to perceive the possibility of making it through to maturity. They realize they've got to be something; so why not a long high reach—the man who cures cancer, the first woman on Mars, a great and famous painter? Children then are also still on the cool side of puberty and can watch the world with a precision of judgment that eros will soon cloud. The boys I knew collected baseball cards or toy soldiers. I had troops of soldiers too; but I also had the faces of ancient heroes, with a few live exceptions. And I had a small museum of fetishes—objects that had come in contact with great, if not necessarily admirable, men. In it were arrowheads that had presumably been made and shot by true Indian braves; a fired Confederate bullet and one of Will's pillboxes with a clod of mud I'd taken from the wheel of Hitler's captured Mercedes, displayed locally in a war-bond drive.

I almost certainly couldn't have told you; but I suspect that, like my baseball-card friends, I was reminding myself of the hardest thing for a child to imagine—that growth toward freedom and control in your life is a possibility, however slow and unsure. I was hoping to believe that a day might come when tall people stopped walking into my room and changing my plans, if not ruining my day, by making up rules on-the-spot that I knew in my bones were wrong and unfair (*fair* and *unfair* are much more urgent for children than *right* and *wrong*).

I know that hope was a part of what propelled me, that continuous prayer for freedom and self-propulsion. And I know I had another hard and driving hope—I already had a thirst to be heroic, to leave my name and face in books and in the grateful memory of the human race. No earlier Price or Rodwell had been known outside the county or celebrated for more than honest reliability (except Will's dead uncle Charles in the Confederate army). But by the time I was ten, valor and fame were my powerful and fully conscious aims. And I thought I'd get them with world-stunning pictures.

So why did I ask, also at ten, for piano lessons? As a result of participating in class visits from our "public-school music teacher" Miss Hobgood, I'd wound up singing solos for a few programs in the school auditorium— Christmas pageants and even one holiday weekend at the packed downtown USO, before dozens of soldiers on leave. Elizabeth had continued to surround herself and the rest of us with radio music. Many times I watched while something as quick as a short dumb song quickly lifted my mother from the depths of a blues that I couldn't budge. She'd catch the first notes, then join with the words of, say, a nonsense song of the time—"Mairzy Doats and Dozy Doats," which incidentally was my introduction to the abstract pleasure to be got from mere language. Will loved to listen as much as she, and I loved to see them join in the kitchen and dance a few steps to some broadcast.

My USO performances had also showed me a crucial thing. Something as simple as a one-note melody, sung by me, could win for a child the pleased attention of a roomful of otherwise bored or lonesome adults (and I already knew what every child learns—all adults are one or the other). I may have concluded that if a few solos got so much attention and worked some gladness, then once my voice broke, wouldn't piano lessons have me fitted for a lifetime run?

I took the lessons, in three towns with three capable women, till I was seventeen. From most points of view but my own, it was a waste of my teachers' time and Will's money. By the end of the second year, I'd become a competent sight-reader of printed music; but once I'd cracked the code, I seldom practiced more than an hour between lessons. Two of my teachers were husbandless though and in need of the cash; and I liked them (they commended my powers of expression, if not my dexterity), so on I went. And in seven years I worked up as far as the two-part inventions of Bach, the *Moonlight* and *Pathétique* sonatas of Beethoven and some of the harder *Images* of Debussy. But the day I quit, after my third year of high school, I rose from the piano bench more or less for good and never missed it a day.

Why had I gone on so long? Partly from childhood inertia, and I've mentioned liking my teachers, and partly because Will and Elizabeth liked the idea. But the two real reasons were big. First, since I seldom practiced, I was always surprised and grateful to find my hands releasing the beauty of certain chords, certain harmonies that invariably waylaid my ear. Even now, rusty to the point of creaking, I can play the first movement of the *Moonlight*, tired as radio and television have left it, and redeem a bad hour. And to have in my mind and hands the secret of something as simple but heart-easing as Bach's Prelude in C is a heady and mysterious power. Every known race in every culture has accorded an awed devotion to music, sensing its nearness to the doorsill of Heaven, its power for blissful good and hot evil.

Second, the piano led me forward in two important ways. It gave me my first usable line of undoubted human heroes, men who'd worked a seam I was working behind them—great composers and their performers. By the time I was in the sixth grade, I had a portrait of Chopin in my room and two small busts of Haydn and Mozart. The actual heads that these busts copied had made the grand originals I played, black marks on white paper. With effort I could copy those marks on a keyboard, pleasing myself and rooms full of others. Nothing but time lay between me and the same kind of work. I would be where they were—if not as high as Haydn and Mozart, higher than I was now at least (chest-height to Will).

And almost as importantly, even in those days before the advent of good phonographs and long-playing records, my lessons opened the larger world of music to me. From the start I loved almost all of it. The radio had Toscanini and the NBC Symphony, the "Bell Telephone Hour," the Longines Symphonette and live opera from the Metropolitan. By the time I was fifteen, my stack of fragile 78s included Toscanini's

Beethoven, Marian Anderson's Schubert and Brahms, Flagstad and Melchior's Wagner, Margaret Whiting's Gershwin, boogie by Tommy Dorsey, ballads by Peggy Lee and chinashop-mayhem by Spike Jones and his City Slickers—my only known aversion was to the hillbilly fiddle. I played them all far more often than I made my own, and soon the artists' signed photographs were joining the other triumphant faces on my wall.

When I was fourteen we moved to Raleigh, which had a splendid concert series. There I heard a majority of the great singers then at work in America, with many comparable instrumentalists and dancers. Normal fare in the 1940s—in a Southern town of fifty thousand, on the main raillines—included Anderson, Flagstad, Melchior, Pinza, Steber, Heifetz, Menuhin, Serkin, Rubinstein, the Ballet Russe with Danilova, a Martha Graham still young enough to dance her own *Appalachian Spring* and world-class orchestras with Stokowski, Ormandy and Bernstein (I only just missed Paderewski and Rachmaninoff but drove to Richmond for Toscanini and the NBC Symphony). The almost incredible fact that most of them would also receive you backstage and give you a moment of eye contact as they signed your program was a chance that only stoked my ambition. The first thing I noticed was their fever-bright eyes. They all looked ready to pierce armor-plate, even a man as glum as Jascha Heifetz. And soon I was bringing my paints to bear on an effort to see them longer and study the secrets of their eminence.

From 1949 till I left for college in 1951, I painted small and intensely detailed portaits of—among others—Geraldine Farrar, Kirsten Flagstad, Katharine Cornell, Ethel Waters, Laurence Olivier and Vivien Leigh. Whatever the troubles of school or home life, I could go to my room, take a sheet of white paper, draw a faithful black-and-white copy of a famous face—Cornell's St. Joan, Olivier's Antony—and then submerge, almost literally drown, in building up with a fine camel brush the hundred colors of skin and eye, each strand of hair, the gold-wire curls of a kingly beard or barbarous gilding on the pommel of a dagger with which Macbeth will now kill Duncan. No drug could have won me such harmless ease. Few hours since have paid better wages of calm reward. And only my later good luck in knowing more than one great artist has equaled the pleasure of those whole solitary days at work in my hunt for manual understanding of beauty and the power to repeat it.

Finished, I'd show the results to family and friends. Then I'd meet my subjects backstage or at the old Sir Walter Hotel downtown, or I'd mail off the pictures and wait for the sight of their kind inscriptions (no one refused me). Vivien Leigh and Ethel Waters, women who'd undergone fairly ultimate brands of pain, went to special lengths to befriend me. Their kindness to my work, and me behind it, went further than they can have known toward validating my hope and fueling me onward. As I'd dreamed for so long, art was propelling me out of the backwaters of adolescence to within seeing distance of the far horizon where a white light vaulted.

Music, dance and drama then were three successive lines thrown toward me in the high seas of puberty. To be complete, I'll regress to the start of that hormonal quake, at twelve and thirteen, and mention another kind of work. I've said that, in my five-year lockable diary, I made occasional line-drawings of men and women engaged in my inexact notions of sexual union. If my early focus on drawing the faces of heroes is a little mysterious, I can easily define my sexual drawings. I was preserving for my private archives a secret blooming at the center of my body. I knew that the happening was historic for *me*, I cherished the fact that it was secret, and I wanted to leave a trail for myself back to this first cave where the thing had started.

Since it was at least twenty years before the average schoolboy could walk to the corner drugstore and buy magazines with desirable humans on full display, I was creating my own set of exotic excitements (another main function of art). I couldn't know my own chief impulse of course, but every cell of my mind and body were driving me on toward actions that no adolescent boy of my acquaintance had managed to accomplish— my body was yearning to make real copies of itself in the visible world, live human babies.

Given the seam-bursting pressure in the head of a boy forbidden to express his sexual need, it remains a wonder, not that so many boys run wild but that far more of them don't explode into orgies of rape and domestic carnage. Masturbation is the valve that spares any town more harm than we know; and with no comprehension of the power that drove me, from the age of twelve, I was turning a whole locked wing of my art into generating the merciful fetishes that helped save my household a maybe gory ending (I've said that our home at the time had been the scene of a real family massacre).

Even so, mighty heads of my steam went unexpended. Except for neighborhood softball, football and basketball, I played no sports; and I never had a strenuous after-school or summer job. Elizabeth and Will were probably too generous with my allowance (five dollars a week); Mac Thornton's tobacco-money went a good way; and by now I was researching the English, Welsh and Scottish lines of my family in the State Library. At first I searched for pure profit; I copied our various coats of arms for the aunts and cousins who'd pay me handsomely at twenty-five dollars a copy. Before long though, the work was not only plumping my wallet and refining my draftsmanship; it was rousing a useful curiosity in my family's history, the narrative of our actual genes as they moved through time and across oceans toward our house and us four moving bodies.

Still I was half-aware of two daunting realities. My drawing and painting were doomed, certainly as a life's work. I was a faithful copyist—people recognized themselves when I drew them—but for whatever cause, I apparently possessed no trace of visual imagination, not of the sort I could set on paper in lines and colors. I'd wind up, at best, a commercial hack, drawing illustrations for other men's stories; and I didn't want to settle for that. I certainly didn't want a lifetime of copying maybe-false coats of arms or waxwork pastels of lawyers' children. My piano playing again was pure imitation of other men's notes; I had no gift for composition or even improvisation. Law and medicine, the ministry and business were unthinkable; and most of science was a world barred from me by my mathematical illiteracy.

What was left? As the sense of an oncoming dead-end grew on me, I might well have fallen into the lethal depression that plagues so many children mired in the powerless, seemingly endless wastes of adolescence (I've often wondered what I'd have done if drugs had been available on the schoolground then as now). But another strong line was suddenly thrown out; it landed on me.

On the raging pitch of sexual maturity, at fourteen, I encountered a teacher who unknowingly gave me the beginnings of sublimation. Her name was Crichton Davis, pronounced *Cray*-ton. We were living back in Warrenton; and Crichton had been a friend of Will's for most of their lives (she has recently, well on in her eighties, sent me a letter that my young father wrote her as she headed for prep-school in Raleigh, nearly as far off then as Boston). She'd left the South at various times, studying at the Art Students' League in New York before returning for marriage and children. And she'd published short stories in national magazines, here and in England. One of them, "Chimney City," is preserved in the O. Henry Prize Stories volume of 1931.

When we met in 1947, Crichton had finished a wartime traveling stint with the Selective Service, the national draft system, and was settled again in Warrenton. I was in the eighth grade, which was then the last year of elementary school—no foolishness about "junior high"—and when my first-semester teacher quit in December, Crichton took the job. Just before we met in early January, I'd written my first substantial piece, a Christmas play called *The Three Wise Men*. I think it arose when I was asked to decorate a classroom blackboard before the holiday. I chose to draw the distant skyline of Bethlehem, rained on by an uncanny new starlight and approached by three large camels with well-dressed riders. The picture, once drawn, worked on in my mind; and during the two weeks' vacation at home, a play about the men came to me; and I wrote it down quickly. Otherwise my graphic activities at the time were rushing down an especially peculiar channel—rank forgery.

For some reason I'd become fascinated with adult handwriting, primarily as shown in the signatures of great men—George Washington, Napoleon, Chopin, Mark Twain and others. I've said that for years I'd been amassing an impressive collection of authentic contemporary autographs. I've mentioned the generals, admirals, actors, musicians and singers. But I was also spending whole afternoons in the effort to copy, and learn to execute as effortlessly as my originals, the precise handwriting of several dead geniuses. It's easy to suggest motives for my painting, the block-building, the crèche arrangement and (in my three Warrenton years of social ostracism) the erotic drawings; but why these blatantly innocent forgeries? I certainly never imagined deceiving the world with a new Chopin waltz or a Washington command.

Wasn't I continuing, on one more parallel track, my fascination with the secrets of human heroism? If I can write enough like Washington, can't I in hidden but powerful ways *be* Washington or at least share in his probity, his discipline and austere strength? To this day I can scrawl out a presentable *F. Chopin*, a skill I learned more than forty years ago. And I honestly think that my childish mimicry of a gesture as small as that signature helped me participate in the brief productive tumult of a tubercular Polish genius whom I'd only recently met in the film *A Song to Remember* and whom I've already outlived by fifteen years. (I also copied Will's signature till I had it so close that he paid me the compliment of saying "Darling, you better hold off on that; might get you in trouble.")

Crichton Davis arrived then in the midst of a flood of old and new forms of miming. As soon as he knew she was back in town, Will told me of her old "liking to draw." So early in our acquaintance, I showed her a winnowed group of my drawings. Previously my kin, friends and especially teachers had received them with praise—any green shoot of student initiative being as rare, then and now, as leaves under snow. Crichton wasn't uninterested. She turned through my portfolio slowly, smiled a few times, expressed a cool interest and returned it. Because I sensed a genuine withholding of judgment, not a frigid or coy refusal, her coolness was irresistible for me. Here at last was someone who didn't leap instantly into my pocket. She'd watch, if I asked her to. She'd even wait awhile. For the first time in my life, here was someone, not to win but to earn. But how? I needed a sustained project.

It was quickly clear that Crichton loved Lewis Carroll. Those were times when good teachers still read aloud to their classes, even in the eighth grade. The after-lunch torpor was a time often chosen as best for both parties in the transaction. We'd put our heads on the desks and be washed by the single reading voice—no one reading to others, or being read to, is in serious trouble (unless the reading matter is a death sentence). The previous year Miss Jennie Alston had won us with a lot of long narrative poems, the Penrod books of Booth Tarkington, and Mark Twain's now despised but very funny *Tom Sawyer Abroad*.

Crichton began with Carroll's two *Alice* books. They were so unrealistic and zany that I'd never taken to them; but the Price sisters had seen that I had copies at home, with the black-and-white Tenniel illustrations, and I'd leafed through them often. That would be it then; a set of *Alice*

Jane Alston—Miss Jennie—at her antebellum home, Cherry Hill, near Inez in Warren County, 1959. She was my seventh-grade teacher at John Graham School in Warrenton, 1945–46; and despite her county-wide fame for strictness, she soon proved one of my all-time favorites and a friend till her death. She taught English grammar as if she'd caused it, but the great debt I owe her is for poetry. She read us good poems by the daily mile and helped us memorize them painlessly.

drawings would catch her. And in a long weekend's work, I copied my favorites meticulously in India ink—creditable facsimiles. On Monday I smuggled them into my desk, as excited as any loaded terrorist with my big surprise. I waited till lunchtime when the other students had left the room, and then I unveiled them to Crichton (who was still "Mrs. Davis" to me). Again she leafed through them slowly. Her finger would go out now and then and trace a certain line—"Nice." But at the end she handed them back with a smile. I'd hoped she'd ask for them or at the very least want to post them for the class. She only said "Very nice. Now why not think about coloring them with watercolor?" I spent the best part of the next night doing that, in the pale tones that seemed appropriate to Victorian drawings. It warmed Crichton a little further; but she was still far from the enthusiasm I craved, and had got so easily in most other grades.

Art instruction was not a part of the eighth-grade curriculum in our school then. But early in the spring, with colored chalks, Crichton drew a huge still-life on the blackboard—a basket of fruit with a stuffed bird above—and asked us to copy it. My careful copy of her original must have pleased her because, next, she invited me to her house on a Saturday evening to join in painting bottles, an activity she'd recommended to the class. A summons from Rembrandt couldn't have tuned me higher.

I spent the rest of the week scaring up appropriate bottles and waiting with increasing delight. Then at eight on Saturday, I walked the long block from our house uphill to hers. She lived in a normal two-story brick house, which she shared with her late husband's brother, Henry Davis. But I knocked with the expectations of an acolyte at the utter sanctum, and in my arms was a grocery bag full of the only interesting bottles I'd found. Since wine and liquor were off-limits in our house, I'd found a pair of the plump ceramic flasks in which Old Spice lotion was then sold and another pair of circular green prune-juice bottles from my aunt Britsy.

Crichton answered the door in slacks, the first time I'd seen her in trousers. A few years earlier Katharine Hepburn had done much to take the lesbian tag off pants for women, and Elizabeth had her own navy-blue pair; but they were far from the general-issue-for-grandmothers they now are. So Crichton's strange get-up and the softer light of evening made her seem a new person at her own door. Though I knew she was Will's

Crichton Thorne Davis in 1947. While we take a test one day in eighth-grade class at John Graham School, I see her drawing intently at her desk, then discarding the paper. Later and in secret, I search the trash can and find her work—this self-portrait profile, a speaking likeness. I'm not unusual, for the time and place, in seeing my teachers as awesome beings (many of them are, in selfless devotion); and this small scrap is an icon for me—a tall kind unpredictable creature in charge of life, able to do many things I envy and willing to share the skills with me.

age, forty-seven, she looked younger and even more self-possessed and elegant than before. I shared the general sense of pupils then that teachers were demigods with bodies free of the usual functions and out-of-class lives as unimaginable as angel grammar. And I'd wondered all week if she'd drop a series of veils and show me the genial and laughing interior I hoped for.

But no, we spent two hours in her normal-looking upstairs, painting flowers on our bottles, with Henry reading his paper beside us. Through smiles and occasional laughter, Crichton told me stories of her days at the Art Students' League, which sounded grander than Plato's Academy. Then she described the time Thomas Wolfe came to Warrenton with his graduate-school roommate Bill Polk. Wolfe saw some of her drawings and wrote prose poems on their backs. That was thinner air than I'd breathed before. Yet Crichton never released her lovely hold on whatever secret room she kept. With her guidance I covered my bottles with respectable-enough gardenias and dogwood. But Crichton's daisies and lilies had a charm and careless flair of quite another order.

I didn't feel trumped in the least. I concentrated hard on watching the economical flair of her hand—the way she could load the brush, then press once, swag downward and have a perfect leaf. Back then I'd never seen a Japanese master calligrapher. When I did years later, in his elegant controlled abandon, I saw Crichton's hand and recalled my longing for the same offhand perfection. When I finally asked how she brought it off, she smiled and said "Nothing to it but *practice*."

When I went out at ten o'clock into a cold moonbright night, leaving my bottles behind to dry, I ran home in the high excitement I'd seek—and find—again and again in my own work. A sane adult, known to my kin as no axe-murderess or child molester (at that point I might have welcomed the latter), had showed me her own hand making its work; she'd also watched mine. At last my fumbling art had been treated with serious attention by a master who wasn't tumbling over herself to overpraise one talented child among a herd of the hopeless.

That was the lesson I took away from Crichton's on a winter night, at age fourteen. I'd finally seen how work could be more than a private game, a secret pleasure. I was twenty-five before I began to teach my own students; but from day-one in my own classroom, I tried to remember

Crichton's beautiful example—firm but not rigid self-control, shared work and laughter and judicious praise, but only when earned.

When Will and Elizabeth pulled our gypsy caravan out of Warrenton one more time in that summer of 1947, I'd had only a six-months' chance to work with the first real artist I'd known, but she'd let me into her private home, and she'd never once scorned me. To the best of my recall, I never wrote anything for Crichton beyond English-class assignments (I was so absorbed in our painting that I can't remember showing her my Christmas play). But her welcoming me as a younger worker into her home, for a single evening, had stamped my mind with a credible enduring imprimatur.

And even now the poem she composed for my eighth-grade autograph book not only gives me pride to remember but shows the enviable invention and dash of her mind. If it only praised me, I'd suppress it here. But how many children's autograph books contain a spontaneous entry like this, an original poem of no slight complexity? Imagine how you'd have felt as its object, set down quickly as it was among the jokes and tub-thumpings rhymes of my classmates.

> And what could I wish
>   For a lad like you
> Who knows how to make
>   All his wishes come true?
>
> For anything wished would surely be vain
> For a lad with a kingdom of wealth in his brain.
>
> But still when you read through
>   Your funny old book
> Give the year "forty seven"
>   A fond backward look.
>
> For friends we have met and friends we will part.
> Farewell, and good going, O! happy young heart!

At about the time of my knowing Crichton Davis, I turned to still another kind of copying. Insofar as we had an archivist, it was oddly

Elizabeth. Will's sense of the weight of past and present made him a natural for the office. But it was Mother who kept a simple camera, always a Kodak, and used it often. Some of her excellent photographs of my infancy suggest the use of an even better lens. But by the time my own interest ignited in the late 1940s, she had a box Kodak with a fixed focus and exposure. It got eight 3 x 5 negatives to a roll of 616 film. At home in family gatherings and especially on vacations, I became the official recorder.

A look at the surviving results suggests that it can't have been simple family pressure that led me to specialize from the start in portraits—kin, friends, pets and heroes. In fact my only other subjects were the occasional natural phenomenon, a mountain or a lake and what I took to be historical sights. There are a number of bald shots, for instance, of those iron markers that line the highways of the upper South so thickly as to constitute a threat to driver attention, though they frequently turn out to mark only one more glade where General Lee paused to water his warhorse Traveller.

The point is that, again for unexamined reasons, I enlisted early in another process of reproducing visible creation. In my adolescent photographs, and in thousands more through the years since, I was concerned to mirror "reality" as perfectly as the prevailing light and my camera permitted. I was never interested in darkroom manipulation or intensification of my evidence—I've never developed or printed a single frame—or in elaborate posing of my human subjects. (Natural objects and animals are always posing, though their occasional tricks and distortions make it worth remembering what Oscar Wilde said when he took up the camera. In 1900 he wrote to a friend "Cows are very fond of being photographed, and, unlike architecture, don't move!")

And from the start I only photographed people I suspected I'd always love and long for or the unloved whom I nonetheless hoped to remember—for beauty, misery or any other feature of what we share: our swiftly vanishing faces and bodies. I dream of doing exactly what primitive peoples fear from the camera—the painless extraction of enough of my subject's soul to remind me forever of the precise feel and odor, the weather of his or her body and spirit. Other subjects, I can buy at the postcard rack.

*   *   *

But my years of pursuing visual copies were limited. Again, by age sixteen my insufficiently abstract imagination was increasingly obvious to me, though I continued to be praised for drawings and paintings that disappointed me bitterly. The failure was large and lamentable; but as time was to show, it was confined to a single department of my mind and may have been partly an inability to work to the fashion of a given era. Strangely I made no effort to correct the problem. Beyond a single studio course in the ninth grade, I never took art lessons; to the best of my knowledge, there were no private teachers in Raleigh then.

And worse, as an American coming to maturity in the 1940s and fifties, I was facing a world of art in which most approved work struck me as bleakly abstract or swaggeringly expressionist. My mind and hand though were hopelessly wedded to the "real" world—the world where you can say "Draw an apple" to fifty people, and forty-eight of them will produce a spherical red object with a small brown stem and maybe a green leaf or two.

Michelangelo and Vermeer were my favorite painters; and whatever each might have thought of the other's work, in my estimation they occupied polar ends of a single spectrum. At the Italian end, creatures recognizable as men gesture grandly or pose forever in an airless self-regarding sublimity. At the Dutch end, women as familiar as photographs of Mother are held upright in a kindly radiance at the absolute instant when God can say what Goethe's Faust can never manage, "*Stay!* You are so beautiful." I wanted to paint for the rest of my life from a point somewhere near the midst of that spectrum. But I couldn't see how, not in my time and place. Except in one or two of my portraits, my hand couldn't paint what my eyes and mind knew.

I did have the peculiar ability, so beloved of onlookers, to catch a human likeness. My hand could transfer the lines and planes of your face to paper. The skill came as early as my set of heroes, so it may have been innate. Or maybe the gift was the Price and Rodwell gift for close watch—the line of her face goes this way, then that. Of all my early abilities, the knack for likenesses was the one that got me the quickest and largest response from kin, friends and the world's great beauties.

And it's the only one I've kept up, from the painting and drawing years. To have the face of a friend pass into my eyes, through my mind, down my hands onto paper and to end with a mutually-agreed-upon likeness is the simplest and maybe most rewarding of all the forms of copying. But as I've said, in the 1950s that lone skill would have doomed me to a life of commissioned portraits—any barnacled matron or rubicund bank-president who could drum up the money.

A few months after leaving Crichton's eighth grade, I moved with my parents and Bill to Raleigh. The state capital was then a likable small green city, not the wallowing present chaos supervised by nothing more thoughtful than greed. I'd visited there on day-trips before, sampling the sparse resources that seemed almost too rich to taste—the Museum of Natural History with its live poisonous snakes, Indian relics and dinosaur bones; the Hall of History with its doll-sized scenes from 1585 (Sir Walter Raleigh's Lost Colony on Roanoke Island in what's now North Carolina), a first-rate art-supply store and at least six air-cooled movie theaters. But the visits were behind me. Now we lived there in a pleasant western suburb named Hayes Barton, for Sir Walter's home in the west of England. The buses that passed the top of our street every fifteen minutes put me in quick reach of all the riches; and I used them at once, especially the movies.

Since I began going alone to movies, at seven or eight, I'd seen at least one "show" (as we called them) a week. But the multiplication of choices set me spinning. Three shows in a summer week was not excessive, except for those occasional months when children under sixteen were confined to their neighborhoods through outbreaks of polio. After a year in Raleigh, I had a lifetime total of more than five hundred films behind me, many of them more than once (by 1951 I'd seen *Gone with the Wind* nearly twenty times, for instance; since I'd begun in 1939, at age six, that was by no means a record). It was nothing in those days of nonstop showings to go downtown with a friend, take a bag lunch and sit through the same film two or three times.

Once in Asheboro David Sumner and I'd gone on Saturday morning with our lunch. Unknown to our mothers, between showings of the film, there was a half-hour vaudeville show. To our incredulous ten-year-old delight, the final act was a striptease dance. In rhythm to our applause, a fine young woman shed her clothing, tossing each piece into a crate marked "Bundles for Britain!" (the timely slogan of a national aid-drive for bombed-out England). Strippers aside, no other art made a deeper impression in my growing mind than the first- and even third-rate films of the forties and fifties, with their allegiance to rapid clear narrative, interesting characters and human faces that held you still and promised rewards you could barely imagine.

My fascination with the medium, its secrets and its stars, also had me clamped to the numerous movie magazines of the time (breathless and unreliable but a lot less trashy than those of today). And for Christmas 1947 my main request was for an eight millimeter silent movie camera. I got it and promptly filmed everybody who'd move in my presence—including Mrs. Woodrow Wilson, Eleanor Roosevelt, Harry Truman and Dwight Eisenhower on visits to town. So in my growing disaffection from painting and with a movie-hothouse around me, it was no accident that by the summer of 1948, when I was fifteen, I'd written a screenplay about Saint Bernadette and her visions at Lourdes. Script in hand I pressed on fiercely with plans for its production. I'd use the dozen neighbor children, all as bored and eager for amusing summer employment as I—not that I could pay them.

A typed copy of the script survives, but I don't know where or when I wrote it or how long it took. I do remember the busy details of a whole summer of location scouting, casting and rehearsals. Sometimes we'd work on location in the sweltering outdoors (since none of us had air-conditioned homes, we were hardened to a heat that would kill us today). Other times we'd work in Ann Shaw's shady new rec-room, where in the breaks between rehearsals, we conducted our homemade anticipation of consciousness-raising groups.

We'd solemnly pore over each other's faults like nit-picking apes; our appetite for humiliation was endless. And the fact that we remained friends after so much verbal assault is more likely an index to a standard youthful assumption of worthlessness than to our moral courage. I remember unnerving the first session by writing down their attacks on me, mainly that I didn't pay certain individuals enough attention. I wanted to have the complaints for later study; they were startled to think I took them so seriously. Or maybe they thought I was keeping a list for future paybacks.

Since my memories of the project focus on such external details, it's plain that my chief emotional investment in a possible film lay in its visual tableaux and in the pregnant actions already achieved in my mind. And my wish to record the loveliness of two of the girls on our street, Pat Cowden and Ann Shaw—my Bernadette and Virgin Mary—was almost as powerful a goad as my growing but secret religious mysticism and my genetic mandate to copy the world in handmade objects of blood and bone.

But as summer ground toward September and school, it dawned on us that the standard bane of films was killing ours. We needed more than a hundred dollars, and none of us had or could get it. My parents cheerfully funded my modest painting and book-collecting expenses; but they balked at a film budget, even the high-toned film I planned (so high-toned apparently that I wasn't prepared to sink all my fall tobacco-money in the venture). So all our plans folded. It was back to the free reliables—rollerskating, then touch football and basketball. Oddly I don't recall much grief at the failure; children are balked far more times than not.

I may even have known I was lucky. The film I imagined was perfect, like my mental paintings; I could lie back at night and see every frame—my raw young friends transfigured to stardom by the new grace I'd found deep in them. But half of me knew it couldn't have worked. So for once I faced the immediate facts and bowed. My untrained friends and our locations on Frank Crumpler's vacant lot, not to speak of my rudimentary script and director's skills, would have stretched us all to the point of absurdity. (In the glimpses of me in those early home-movies, I look well past rescue—gruesomely self-conscious in the classically scornful adolescent way—and most of my friends give the usual version of goofy unease. Pat Cowden has not only the face but the inner stillness that a camera worships.) A failure in the presence of so many friends and parents might have shamed me too near the lucky meeting that lay just ahead.

What I didn't know luckily was that my mind was already yearning for the form where such a perfection of concept and performance is sometimes possible—the novel. If I'd known I might have lunged and failed too soon. A very few novelists have responded early to that need and produced stacks of adolescent narrative. By then I was reading good novels voraciously, but my own first attempt would wait ten years.

* * *

In the remains of that summer, I continued to read—I recall a first overwhelming encounter with *Madame Bovary* and the slower but vastly greater power of *Anna Karenina*. I continued my heated diary, and I painted portraits of Ingrid Bergman as Joan of Arc and Vivien Leigh as Anna Karenina. But I also wrote my first piece of narrative prose built on adult characters. My cousin Marcia and I had begun a co-authored novel when we were ten. It was about a boy-girl pair of children on a boat trip to Europe, and it never got past an early scene in which one of the children nearly drowned in the ship's pool. But that first short story was called "The Ring," and the plot was stolen from a lurid radio drama I'd heard years before. A man named Laurence gives his wife Elaine a cursed emerald ring, and a supernatural action ensues.

Once finished, I bound the typescript in a stiff folder, painted a ghoulish portrait of the dead Elaine for the cover and read it to the younger neighbors. They viewed all my efforts with healthily unawed wit and baldly critical eyes. Then I filed it away, with no try at publication. After the movie debacle I'd bolstered my suspicion that the powers of an even better copyist were cooking deep in me. But however much I longed for perfect works and the attentive love of audiences, I'd read enough good novels and plays and seen enough good films to know that my junior productions were way below professional level.

Again I might have despaired of a chance and hitched my wagon to another star—like medicine, law or the ministry. It was a decade when, thank God, a great many high-school graduates were realistic enough to have no plans for college; and at school we were beginning to get counseling in the imminent matter of jobs. So I was reaching the career-choosing age; but my reading, the lazy fun of suburban childhood and my increasing trust that a benign destiny had me in hand buoyed me pleasantly onward toward the falls.

The falls were a woman named Phyllis Peacock. With her college-professor husband and young daughter, she moved to Raleigh in 1948 and began teaching junior English at Needham Broughton High School. I had a sophomore biology class in a room in which she taught the previous period; and we were always amused and a little spooked to see the

Phyllis Peacock at Needham Broughton High School in Raleigh. The picture shows her in 1959, ten years after I first worked with her—that's my brother Bill at eighteen, on the right—but her face and vigor are nearly the same.

crowded blackboards of grammar exercises, diagrammed sentences and barbed epigrams that the new teacher left in her wake, all in mysteriously coded colors of chalk. In her first month she put not only her own students on notice but the next generation as well; we were helplessly bound toward her.

And just as I'd come to the sad conclusion that my painting and filmmaking skills were thin and doomed, I landed in Phyllis Peacock's junior English class. At close view that first week of September 1949, I could see at once that she was not only a formidable guardian at the gates of good old censorious, rule-ridden clear English. She was also that rarest of unicorns—a magical teacher, the kind who works an inexplicable and unrepeatable voodoo. The magic proceeds from a combination of effortless command of the subject, the discipline of a field marshal, the theatrical skills of classroom mastery and, most crucial, a fervent belief in the life-or-death importance of her subject.

Phyllis had them all in spades, especially the fervor. Class after class, she flung herself on the day's point—uses of the semicolon, a sonnet of Longfellow's, a story of Jack London's or the absolute demand for courteous behavior, in the classroom as in life. She was an unblinking reader of faces; so she must have known that we found her heat more than a little comic, till it turned on us. I've said that I had fine luck in teachers right along, but Phyllis was in a new league of exotic excitement. This woman plainly knew that poetry mattered like blood or money. I didn't know I'd been waiting to hear that. It turned out I had, though like my classmates I laughed awhile longer.

Since each year of my life had brought me fresh reasons for feeling outlandish, I began to warm to her sooner than most, though I continued perfecting my imitations of her manner—the instant smile that collapsed into the direst of frowns, the frail voice of pathos that descended and swelled to an iron contralto of scorn. By then I and my classmates were sixteen or seventeen. We were physically adult, however infantile in behavior; but we'd yet to encounter a teacher who expected us to *be* adult—to be impeccably punctual, reliant, no eyesore to look at, prepared and courteous. When we failed we were informed in terms that would have been equally appropriate at the burnt-out end of a marriage or a failed disarmament conference.

Life mattered, the smallest act was an important component of life, *get serious!* Strange to say, we did—with almost no exceptions. Then she said something even harder to believe—we were men and women, not boys and girls. Expect no allowance for tender years. Yet with all her rigor, she laughed at herself when we least expected and could exercise mercy appropriately. Phyllis Peacock was the only teacher I've known who simply refused to let a sheep wander. He might not make an A, but he'd damned well better earn a B-minus or demonstrate some dreadful handicap. (The *damned* is mine. She'd have scorned my resort to the shorthand of mild profanity to express a meaning for which I should have worked to find a decent but forceful equivalent. Luckily for her, she retired before children began to use, every sentence, the oldest obscenities and blasphemies till now they have a language incapable of verbal outrage when needed.)

Eleventh-grade English concentrated on American literature, and Phyllis began to reach me powerfully when we moved into the reading of Emily Dickinson. Though the complete poems were still unavailable in a trustworthy edition, I'd for some time owned a Modern Library selection with Conrad Aiken's useful preface. Like all Dickinson's readers, I was partly seduced by the legend of her chosen cloistered life—a choice I suspected was possible for me—but I'd also read all the poems in the volume. And in them, for the first time yet, I discovered an angle of sight and a voice that chimed uncannily with my own (later in the year I discovered the next blood-brother, Ernest Hemingway; and Phyllis proved her mettle by meeting his harsher texture with never a flinch).

She'd stand before us in a normal-size classroom, this small narrow-hipped woman as bare of fat as a steel bar and as coolly wild as Emily Dickinson, and read out

> *This is my letter to the world*
> *That never wrote to me....*

In the act of reading alone, with no explanation, she'd make us see that it was not merely metrical language or a pathetic admission from one more dry spinster (of the sort most of us had several of in our huge families) but a not-quite-infinite shaft opening onto the adult world of knowledge and power, a glimpse of brands of feeling even more intense than our own and far more potent in the world than our pubescent howls. That first year with Phyllis Peacock taught me what I still believe—that Auden was badly wrong in his claim that "poetry makes nothing happen." Nonsense, poems change whole lives—mine for one, as the poetry of Hardy and Yeats changed the young Auden's.

That brief lyric of Dickinson's, and hundreds of others like it in her work and the vaster world of all poetry, was a true copy of a brave life's understanding. It could serve more purposes than a fifty-dollar Boy Scout knife—as shield, sky-scope, ice-axe, lantern, entertainment event and, maybe above all, as a hook for love. Phyllis convinced me that enduring literature was made by individual men and women much like us and that, for their pains, those heroes were due our endless praise and love. She was that romantic, that right.

I showed her some of my drawings, which she liked too much; and she soon asked if my vocation wasn't for the ministry rather than the desk. But by Christmas vacation of that first year, silently and in no one moment, I'd signed on in earnest for the life I thought lay behind the poems she read and we studied. I've said that, for my first prose theme in her class, I wrote a half-page sketch of Marian Anderson's recent recital downtown. And a few days later I wrote a short reaction to Olivier's film *Hamlet*. Phyllis responded with praise but she also let me know that the pieces might have been more fully imagined, more strongly braced with visual detail and less outright statement of the unproved truth I propounded so quickly.

Without quoting Conrad's famous claim that the prose writer can do nothing but make you *see* ("That—and no more, and it is everything"), she helped me begin to teach myself that no narrative can hope to succeed unless it takes invisible pains to make its story as visible to the audience as a good *clear* movie. Her insistence on clear communication also began my eventual discovery of the next basic principle of narration—you can't tell your audience a story that (A) it either doesn't already know or (B) it doesn't want to hear. And each of those implies that your story had better be a good and familiar *copy*. You can tell no unprecedented stories about incomprehensible, emotionless life forms from Pluto or about Earthlings too revolting or boring to meet or watch through a two-way mirror.

And at a time when the more obscure works of Joyce, Eliot and Pound were fanning a high roar of narcissistic obscurity in so much American writing, Phyllis taught us otherwise. Now and then in a poem, she'd allow a little mist. But in narrative or critical prose, her own taste brought me to see how a writer must assume that his reader is a literate human being of good will and a reasonable degree of patience but of no special training or automatic allegiance to the writer. In short, she expected straightforward American English, stripped of shorthand, jargon and code and as lucid and entertaining as the complexity of the subject allowed.

In later years when I've sometimes known that my prose was clouding or clotting, I've pictured the frown on Phyllis's brow. And while I've occasionally slogged ahead, convincing myself that murk was implicit in my theme, I've never doubted the rightness of her principles and never regretted for an instant the fact I found in her as hardnosed an early reader as any suspendered city-editor from the grand dead days of American papers. (To be accurate and just, I'll add that Phyllis was preceded in my schooling by at least eight other English teachers, all women and five of them never-married, who inculcated principles that had been in force since the time of Samuel Johnson and are serviceable now. In thirty years of college teaching, I've met no more than a half-dozen students who've worked with teachers as firmly grounded.)

After that Rubicon experience in my junior year, I joined Phyllis's brand-new creative-writing class in the twelfth grade. By then she'd long since noticed my direction and urged me onward with poetry. Under her bright eye then, for another year I poured out verse. The metaphor is accurate, *poured*. However young and derivative, the lines that survive came down the fingers of my right hand with little more effort than it took to walk to the desk and hoist a pen.

That's not to deny that I often spent hours discarding worn thoughts or obscure language—Phyllis was one of the rare teacher-readers who could courteously say that she was confounded or bored (if more writing teachers could admit the frequency of their *boredom* with student work, what better books we'd have). But partly because of the groundwork of structure and logic built under me by Phyllis, her predecessors and a few who came later, the initial act of producing my work is mostly an occasion for excited ease, then relief and thanks. Only later, and colder, do the principles come back as battering rams to try if the thing can be breached.

She did me many more useful turns. In secret she sent my portrait of Olivier's Hamlet to the man himself; and back it came with a quote from the play and his signature. She and her buoyant husband Lee, who taught American literature at Meredith College, took me to New York for my first visit at age seventeen (New York then was a long way off). That was when we saw Ethel Waters and Julie Harris in *The Member of the Wedding*. In the same long Thanksgiving weekend, we also saw John Gielgud and Richard Burton in *The Lady's Not for Burning*, *Don Carlo* and *Manon Lescaut* at the Met. And I was addicted for thirty-four years.

None of her gifts lasted longer though than her endorsement of my sense, growing from the age of six, that all work which we agree to call beautiful rises from our early dealings with the unseen world of power, as the Mississippi rises in Lake Itasca. She let me know how she shared my belief that serious work—poems, mitered joints, sung songs, good bread—flows in a circle, whose final closure we cannot see, back to its source in an endless hoop. And in that closure all visible works will ultimately vanish.

Because of Phyllis's unremitting force—and other forces I'll speak of later—by the time I left her classroom in June 1951, I'd begun to suspect that every art I courted from stick-figure elephants to sonnets and stories was a facet, however fractured and cloudy, of a mirror aimed from various angles at the all-but-blinding face of a light that willed my reflected fragments into being, as it willed all else: me and the world I was helpless not to copy from here to the end, if it plans an end.

As befitted a young and fairly humorless priest, I centered for some years more on the writing of poetry. From meeting Phyllis Peacock in 1949 till the fall of 1954 and my senior year in college, I wrote maybe thirty poems, enough of which survive to give a sense of what a limited amount I was good for. That I wrote them at all was unusual for the time and place but not jaw-droppingly odd (there were several dozen other writers in town). So I went on through high school, enjoying my numerous friends, almost none of whom wrote poems or gave signs of thinking me a cause for neighborhood alarm.

Again like many of my schoolmates, I'd read thousands of lines of

Ethel Waters as Bernice Sadie Brown in Carson McCullers' *The Member of the Wedding*. I finished this portrait in 1950 and, on my first trip to New York that November, I took it backstage to Waters after a performance of the play. Her fading inscription says "Words fail me in finding the right things to say to this beautiful tribute paid me in this moving and spiritual picture. God bless you and may I always prove worthy of such love. Ethel Waters."

poetry at school and memorized hundreds. But most of it had been the traditional favorites of late-nineteenth–early-twentieth-century England and America—Wordsworth, Keats, Browning and Tennyson, Emerson, Dickinson and the lesser poets of the First War. Except for a long romance with T. S. Eliot, who'd won the Nobel in 1948 and was suddenly famous, I'd read almost none of the poets at work around me. In fact by the age of eighteen, I'd read far more good fiction than poetry. And I'd begun my own writing with a play, a screenplay and a short story. Why then did I spend all of high school, and the better part of college, in writing poems—mostly short lyrics?

Surely the reason is simple. For beginners, song-like poems have one enormous advantage over narrative prose. They're short. When you're sixteen, or a term-paper-ridden college junior, the prospect of even a ten-page story can seem unimaginably forbidding. But a ten-line poem is often possible, maybe awful but possible. In addition good fiction requires a complex fund of carefully witnessed, stored, marinated and transformed memory of creatures, things, places, thoughts and feelings. And again such a fund is only acquired and transformed into usable shape with time, substantial stretches of well-spent time.

Almost no really young human beings have managed to produce good short fiction. Superb music, mathematics and public performance, yes—often dazzlingly so—but not prose stories or novels. Fine lyric poems, however, have surfaced in the teens of several men and women like Arthur Rimbaud and Edna Millay. And the recent American experiments in poetry writing in grade school have produced some impressive results from schoolchildren. In such quantity they give strong indications that the lyric and meditative impulses at the root of poetry are present in more minds than we'd guessed. The motor impulse of lyric verse lies near the child's springs of wonder, awe, innocent detachment and equally hot passion, even violence and ecstasy.

So with the normal limitations of my age, and with a few exceptions where prose was required for a class, I kept to brief lyrics. I wasn't writing daily or even weekly, and most of the results survive. If I read them now, after thirty years of counseling young writers at a university, I can see my often comic errors—the taut-browed earnestness, the predictable emotions, the self-dramatized lonely heroism, the lack of technical con-

sistency and variety, the laziness. Yet a patient teacher might also see
that those faults are the underside of the core materials of most good
poems. In short, none of my early lyrics stands alone as a mature poem;
but they do show tendencies that a watchful teacher might recognize as
hopeful (I've given a fair sample earlier, in "To a Negro").

First, the boy is a born witness or spy. He's helplessly fascinated by
the ritual power of language—the tone and weight of single words,
their architectural relations in a sentence and the broader structures of
rhythm and total meaning and their potential for evoking human response. And he seems to have a raw flair for metaphor. Yet just as he's
never painted an abstract picture, he almost never writes a surreal, abstract or obscure poem—one in which words are used as sculptural or
musical objects, for their look and sound, or as private code. He's bound
as tight as Homer to the imitation of appearances and to sequences of
cause and effect, the look of creatures and things and the actions of time.
All of which is to say, the boy may not trust the visible world; but he does
it the honor of watching it closely. When he can muster the patience
and courage, he lets the world be itself in his presence. Then he filters it
to us through his eyes and mind.

Thomas Hardy said that literature gives us reality seen through a temperament. I'm not sure that, then or now, I'd agree to use *reality* so
loosely—who's to discern the base line of *real?*—but the boy I was had
sensed Hardy's point. Again he was no prodigy; and for someone raised
to be courtly, he was far too ready to commit profound discourtesies on
the shaky ground of artistic license. *The gods have sent these words and
rhythms; who am I—who are you?—to ask for more?* In my better days
though, as more good readers read me and wondered, I knew I must train
my eyes at least to meet the world. And I never doubted I must pour
whatever new sights I found into legible messages intended for others,
most of whom were no more used to reading poems than Will and
Elizabeth.

As one more exhibit, here's a poem I pulled from the blue in my last
year of high school.

> *In triumphant gray procession*
> *On my soul of woe,*
> *Companies of stately angels*

To their heaven go—
Bearing what I could have done
In a long locked box,
Leaving what I did in state,
Chanting unrelenting spurn
And my heart's still flaming ashes
In a silver urn.

If one of my present students wrote it and asked my opinion, I'd probably say that I couldn't fail to notice how the poet was advertising his youth (that "soul of woe" and the baleful guilty tone). I'd notice too that, even in a short space, he's told a story—it's a narrative lyric—and that both his image and his burden of failure show clear signs of religious training. The beat of a thousand Protestant hymns is stamped in his ear; and his guilt, like most churchly guilt, is self-absorbed—notice that his burnt heart deserves a silver urn.

But I hope I'd also have the sense to thank him for the ring of his passion, a sane-sounding hunger that plainly aches for the bit of control. That brand of need is not a trait that's overstocked in any decade, even in a big warehouse of writers. I'd urge him to break that horse to the bridle, then take his seat firmly and let it run.

But why did I write it and the years of others since—poems, novels, stories, plays, essays? Assuming the question has a possible answer, it brings me back to the starting gates. Why do living creatures copy their worlds? Why have we, since the caves at least, tried so consistently to copy, not only the visible world but the unseen world—God or the gods, the black hole we now call evil and the ring of light that circumscribes it? The simplest answer is that all such copies are a copy of the commonest action on the face of the Earth. The whole of organic nature is involved in the steady physical effort to reproduce itself. Some ninety percent of the American population copies itself in living offspring—the actual infant who arrives with Grandfather's ears, Aunt Ella's eyelashes and its mother's temper.

Since it's gospel for atheists, agnostics and believers alike, it can firmly be said that sexual reproduction continues, not so much because it's pleasurable but because it's supremely useful (or was in less crowded times). It renews the species and provides the world with the necessary workers, soldiers and with the next relay of copyists. But can't we also say that some ten to fifteen percent of the human race is childless because that is also useful, a check on crowding and the freeing of a few observers from the task of propagation and nursing?

It's the stuff of cruel jokes; but it's also the view of many sane observers that a remarkably high proportion of unmarried persons, in America at least—bachelors and spinsters by strong choice or accident—are involved in the other kind of copying. It's a work that might, unpleasantly but accurately, be called dry reproduction. And it issues in a broad stream of teaching, priesthood, and those million works of visible art (in all the forms of useful design) that are borne for the world and delivered to it by otherwise barren artists.

To speak for myself, after thirty years of a life barren of all copies but a long shelf of books and two generations of the students I've taught— most of whom absconded with no thanks or blame—I can say without irony that I'm at grateful ease with my own progeny, my copies of the world. I don't bind them in protective wrappers, I don't let myself be photographed with them, I don't hang their prizes on the walls of my office like antelope heads, and I seldom read a page after it's gone into print, but I'm glad I bore them all.

That's not to say I think they're flawless or equally strong—though it does partly say that I have few friends who claim as much of their flesh-and-blood, part-copy, part-original children. But I do take an artisan's pride in their making and lasting. True, the oldest of my books is now only twenty-six years old, and John Keats's life only lasted that long.

If you'd asked me though, at high-school graduation to explain my aims, could I have answered so volubly? Surely not—I knew I'd yet to write an adult poem or story—but as I'd known I was married at three, at sixteen I dimly perceived a long vocation. So walking off-stage in June 1951, diploma in hand, I think I'd have tried to say this much. I believe I write because I can, and I *can* because it's my one big gift. Some of my friends can take up a bat and hit every pitch with a native grace that I fail to get. Some others can soar through the higher mathematics, where I'm excluded in cold blank terror.

The chief hero of my adolescence was a friend my age who could dive into pools of water with a dolphin's flawless playful power. In all that world of bodily grandeur, he far surpassed me. And I worshiped his gifts, unhampered by envy. For even as a bumbler with almost everything to learn, as I watched the graceful arms or mathematical minds of my friends, I could feel a parallel gift within me. I already knew that writing was an automatic faculty of my eyes and mind, my strong right hand (that had trained as a forger).

I had a crowded and ready memory, a natural bent for the English language, a hunger to hoard more and more mental pictures of the world. Best and most dangerous of all, I had an enormous hunger to love and be loved—though for some old reason, maybe another legacy from home, active loving was then more urgent for me than being loved. I was betting I could win that kind of notice with nothing but words. Thirty-five years later I think I bet right, though what I couldn't know at the start was how I'd eventually happen on rewards even better than human love.

I've lately been given the high delight of work for its own sake, work for the pure pleasure of working, work that's again like childhood play—imitative but innocent, utterly gripping and entirely satisfactory since it eats and digests all hours of the day and tires me for night. And one of the largest pleasures of my life has been the recent discovery that such apparently private work has pleased more readers than I'd pleased before.

When I left home for college in September 1951, I left for good. I returned for two summers, a scattering of holidays and later a night or two. I first went twenty miles west to Duke University; Will died while I was there. His own tastes in art were different from mine, but he knew what he liked, and I could share all his likings except in music (he loved the soupier big bands of the thirties and forties, Guy Lombardo and Sammy Kaye). He read my high-school poems and stories carefully, with an occasional question about meaning; and he always said "That's fine, son." But he was fifteen months gone before I had even two mature short stories to show, one of which was made from his death.

After four years at Duke, I went east to England for three happy years of further study; and that cast the lot. There I wrote two more stories I can stand behind still, and I laid out the plan for a first novel. Then I came back to Duke to write and teach, moving at once to the country crossroads where, thirty years later, I'm still at work. From here I saw Elizabeth at least twice a month and more often once her last illness struck, when Bill was in the Navy. Though the sight of her pain and blindness was awful, she'd watched me through worse. And the unself-conscious spectacle she offered, of laughing courage, made the time instructive.

With her lifelong need to lunge for the truth, she let me know her disappointment when my first book wasn't dedicated to her. But once I tried to explain the reason, she took her old open pleasure in its luck and its contents—she knew the places and the kinds of people in it; she heard many echoes of Will, her family and her own rich patience. Among my writer friends the sad rule seems to be that sooner or later their parents and kin are offended by their work. Their elders sense that they're the things being copied, the unwashed apples in the child's bold painting; and they balk at the sight. The fact that all my family have liked my work—or in the case of my non-reading kin, have been politely indifferent—has been a liberating relief. When I've sometimes wondered if it's meant the work was too kind, I've reminded myself of their toughness. (My fifth novel, *The Surface of Earth*, bore a few likenesses to Price-family history. After its publication, only one of Will's sisters—Lulie—was alive, though badly crippled by arthritis; and I wondered how she'd take it. At my next visit I noticed a copy on her chairside table. We talked for a good while with no reference to it. But at the first lull, Lulie's eye fell on it. She laughed and tapped the cover with a firm forefinger—"Well, you've done *us* to a T!")

That brand of level welcome has meant above all that I've never been forced to hate my homeplace, as many of my writing friends came to do. Their inability to live near their homes in a racially divided region compelled them to sever the feeder-roots of their work, with tragic results—their work underwent the slow death of cut flowers. Whatever my staying cost me in immediate pleasure and international glamor was offset, for me, by the chance to stay in a place that I knew like my hand and to watch it slowly till I'd seen it move and change through decades. The absolute subject of large works of art, from epics and novels to Sistine ceilings and symphonies, is finally time—the movement, the gifts and tolls of time. And that central movement, far slower than the turn of plants toward light, can only be gauged by eyes that are near and entirely at rest.

Elizabeth died seven years after I was back. By then I'd given her a more-than-earned part in the dedication of my second book. Those were early stories that owe so much to her ready laughter, her quick tears and—in the face of her clear-eyed counting of the world's bitter cruelty—to her unquenched taste for the unknown day and the strangers in it. By the time she died, I was in my early thirties, braced by helpers on three continents. With both parents gone—and Ida, Mac, Grant and more—I was lone and free, before most writers, to dismantle the screens I'd raised to keep my work from wounding the few who'd made my first world spacious and crowded, then had held it toward me with hands more generous than any hands since and watched me take it through knowing eyes with no trace of blame.

Macon, the room I was born in on the left and the oak tree struck by lightning years before 1933. Its death was expected all through my childhood; but now, sixty-some years after the shock, it goes on, raining down acorns by the bushel.

7

CREDIBLE LIGHT

WILL AND ELIZABETH PRICE, PATRICIA
COWDEN, HOWARD POWELL AND MORE

WILL LIVED FROM 1900 TO 1954; Elizabeth from 1905
to 1965. If you'd asked either one of them, at any point in their adult
lives, to tell you their religious convictions, they'd have eyed you aslant.
They were not chilly, mink-stole believers; neither were they the clapping-
and-shouting brand. And anyone who asked such questions in America
even then was more likely out for your money, not your soul. But if my
parents found a reason to trust you, they almost certainly wouldn't have
said *Christian*. They'd have answered separately *Baptist* and *Methodist*.
And unless you grew up near them, in the same stable white-and-black
agrarian society, you wouldn't have heard the ominous rumble in those
two names. It was more or less all that divided them.

Will's family began the division. His Welsh-English-Scottish father
was Episcopalian; his Scottish-French mother was Baptist. The two
churches stood on Main Street in Warrenton, less than two blocks apart
in distance but a good deal further in appearance and atmosphere. Emmanuel Episcopal was a brick Gothic Revival structure with good
nineteenth-century stained glass, narrow pews with kneelers and a slave
gallery. The small congregation consisted in large part of the town's
older and better-fixed families (in Will's boyhood, only forty-odd years
after the Civil War, there was almost no real wealth in town; but there
was no shortage of prideful memory). The services were decidedly low-
church, as Episcopal rites go. But compared with other Protestant rites
in eastern North Carolina, they were papist—processions, candles, vest-

ments, rote responses and book-read prayers followed by short dry sermons. Two of Will's three sisters and his two older brothers attended Emmanuel with their father, all regularly but with no visible ardor.

Again Will was the youngest son; and with his youngest sister, he clove to his mother's Baptist persuasion—Lula McCraw Price's. Despite their Scottish lineage, Lula's parents—a McCraw and a Solomon—were staunch Baptists. The church that stood in Will's youth was replaced before I saw it. But its red-brick successor had the bare-walled scrubbed rigor of the original, plus opalescent non-pictorial windows. In his boyhood Will had acted as sexton or general caretaker for the old church. In later years he often admitted that he'd taken the job because it also comprised the office of bell-ringer and that his mother said "Will's religion lies mostly in the bell-clapper."

I was too young to measure Lula Price's degree of piety; and though my grandfather Edward ("Cupe") Price died before I could know him, he left no churchly odor behind. No doubt in religion, as elsewhere, they were both kept from fanaticism by unquenchable wit and a keen awareness that "church" in a small town was at least as much a social as a spiritual reality. And Will's imitations of old Dr. Taylor reading the lesson or of Mrs. Pendleton singing a hymn were frequently requested and gladly repeated at family gatherings.

One repeated story may well preserve the heart of the nature of my grandparents' piety. One winter night, when they both were old, Cupe and Lula had sat up unusually late for some family gathering. When they at last undressed and knelt on opposite sides of the bed for prayer, each went promptly to sleep. However much later in the frozen night, Cupe woke disgusted. He struggled to his knees, went round to Lula, shook her and said "Wake up, Lula. Damned if we haven't been praying all night!"

But I did know Lula's sister Annie Belle McCraw, "Sis" Belle in her asthmatic old age. The youngest of three girls, Sis Belle was much the least attractive. And though she talked volubly, she occasionally stammered—the result, according to legend, of a spider bite in girlhood. She remained a spinster, outliving her own generation and surviving as an increasingly querulous and unwelcome legacy, in the Price family home till I was in my late twenties; and she died there (as sad a death as I'd known, with no one to mourn her). In earlier days the best description of her truculence came in a retort of Lula's when Sis Belle had corrected her on the fifth minor point in a story she was telling, "Belle, if I said Jesus Christ was crucified, you'd say 'Ah ah, Sis Lula, he died of a sore throat.'"

Sis Belle was what was called a hard-shell Baptist, loyal to the death and disdainful of rivals. She believed, and proclaimed to her Episcopalian kin, that Jesus himself founded the Baptist church—end of argument. When they delightedly asked if he hadn't also founded their own, she replied with more than comfortable accuracy, "The Episcopal church was founded by Henry VIII." She came by her certainties honestly. One of her and Lula's uncles was Josiah B. ("Unc' Joe") Solomon, a famous Baptist theologian, preacher and exponent of the baptismal doctrine of total immersion.

Without questioning the passion and solace of my great-aunt's beliefs, I can honestly say that her professions of faith were symptoms of a regional trait. The four main streams of Southern white Protestantism—Baptist, Episcopal, Methodist and Presbyterian—were as distinguished for hot domestic politics and home theatricals as they were for rigor and charity. In households like Elizabeth's, where all members belonged to one sect, amusing and instructive quarrels might develop on minor points of shared doctrine. For instance when Jesus mentions the Unforgivable Sin in Matthew 12:31, is he referring to murder, pleasurable sex, card playing, dancing or whatever else? Hence the old joke, "Why won't Baptists make love standing up?"—"Because somebody might think they're dancing." But in deeply divided families like the Prices, cross-denominational scorn was one more weapon in the elaborate arsenal that stood ready for use at unpredictable moments of internal crisis. If you got mad at your Episcopal sister, you could always remind her that she wasn't really baptized and was thus bound for Hell, which you weren't—though you'd miss her in Heaven.

Baptism above all was the coal most likely to flare at family gatherings. Southern Baptistry shared with its rival sects an emphasis on the dire necessity-for-salvation of the rite of baptism. Baptism alone washes us of the birth-taint of evil which we inherit so inexplicably but obviously from Adam and Eve, our first ancestors. Baptists however were unique in the intensity of their insistence that a valid baptism required

that the body of the recipient be submerged, head and hair, in water—
thus their doctrine of "total immersion." And because Jesus was baptized
in the Jordan River, which flows south from the Sea of Galilee to the
Dead Sea, there were even Baptist sects that demanded immersion in
running, not still, water. Further, since Jesus sought baptism as a full-
grown man, since the unwashed soul must consciously will its salvation
and since infants can't safely be immersed—though they've been most
deeply dunked in the Russian Orthodox church for a thousand years
without noticeable loss—then the only baptism pleasing to God is available solely to those above the age of reason and only at the candidate's
free insistence.

Well before adolescence I witnessed dozens of intramural family debates on the question. At Will's home the tart Episcopalians would
wrangle with the blunt but grandiose Baptists. In our own quarters Will
and Elizabeth would contend. And sometimes at the Rodwell home in
Macon, Will would contest the whole of Elizabeth's undogmatic family,
who nonetheless loved a good tug-of-war.

Whatever Baptists were present would begin quite properly by pointing out that in the first gospel account of Jesus' baptism, Matthew says
that "he came up out of the water." Then they'd drop their H-bomb—
can anyone seriously propose that a grown man waded out into the midst
of a flowing river only to have a few drops sprinkled on his head? Nonsense. And in Will's words, "The foolishest thing about it is you all's
pictures of him standing chest-high in the river, with John the Baptist
pouring water on his head out of a damned seashell! Where was the *sea*?"
He'd be rosy with triumph.

But the Methodists—and most other sects, Protestant or Catholic—
would reply that the Old Testament abounds in descriptions of ritual
anointings and purifications by sprinkling:

> *Purge me with hyssop and I shall be clean;*
> *Wash me and I shall be whiter than snow.*

(Hyssop was a wild plant, handy presumably for sprinkling water over a
dusty or sinful body.) Then they'd call on the always-limited Baptist
sense of mercy and assert the necessity of purifying infants of original
sin by the rite of baptism—and a baptism that does not threaten their

lives, thus sprinkling on the crown of the head but not immersion. The rite was called *christening*, from the Greek word for *anointing*.

Unless the dinner bell intervened, the ante in the game would rise to its next hotter level with the Baptists' rejoinder that christening was no more a substitute for baptism than a quick hand-wash at the pump in the yard. The sinless Jesus, by accepting total immersion from his cousin John the Baptist, had thereby required the same of all who proposed to follow him and claim the grace of his salvation. All who did otherwise would see their error when they rose from the grave on Judgment Day and smelled the scalding sulfur of Hell.

And so on. Many families quarreled far less zestfully than mine. In extreme cases, homes shattered on the anvil of the question. And reams of eighteenth- and nineteenth-century letters tell that, in divided families, the saved parties suffered agonies of fear for the safety of their kin— especially for the numerous unsaved young men, so steadily tempted by sins of the flesh in a slaveholding world. In the Price-McCraw household in Will's lifetime at least, faith in the mercy of God was strong enough to preclude such anguish in all minds but Sis Belle's. And all of Elizabeth's Methodist kin were easy riders in a similar faith.

Maybe that ease was the reason, or maybe a courteous temporary standoff between Will and Elizabeth; but I was not christened in infancy. And as my religious hunger grew in late childhood, a distressing crossroads loomed—Methodist with Mother or Baptist with Father? Till that hard moment my sense of God had grown freely and painlessly. And by the time I reached the age of entry into full church membership, the middle teenage years, I'd brought myself to a secret homemade mysticism. It was no private magic-set or the threadbare mumbo-jumbo that passes today as New Age mysticism but, unknown to me, I'd stumbled on a downright traditional mysticism. Before I entered school I knew one more untellable thing. In the midst of my family, our strong triad, I was nonetheless also a solitary soul, in what I thought was direct touch with the unseen blazing center of things, the uncreated creator of all.

My boyhood entry into such a strange and glowing world began in simple, apparently accidental events. Will and Elizabeth were not regular churchgoers. Their amused tolerance of human folly sat awkwardly among the puritans-of-all-sexes who dotted the pews. And while they occasionally took me to Sunday school, they mostly relied on home instruction in the underpinnings of Christianity. To be accurate Elizabeth had little to do with it; she limited her teaching to unceasing demonstrations of selfless care. It was Will and his mother who started me. I've said that Lula Price gave me a Bible-story book in 1935, six weeks before my third birthday. It was *Wonderful Stories of the Bible in Words of Easy Reading* by Josephine Pollard. Despite its cover picture of Jesus, surrounded by children from every race and nation, all the stories are from the Old Testament and are illustrated with black-and-white drawings that have some of the stark force of wood engravings by Dürer.

Since the book was a present from his mother, Will may have read me a few of the stories; again I have no memory of it. But I have strong impressions of poring alone over the no-nonsense pictures and wondering at their secrets and causes. And by the time I was four, Will had bought me a much thicker, mock-leather-bound volume, *Hurlbut's Story of the Bible* by J. L. Hurlbut. That source gave me the major stories of both Testaments, with no expurgation and with numerous DeMilleian illustrations, mostly German, of hefty voluptuous women and hirsute heroes. By the time of the gift, Will had succeeded in giving up drink. Was the book a sign of his growing interest in me—concern or thanks or just a new ease—or was he fanning what he hoped was an ember that would ultimately call for the fuel of Baptist answers?

Whatever, since I was so often alone, I spent a lot of time thinking about those crowded pictures. A few were especially magnetic. I looked long and deep at Abraham and Isaac trudging toward the sacrifice, at Moses smashing the tables of the Law, Samson languishing at Delilah's and at Jesus spookily transfigured with Moses and the prophet Elijah. Nothing now tells me that I felt spiritual emanations from the pages. And unless I'm to claim an early pull from God, I have to guess that my attraction to the book was one more exhibit of child's curiosity. By storing the rich information packed into so many teeming but safe pictures—people dressed to the eyes, people naked as grapes but each one burning at white-flame heat—I was learning the lines of passionate life in a world where the least move matters. I'd never again sit still for the milk pudding of most child's books.

I'm speaking now of the years before school. And not to claim boy-sainthood, I hasten to add that I was equally fascinated by most other worldly spectacles. I was fair game for any available sight—the acts of my high-strung and energetic parents, the black woman singing in the kitchen, my grown kin with their unfathomed highs and crashes, my few young friends (mostly girl-cousins, as baffled as me); and those two dogs there on the sidewalk, stuck together for some weird reason that called for witness.

I've looked at similar traits in my parents. Any mimic as good as Will must watch his subjects with a minute closeness, and at least a third of Elizabeth's pleasure came from her hunting orphan-eyes. The longer I've lived, and especially the longer I've observed college students, the more convinced I am that most people—most Americans anyhow—are functionally blind. They proceed through the world with a phenomenally limited visual curiosity. And through self-absorption or self-satisfaction, they miss upwards of ninety percent of the interesting and instructive sights they pass. So I was all the more fortunate in one more of my parents' legacies, their gift for attention. That steadily prowling watchfulness began early to bring me a good deal more than the billion sights of the daily world.

There's a photograph of me at age three in lightweight Sunday best—maybe Easter? I'm sitting in clear sun on the front ledge of our house in Roxboro. If I don't recall the exact occasion, I can explain the piece of folded paper in my hand. It's a Sunday-school bulletin. Will and I have just returned from Baptist Sunday school, and he's recording the fact on film. From those early years I recall a few more such outings with him, to the Baptist church in Asheboro (where the minister was also named Price).

And I know that, on trips back to Macon, Mother and I would attend the Methodist church of her childhood. In hot August we'd sit on hard pine pews; and I'd crane all ways to take in these country strangers, farmers with buxom wives and their stair-step children. It was there that I, a bottle baby from the start, first saw breast feeding. A child cried; a farm wife popped her breast out like a big white fruit from its hull and pressed it to the baby who at once shut his eyes and suckled in rapt ecstasy. Another Sunday a baby cried and, when it kept going, Ed Bullock

Home from Baptist Sunday school with Will in Roxboro, Easter 1936. He may be taking this picture for his mother, to prove we went.

said—behind us but loud enough to hear—"What that baby needs is a bust in the mouth." And that was my discovery of puns, the first word game I'd noticed.

Otherwise those Methodist and Baptist churches offered little else for a child to watch, unless it was the wasps that flew freely in and out of the flung-open windows. Adult Southerners, in those days before air conditioning, dreaded heat prostration worse than poisonous stings. Children never noticed the heat but were skittish of the wasps. And another child activity, which Elizabeth taught me, consisted of leafing through the hymn book and silently reciting the names of hymns with these words added, "Under the cover." You'd come up with, say, "Rock of ages under the cover" or "Onward, Christian soldiers under the cover." But that was likely to produce giggle fits.

Still church as a weekly habit was never a part of our lives. One cause for that was Will's and Elizabeth's differing allegiances. As much and as steadily as she loved him, and as relaxed as her own commitment was, Elizabeth never thought of joining Will's church. She explained it to me as a matter of loyalty to her dead parents. And as long as his Baptist mother was alive, Will could never consider joining with Elizabeth. Again that difference was the one gulf between them, and now I can guess that it also owed much to their unconscious needs for at least one wide external breach in the midst of so much union.

Even more important, they had mystical tendencies of their own. I stress the word *tendencies*; they were almost certainly unaware of them. They went to their graves thinking that *mystic* referred to nothing more serious than gypsy palmists and vaudeville mind-readers. Neither of them talked faith for more than ten seconds at a time or, God forbid, theology (beyond the ongoing great baptismal wrangle). But there came the moment, every night of the years I knew him, when Will knelt and prayed for upwards of ten minutes. On nights when he stayed down extra long, we'd mouth questions over his head—"What's he worried about now?" But we never snickered. And though Elizabeth's prayers were silently dispersed as needed through the day, she kept a set of devotional meditations called *The Upper Room* at her bedside and read from it nightly, along with her scandalous novels and the latest issue of her favorite magazine, *Sexology*.

Their endless, often self-depriving charity appeared so natural as to be reflexive. But I know that their care was also impelled by family devotion, a broad humanity and a Judeo-Christian inculcation in Good Samaritan ethics—ethics which, again, were blind to most racial injustice. Perennially strapped for funds, they more than once spoke of wishing they had enough money to tithe, to give ten percent of their income to charity. And they'd always point, as their example, to Hawkins Gilliland, a prosperous Macon grocer who was known to tithe, "That's what makes him as successful as he is."

I'm sure that, through the years, they did give away to friends and family more than a tenth of their money and goods—they were surely prodigal with their time and strength. If Elizabeth had five dollars, she managed to smuggle two of them to a jobless nephew. When we returned from Macon visits with a car full of produce and smoked pork, a good half of it was distributed at once to neighbors. Even when she was approaching sixty and plainly dying, I'd give her a check for new clothes, only to find that it had gone to buy Joel Jackson a set of books he wanted. The giving was plainly so natural that no one accused them, poor as they often were, of extravagance. And neither of them ever preened themselves for the charity involved. I doubt they thought of it as good works. It was something not only natural but that they liked to do, a return of thanks to a world they enjoyed. Their few surviving friends recall how little they expected by way of recompense.

Yet unless I misread them, Elizabeth was more nearly satisfied by the world as it lay before her. Her best rewards came from her marriage, her home and the larger family of sisters, brothers, nephews and cousins. I can't speak for the years before my birth, when she faced Will's drinking. But in the years I watched, she seemed most concerned with God toward the end of her life. Then she was mostly alone, going blind and suffering long nights with trigeminal neuralgia or *tic douloureux* (pronounced in the South, *tick dolly-rue*). It's a condition notorious for agony; and I once heard her say "If you were prising bones out of my skull with a crowbar, it wouldn't hurt bad as this." Surely those nights were prayerful and baffled—"What have I done, to suffer this?" She may have known but I didn't, and don't.

I know that in 1963 when Bill and I entered her hospital room, hushed with dread, minutes before she was to be wheeled to brain surgery, she caught sight of us, snatched off a bandanna—revealing her freshly shaved head—and cried "Khrushchev!" (the bald and menacing Russian premier of the time). Then she half-laughingly told us that she hadn't slept much the night before, "I kept trying to recite the twenty-third psalm, but I couldn't get past 'He leadeth me beside still waters.' How *does* it go after that?"

It makes a clear emblem of her spirit and trust. She recalled at least that guidance would be there when needed. And it seems to have been. She suffered and died with unspeakable bravery and laughter.

I always assumed that Will leaned harder than she on his transactions with what he took to be God, the power that had made him and that willed him to live a just and generous life. Elizabeth was a natural self-spender, tirelessly burning the fat and lean of a restless life. But the major virtues were hard work for Will. And though he achieved them to a degree I've seldom seen exceeded, he often showed flares from the jealousy, anger and self-absorption that were also part of his natural state. Once he'd won the struggle with drink, he had an abiding hunger for rest; and whatever blocked his taste for peace distressed him quickly.

But he lived with a vivacious woman who subdivided her love many ways outside marriage (I'm speaking of family and friendly affections, not adultery). He fathered two sons who suffered unusual dangers in infancy. And his work as a traveling salesman required him to spend hundreds of days and nights alone in sad hotels—when his fears for health and safety, and his longing for human warmth, made him crave patient company. In all those straits I suspect that Will got from his union with God the strength to proceed on a way that yielded slim rewards. The fact that his laughter and his well-laid jokes endured to within three weeks of his death seems proof enough that, under the fear, another strength surged up to renew his taste for the treacherous world.

Since he and I never discussed religion after I was grown, I can only guess at the terms of Will's prayers and his steady awareness of a watchful Heaven. He trusted in an ultimate goodness because his mother trusted and all his other kin and because, in the trough of his drunkenness, he asked for help and was sure he got it—a slow but mammoth new help that could not have come from within and that lasted a scared man the rest of his life. That was all Will knew; he was no Bible reader, no student of doctrines.

I've said that when I took him my early questions on God, Jesus and immortality, I got brief answers and frank admissions of ignorance. What he knew was basic—God was God and Christ was his Son. You could ask; they would help you. No further details, barring total immersion. From the age of thirty-six, Will believed because he'd witnessed miracles beneath his own roof, in his own mind and hands. He hadn't needed more. Anyone could have it (what he couldn't know was his own broad power, the power to seize the jolt of grace and let it burn him on to the grave).

Still when I was ten, and beginning my series of hero portraits, I asked him if there were any pictures of the way Jesus really looked? I'd noticed that the available pictures shared little more than dark eyes and a brown beard. Will's answer revealed a genuine lack of information. But it also goaded me to spend hundreds of hours of fruitful search, through childhood and after. He said "Yes darling, they have his real picture in student Bibles." I'm sure he believed himself. When I asked where I could get such a fine source of knowledge—at that point I had a tidy book budget, composed of birthday checks—his answer would have gladdened Sis Belle's heart, "The Baptist Book Store in Raleigh would have one."

Before my quest began to center on the face of Jesus, I'd undergone two serious and uncanny experiences away from home. Again from the age of six to eight, I lived with my parents on the rural outskirts of Asheboro. And without nearby playmates or brothers and sisters, I spent long afternoons roaming the woods. My reading interest at the time was American Indians; and I'd seen several Indian movies, especially *Drums Along the Mohawk*, where Indians were the official villains but not for me. And slowly with no knowledge of Wordsworth, Thoreau or the other pantheist nature poetry of England and America, I came upon a faith of my own, parallel to theirs but newly found. The other possibility is that such a faith was extended to me by an unseen mind that willed my attention.

I'm as certain of this as of the floorplan of my elementary school—on the afternoon of a gray fall day in 1939, I wedged my hunting knife into the soft bark of a pine tree. I pressed my lips to the dull edge of the cool blade. In that moment as I felt the tree's life in the steel, I knew that the world beyond me—every separate thing that was not Reynolds Price— was as alive as I. Through means that, then or now, I couldn't begin to explain, I knew that all matter was alive and aware—listening, seeing, hearing or feeling in its own way.

Every thing knew, or knew of, every other thing; and each understood its kinship with all. In some way that went past the fears I'd been given by Will and the world, I knew I was safe and could go on watching. But I was far from suspecting with many nature mystics that the world of trees, rocks, water and beasts is actually made from divine energy and is thus unreal as matter, precisely because it is somehow God or a set of God's masks. My boyish conclusion was in direct opposition.

I understand that it's hard to credit the distant memories of self-defined prodigies (Wordsworth says that, as a schoolboy, he sometimes ran to embrace a tree, solely to prove to himself that it had real substance and was not all spirit, as his mind had suspected). I can also see how easy it would be to credit my own experience to the loneliness in which it occurred—an imaginative boy with few playmates invents a kindly universe of unseen companions. Many children have phantom playmates for whom they invent personalities of sometimes frightening complexity.

I went another way. I had no sense whatever of invention. I perceived an immense created being, dispersed in millions of things. And I worked to press myself toward the being. I wanted it to know me as fully as possible and for me to know it. Since I'd heard a lot about God, I assumed God had made this single thing. But I knew God wasn't it—God was not a rock, and he surely wasn't me. He was watching us though, with hope and a set of powerful rules that I needed to learn. All I knew then was, they were rules for dealing with every other thing. They were hard rules but serious as a heart attack.

Even at the start I didn't expect flowers or lizards to speak to me like characters in Walt Disney movies (I'd seen *Snow White* at four and been properly terrified by those rapacious trees). My sudden knowledge of union with nature was bare of condescension and sentimentality. None of this was tame, charming or adorable. On the contrary I thought that most of nature was superior to me and my race. Most of what I could see

Near our Asheboro home in Dogwood Acres, the summer of 1939. Johnny
Weissmuller's Tarzan is my reigning hero; but the model here is Jon Hall,
co-star of Dorothy Lamour in South Sea Island romances. The first grade of
school is still weeks ahead, and the woods behind me are where I feel my
early way into what seems the living heart of things.

was plainly better than me—in self-possession, reliability, endurance and beauty. I recall long waits on the bank of the creek below our house. Once I discovered the haunts of the ghostly crawfish that were the color of my fingernails. I'd wait to see their cautious sallies and their courtly meetings with one another. Far down as I knew they were from us, they seemed perfected in a way I could learn—still silent to me and peaceful, with their own ample knowledge that I hoped to share. Someday I thought, if I listened hard enough, I'd know that nothing on Earth is silent. From crawfish to rocks in the hearts of mountains, everything speaks. And its language can be learned.

As a single example, at the time of that moment by the pine tree and for more than a year afterward, I had a German shepherd dog named Bill. Bill and I knew each other so fully and communicated our sympathy so perfectly that even strange adults noticed us—the way our eyes were constantly meeting, the way Bill understood my every thought. He was my main companion and, in most ways that mattered, my main consolation. And I knew Bill shared the feeling. Our union was so near-total that when I was eight and my brother was born—and came home, named Bill too—Will and Elizabeth soon had to persuade me to give my dog away.

I saw their point. Bill the dog was full-grown and formidable by then, and he showed clear signs of resenting the preposterous interloper into his and my world. The niece of one of our Macon friends had been savaged by a dog of Bill's kind and size. It was a key to my hopes for a younger brother that I let the older Bill go. It was also the first knowing sacrifice I'd make for what I then hadn't learned to call my fate. A brother would almost certainly speak my language sooner than a dog, even Bill. So I banked on that.

That young, I made no other effort to think through my knowledge. I had nothing like the conscious intelligence to explore its implications, if intelligence was what I'd have needed. I've since learned that a similar knowledge is shared, not only by most primitive peoples and by all American Indians but by many others who've also had my good luck—a lonely childhood in uncrowded countryside. Most urban children literally can't hear or see the fact; too much of what they see is manmade and hideous if not harmful. But at six, seven and eight, I thought I was alone in my insight.

And I soon realized that this understanding of the broad web of nature placed heavy duties on me. The interesting question for me now is this— if at six I was merely inventing a world of benign companions, why did I bind myself with the duties and burdens that my world demanded? Why didn't I push on to hallucinate the thoughts and voices of things, whole speeches from hawks on the joy of solitary flight? I only thought I must work to decipher the life of things different from me and mine; then I must honor them.

I also knew—and this was the heart of what seemed then and now a revelation—that everything, watched long enough, was good. I felt at once that the news made me happy; I likewise understood that the news stopped with me. No one I knew, however much I loved them, would sit still to listen. And if they sat, I couldn't tell them. The knowledge wouldn't fit into words, not now at least—not without turning me into a fool, which I knew I was, too much of the time already. How could I guess I'd spend a lifetime trying to say it?

I would be nineteen before I met anyone else who admitted knowing the same. It was then, in a sophomore course in English poetry, that I encountered Yeats's poem "A Dialogue of Self and Soul" and was wildly elated to see my secret in black on a page, endorsed as the conclusion of a great poet. I've since read poems that have meant as much to me, but no poem ever struck me so instantly with its soaring rightness. I read the last lines with a sense of reciting them, my first case of that best pleasure, the feeling that I'd written the lines myself.

If I'd been older and already a writer, I might have resented Yeats's prior claim on a truth I'd thought was mine; I was still too young to be less than glad of the brotherhood. The secret truth remained that, well before puberty, in the developer-threatened woods of Randolph County, North Carolina, I discovered or was shown the heart of Yeats's ecstatic adult conclusion. I was soon to learn that it's likewise the conclusion of most of the world's mystics—Hindu, Hebrew, Buddhist, Christian, Muslim—and a line of poets from St. Francis to Auden.

We must laugh and we must sing,
We are blest by everything,
Everything we look upon is blest.

How I merged that revelation into a particular creed and, for a short while, a particular Protestant sect is a wide strand in the story of the remainder of my childhood and early maturity. What it involves next is the second experience I mentioned.

I found a first home for my knowledge. In Dogwood Acres, three blocks from our house, stood the single church in our part of the county—the Episcopal Church of the Good Shepherd. It was a plain stone building with flagstone floors and little of the glamorous decor permitted to that denomination. By what seemed too good a coincidence, the young rector's name was William Price. And by a process I no longer recall, I began to go there to Sunday school. I've also mislaid whatever thoughts I had on the relation of my lone revelation to the different world of church, with its noisy outskirts of friendly chatter and income-counting.

But I went most Sundays. And soon I was serving as a candle-lighting, cross-bearing acolyte. I doubt I must stress the importance for an early mystic of such close assistance at beautiful acts which bowed to the unseen face of God (or the obvious fact that an acolyte is also an actor, a highly visible player in the rite). Then in 1942 I was presented with my first actual Bible, a King James translation of the New Testament. The inscription says "for bringing a new member to church school. You have made a good beginning. May you continue to serve well in His name." And I began to read it, especially the words of Jesus, which were printed in red and were far more interesting than the words in black. The red not only showed what was law but also that Christ was much smarter than Matthew, Mark, Luke or John.

Though again I don't recall how, some combination of those forces brought me to ask for the baptism I'd never received. And in 1944 when I was eleven and Bill three, the two of us were baptized at last—christened together in the presence of both our parents. My only clear memory of the moment is not spiritual; I can see myself cupping a hand to catch the stream of water that poured down my tan coat-sleeve. I also know that some of our cousins were there and Will's boss, who was a pillar of the church and whose presence may have helped ease or cover the regrets Will must have felt.

For the religious friction between Will and Elizabeth had only grown and was a potent factor in my hewing a middle course for years to come. Mother was pleased at the apparent compromise; and since it was the church of Will's father and five of his brothers and sisters (his one Baptist sister had joined the Episcopal church with her husband), Will at first seemed accepting. But a few months later, he erupted; and in an instant, he and Elizabeth were deep in the worst quarrel I remember.

I never knew what lit the fuse, but I know the charge exploded on a Sunday afternoon. I was in my bedroom reading. Then the quiet ended with their slowly rising voices, just across the hall. Like any child I listened for my own name and my blame in the matter. Soon I could hear even worse news. Bill and I were not simply involved; we were the cause, mainly me as the elder son. And Will was loudly accusing Elizabeth of steering his sons away from his family to hers. He even said that Ida, to whom he was otherwise devoted, had taken too much of Reynolds's love.

I was old enough to realize that, like most American wives, Mother had managed to move us her way. Our visits home were always centered on Macon and Mother's family. We'd stop by the Prices' on our way out of town for an edgy hour, and neither Bill nor I had more than a joking relation with Will's sisters or poor Sis Belle. Elizabeth threw back that Will had agreed to the arrangement—he plainly enjoyed her kin more than his own; he couldn't wait to put his feet up on Ida's porch rail and eat at her table. But next he was blaming her for leaving Reynolds so confused in the choice of churches that he'd gone off on his own and chosen a crowd as pale and peculiar as the damned Episcopalians. (I'd been baptized there, to be sure; but I wouldn't technically be a member till confirmation, at thirteen or fourteen.)

I'll go on wondering if I heard similar quarrels or worse, in my infancy. But that hot day in 1944 was the only time I recall lurking on my bed in genuine fear that my parents would soon come to blows. It was maybe only the third or fourth time I experienced the dread of so many children—in a few minutes now their voices will dim, but Mother will come in and tell me to pack: "It's over. We're leaving your father for good."

One more time, it didn't go that far. In their volcanic way, they slowly subsided and were cool if sore by suppertime. But from that afternoon I knew more certainly than before that another oncoming choice of mine was tautly sprung and bound to harm one or the other of the two on

Earth who were most precious to me, without whose steady presence and consent I could not imagine life.

Shortly after that ominous Sunday, the better job I've mentioned for Will took us back to Warren County. My recollections of those years show that, with no further urging from either side, I chose to split my church time three ways. By then my voice had strengthened without breaking or sinking, and soon I was in modest demand through the county. The most frequent request was "Beneath the cross of Jesus, I fain would take my stand." I was drawn to it by the second line. It called Calvary, the hill where Jesus agonized, "The shadow of a mighty rock within a weary land." I'm not sure why it reached me that young; but it was a line whose echo I heard again years later in Eliot's *Waste Land*,

> *(Come in under the shadow of this red rock) . . .*
> *And I will show you fear in a handful of dust.*

I attended summer-vacation Bible school, where we made Hebrew houses from flour paste, and occasional Sunday school at the Baptist church. I sang more than one solo with the children's choir at the Methodists'. And other times I attended Sunday school and served as an acolyte at Emmanuel Episcopal in the presence of my aunts and the two boys who were my weekday tormentors in school. But there in the lurking passive years between self-sufficient childhood and passionate youth, my mysticism was in hiding. The cause may have been simple—in our three years in Warrenton, we always lived in town, though open country was never more than a short bike-ride away.

Except for occasional outings with Mac though, and the two or three times Will and I went squirrel hunting (so I could use my new .22 rifle), I recall no more lone wanderings in nature. I did my schoolwork and enjoyed the bused-in farm children. In spite of the ongoing ostracism, I enjoyed my family, took my piano lessons, read my way through the good town library, drew faces and forged the signatures of great men, went to two or three movies a week and watched intent as the furious tide of puberty took me like a hapless promontory. Despite my unhappiness about the tormentors, there was apparently little time, and less force, for private soul-searching.

From here it seems odd that the torment and its resulting rejection, which gave me so much loneliness, didn't move me—as it does so many American and European adolescents—to throw myself on religion for the refuge and satisfaction that the daily world denied. Maybe my old familiarity with solitude satisfied me more than I knew. In any case, sealed up in myself, I was lucky to avoid the rocky shoals of overheated teenage religion.

To the left lies the danger for low-church, bare-wall Protestants—a plunge into self-righteous puritanism, with its damn-you-to-Hell view of most others. To the right is the danger for high-church others (Episcopalians and Catholic converts)—a warm bath of voluptuous aestheticism, a "bells and smells" snobbery which is often seasoned with a self-flagellating masochism that masquerades as union with the torn and bleeding Jesus.

Aside from my prayers to be better liked, for the healing of face pimples and the sane management of masturbation, in those years the world of God meant little more to me than a wide array of possibilities for social life with other church members and for theatrical self-dramatization (me in vestments at the altar again or solo in the choir-loft). And again every move was complicated by the armed truce between Will and Elizabeth.

I know I never entertained a doubt of God's existence or his constant scorekeeping; but since my lost days as a boy in the Asheboro woods, I'd felt no direct divine breakthroughs, no leaning on me from behind the sky. I heard no calls stronger or stranger than the voices of family friends and my mindlessly evil tormentors (I still can't think that *evil* is too strong; they knew what they did, and they did it for years). Strangest of all I have no memory of praying for them to like me again. Whether I prayed or not, my waking mind worked hard at detouring past their hatred, with no awareness of help from the sky. And I can't recall regretting the silence. In those years like most children, the last thing I wanted was an external hand to jerk me up in naked rawness and expose me to view too soon, unready.

I was fourteen when we moved to Raleigh in the summer of 1947; and for whatever reasons, I at once resumed my quest for the actual face of Jesus. Those were days when the publisher Bennett Cerf could jest truthfully that in many states there were more blacksmith shops than bookshops. The state capital of North Carolina, down into the 1960s, had only three; and in only two were books more than a sideline. Still I frequented the Baptist Book Store, Alfred Williams Book and Stationery and the shop by the old State Theater. I never found Will's promised "student Bible," but I did discover a packed anthology of guesses at Jesus' face in a thick book called *Christ and the Fine Arts* by Cynthia Pearl Maus.

It offered dozens of portraits of Jesus and scenes from his life. They ranged from the sublimity of Leonardo's sketch for the central head in his *Last Supper* to the eunuchoid-androgynous genetic mishaps of so much modern Christian art. Even I could see the difficulty of the quest, but I studied the book as another might have studied baseball statistics. And though I soon learned that there are no sure portraits of Jesus from the life, my hunt continued.

I see now what an odd hunt it was for a naive boy in mid-twentieth-century America—the product of religious but hardly ardent families. Yet the fact is that till I left home for college, I was seldom not at work, copying one of the faces in a long line of drawings and paintings. The crucifixion with its fast high drama was the main event I studied— Christ bearing the cross, Veronica's bloody veil with its print of his mangled head, his nailed hanging body, his grieving mother and his young friend John at the foot of the cross. For lack of reliable historical data, my hunger was never quite filled (and I was troubled by an early Christian tradition, based maybe on a prophecy of Isaiah, that the Messiah was physically unattractive).

It was in the late 1940s that I first saw a photograph of the vastly imposing image on the Shroud of Turin, a long piece of ancient linen with its faint markings that, in photographic negative, resolve as the clear but inexplicable print of a crucified man, from head to foot, front and back. From that moment, whatever the solution to the mystery of its origin, I had a sufficient face, and a credibly assaulted body, that seemed as near as I could hope to advance toward the original. For me the face on the Shroud was the image that seemed no guess at all but the thing itself.

At once it surpassed the variously moving guesses of artists in the Roman catacombs, the Byzantine mosaicists, Mantegna, Leonardo, Rembrandt and Rubens (most others were too bland to say the more frightening words of Christ, *"Before Abraham was, I am"*). Carbon dating now concludes that the linen is medieval in origin, with the corollary that the image was somehow made by an artist. But no one has shown how a fourteenth-century artist produced an object so complex in historical accuracy and still so mysterious in its physical properties. Meanwhile the battered calm face on the Shroud goes on seeming a worthy cause of the cataract of music, art, architecture and mystic rapture that artists and saints of the past two millennia have poured in honor of Christ and directed toward him. And all the Christs I imagined thereafter began in the unanswerable eloquence of the Shroud.

In those last years of childhood, several other forces worked to increase the magnetic draw of Christianity on my original insight. Shortly before we left Warrenton, in a conspiracy of more than usual meanness, Will's Baptist church rudely forced the resignation of its pastor of more than twenty years. He was Robert Brickhouse—the one other human being besides Elizabeth, me and maybe Grant who'd helped Will through his struggle with drink.

Will had done all he could to prevent the ouster, and when he failed I recall his saying "I believe in retribution. God is not mocked. The men who did this will eventually pay." In only a few years, the ringleader—a longtime superintendent of the county schools, who was also an internationally honored Mason—was convicted of embezzling state funds and sent to common prison. But well before such vengeance, the old Baptist fire went out of Will's soul. And though he joined the First Church in Raleigh and often went there (I often went with him), he also silently surrendered the hope that his sons would choose allegiance with him. And one of my hardest quandaries dissolved in his own disillusion.

Simultaneously Elizabeth's minister from Asheboro came to Edenton Street Methodist in Raleigh, then the largest such congregation in the state. Soon Mother and I were there to hear him on Sundays. Howard Powell was a full-scale pastor, a reliable friend and a superb preacher in a polished version of the old style of Southern pulpit oratory (he'd been reared on a tobacco farm in Sampson County and never forgot his plow-boy youth with its raging soothing sermons). And though he incorporated enough fire-and-brimstone to remind you that God the Father meant serious business, he mostly preached with a searing eloquence of the ultimate mystery of God's dangerous love and mercy. Soon too he took an interest in me and my questions. I often drove him on pastoral errands to other churches. And through my coming four years of high school, he showed me how one convinced man met a world where the divine love he trusted so often buries its face in pain and evil.

Our two-doors-uphill neighbors on Byrd Street were the Cowdens, an Irish Catholic family from Pennsylvania. The parents were good laughers, welcome and punctiliously devout in the unreconstructed old Catholic way. Their younger daughter Patricia, who was nearly my age, quickly became my close friend. The fact that Pat was one of the great natural beauties I've known hardly diminished her draw on me. She was the first person I'd met who could silence whole rooms by walking through. And she literally never noticed—a case where myopia was good for her soul. More than any beauty I've known, Pat's radiant exterior was steadily beamed from a core of goodness. Even more surprising, she could be counted on to cast a salty blanket over my ecstatic flights at the moment of peak efficiency.

I went to public school; and Pat went to Cathedral, then the only parochial school in the city. Her teachers were classically habited nuns, in the flapping black robes and marble-stiff wimples that were so much a part of the power nuns wielded before they took to miniskirts. Another few million volts came from their names, sounds as grand as Sister Jeanne d'Arc and Sister Benigna Consolata. When I went with Pat to Cathedral one night for a play, I met her favorite priest Father O'Connor and some of her teachers. I was glad to confirm in person that her music teacher Sister Jeanne d'Arc more than earned that ringing name; her scrubbed young face was as beautiful and strong as an unadorned two-handed sword.

Some of the other names sat a little oddly above cheerful or sour Irish-potato faces but I didn't laugh. In hindsight I think I was hearing a firm announcement from even the palest face. They sensed the dignity conferred upon them by their outlandish courage in departing from the human family of marriage and childbearing. As brides of Christ they were literal outlaws in our Protestant world, and they used that air with a knowing power. If any one of them was unhappy, damaged, cruel or ignorant, she escaped my eye (and Pat's). At fifteen I thought they were living with undeniable elegance on whatever outer rim God allowed them for work and prayer—which is also work, as Pat was the first to teach me. All the deeper then, Pat's good-humored but intense devotion to the Holy Family, especially the Virgin and the suffering Lord, and her loyalty at confession and mass were reaching me powerfully.

Unlike many Southerners my parents were not automatically fearful of Catholics, though they shared the local misinformation on Catholic doctrine and practice. So they were not alarmed when, long before coming to Raleigh, I began to show an interest in two Catholic saints—Joan of Arc and Bernadette. I'd been fascinated by Joan and her visions since the age of four, when I was given a book about her. My awareness of Bernadette came in 1945, with the film of Franz Werfel's *The Song of Bernadette*. I've mentioned my interest in the wretched peasant girl from Lourdes who in 1858 experienced a series of visionary encounters with a Lady who eventually identified herself as "the Immaculate Conception."

I searched in vain for a boy visionary. But the odd fact then was that there were no such boys of sufficient fame to inspire children's books or movies—are there yet? Somehow the young Francis of Assisi was ignored, maybe because of the scene where he stripped himself in public of all his father's possessions, including his own clothes. So I continued reading all I could find about both women (to later effect maybe—my fascination with peasant women as spiky but transcendent as Joan and Bernadette was a force in the creation of interesting but credible good women in my later fiction). And when we settled in Raleigh, my interest was deepened by the nearness of a flesh-and-blood gorgeous Catholic girl who poised, in my mind, on the real but sublime edge of sanctity. Not by coincidence, she shared my interest in the two young saints.

Pat and her mother Mary shared, in fact, a prior devotion to Bernadette. And early in our acquaintance, they received in their home for three days, like a noble guest, a traveling statue of Our Lady of Lourdes. By then I'd seen enough good art to know that most modern Catholic pictures and statues were vapid if not revolting. But I remember that Lady as a beautiful presence in the Cowdens' crowded dining room—a two-foot-high woman in flowing white with a sky-blue sash and a long pearl rosary. It was a faithful copy of the statue, carved to Bernadette's

Patricia Cowden, Raleigh in the early fifties. The friend and partner whose beauty and mystic conviction were weighty in my high-school years and, in memory, still are vivid and strong.

specifications, that stands on the actual rock in Lourdes where the Lady appeared. And at this Lady's instructions, Bernadette had unquestionably dug up with her hands the spring of water that's flowed ever since and healed so many. I wanted to kneel in the room with Pat, but our already-keen sense of the gulf between our churches stopped us.

Still the heat of our spiritualized relation endured—partly fueled in me, to be sure, by a crackling draw toward Pat's growing, near-but-distant body. Though she taught me the prayers and meditations of the rosary and though we talked of St. Jude and novenas and other forms of magic-working prayer, I don't recall that we said so much as a benediction together. We were like two souls imprisoned for the same offense. We could talk and wave between our cells, but they never let us touch. It bound us all the closer of course. (To balk the suspicion that we were repulsively pious or deranged in our long talks, I'll add that we spent a good deal more time in playing roller bat, basketball, bridge or in skating as we dodged polio in those five threatened summers of the late forties, early fifties. And with the boys on the block, I spent further hours in dirty-joke telling and elaborate, if often misinformed, anatomical speculation.)

But if we never prayed or communed together, Pat was my smuggler for the two Catholic objects I'd wanted for years—a crucifix and a rosary. It's necessary to say that, in general, Protestant churches display the bare cross, however stylized. They mostly avoid the more realistic crucifix with its copy of the dead or dying body of Christ. For them it's a distressing half-truth. I'd asked Howard Powell about the difference, and he gave what I later learned was the standard argument—Christ didn't die for long; why stress those thirty-odd hours of agony and death? But for whatever reason I'd been on the Catholic side of the argument for years—it's another half-truth to deny the intensity of Christ's saving agony. Early in our friendship Pat and I discussed it; and on my next birthday, she gave me a handsome crucifix "blessed by Father O'Connor."

Then she lent me a rosary. My parents adored Pat, and liked all the Cowdens, almost as much as I. But at that point Mother gently mentioned that I didn't want to get too involved with the seductive giftware of Catholicism. She'd got similar gifts years earlier from a priest in Henderson, who brought her presents from the Holy Land and then began a

drive to convert her. I assured her honestly that the dogma of papal in-
fallibility, if nothing more, would keep me Protestant. And I explained
my need for the rosary by saying that I was making the prop-rosary for
the Virgin in my Bernadette movie.

That far at least, I was honest. I did go downtown to Woolworth's and
buy the fake pearls with which I copied the original in Lourdes. But once
I'd finished and returned the model to Pat, I went on secretly for years
in using my copy for hours of prayer to the Mother of God. I implored
her help in numerous needs and fears—a chemistry test, a romantic crush,
a trip I hoped to take, the fate I imagined: a man in control of his life.
(Years later I bought a smaller black rosary in Rome, but I'm glad of
those hours on my fake-pearl beads. They bridged a way through one of
my early quarrels with my own church. Many more Protestants than I
agree that the all-male and often bullying atmosphere of so much Christian theology and worship is in serious need of a powerful *other*, some
worthy but tender counter-energy to the firebreathing, waste-laying God
of Sinai or the equally threatening Father in the letters of Paul, with
his righteous pounding.)

What were they about, my hours of secret meditation on the various
departments of God? Was I coping, in classic Western adolescent fashion, with the guilts and fevers of puberty? Was I grooming myself for
the priesthood? Was I responding to an external draw from divine grace?
Or was I yearning for sainthood? Even at the time, in my raw innocence,
I believed I was doing all four. And I was doing so in awareness of a
maxim that Pat often quoted, "Those whom the Lord loves, die young."
I'd changed since my early teens; now I expected and maybe wanted to
suffer for my ardor.

Again that kind of self-dramatizing masochism, even to the point of
suicide, is common in adolescence. Children on the verge of maturity
have after all watched the adult world with the locked attention of the
hunted. Better than any adult, they see the fragile alliances on which
adult happiness depends, the endless sell-out of daily life. They know as
if by instinct many gleaming painful truths about life, truths which they
seldom import into their maturity. And the heaviest of those burdens is
every child's ability to see, with merciless clarity, the million ways in

which human beings are dauntingly responsible for one another and how the sacrifice of one life for another is often called for and is not heroic.

In those years near Pat, I was still marooned in that unconscious wisdom of childhood. And before I moved into the adult state of necessary but tragic amnesia, I was drawn and pushed to focus huge charges of my energy on *effort*. I saw myself on an unflagging march toward victory in the few skills I could manage, those I'd been given and must give back with interest.

I'd be the best student in the state, the best visual artist and writer (though I lost the only high-school writing contest I entered to one Charles Kuralt of Charlotte). I'd be the best friend and support to all who needed me and, above all, the best local servant of the power that drove me. But I'd do it all unrecognized. For the first time I wanted to serve invisibly. Laser-hot as the energy was from sixteen to eighteen, I kept its source hid, confiding it only to my still-locked diary, alongside my sexual records. Where else in those drugless days could a boy, impelled by grace and his own immense hormonal fuel, turn for refills and guidance?

I turned like my father to prayer. And as none of us ever knew what Will thought on his knees each night, no one—even Pat—knew what I said and heard in my hours alone. But the puritan goals of success, prosperity and virtue in the eyes of one's community were by no means the point of my devotions. I'd of course mention the upcoming geometry test in my prayers, but it's not a brag to say that the Honor Roll was easy for a boy with the genes of two families rich in linguistic skills and with acres of time for homework. Some much stronger craving worked in me and cried for help.

A sophisticated agnostic might imagine any number of adolescent neuroses, Oedipal turmoil and guilt. And in my own teens, I played the amusing parlor games of Freudian analysis like everyone in school and elsewhere. For a year or so there, I could watch you for a day and pigeonhole you forever by sundown into a tidy set of hopelessly airless and inadequate slots. You'd have escaped me entirely, with all your best secrets intact; and I wouldn't have noticed. But a century of such simplistic analysis has now led careful thinkers to see its threadbare imaginative and scientific resources. If nothing else, recent studies of heredity and brain physiology have shown that the mind and the life it generates are far more intricate in motive and performance than an outmoded symbolic logic, like that of classical psychoanalysis, can allow (not to mention the quackery of amateurs).

If I conclude that, in mid-adolescence, the Hound of Heaven had begun to bay me—that the central power was hunting me—and that I was slowly being exhausted and forced to turn from my useful but incomplete boyish pantheism, I can't expect many readers to believe me. But—and this is crucial: without thinking for an instant that I was alone in being the prey of such a hunt—that's what I conclude. What the hunt turned me toward was a costlier understanding. The world consists of two things, not one. Those things are a creator and its creatures. For the first few decades of the hunt, my only contribution lay in knowing what was after me and in turning to face it in moments that, however scared and badly managed, began to show why it hunted *me*.

The single worry that I spared the Virgin, there in my self-painted deep maroon-and-gray second-floor Raleigh bedroom, was another lone activity—my sexuality, with its rollercoaster joys and miseries. My puberty virtually coincided with the publication of the Kinsey report, the first systematic look at American sexual practices. Till Kinsey surprised us— delighting millions, appalling as many (one percent of all American sexual pleasure came from "animal contacts"!)—there had been no public understanding of the fact that American males reach their peak of sexual capacity in the mid-teen years when the wretched boys are, or were in my time, most strictly forbidden to perform their need. Worse, we were silently instructed not even to admit the need, certainly not the fact of our endless stamina. We could outperform monkeys in zoos.

The first tides of puberty swept over me in Warrenton, where I had no male confidants. So I was left without counsel to wonder at the medical and moral implications of this apparently inexhaustible self-administered delight and solace (I say *apparently* since it was one of the fears of my ignorance that I would break something in my body and be ruined for life). But even in the religious doldrums of my early teens, I knew that anything so immense in spiritual power as this—anything so deeply grounded in my flesh—had to be watched by the sky. And good

or bad, the whole point of solitary pleasure is weirdly compromised if
God is watching, or some angel deputy, not to mention that actions with
such quick and eruptive results seem a lot more violent than a loving
God can want.

I'd heard occasional, not especially strong, home-warnings against
masturbation, always from Mother oddly—maybe because she'd grown
up with three boy-kinsmen in the house. Once she claimed to know of a
boy who was driven to Dix Hill, the state madhouse, because he did it to
the point where he literally couldn't stop and went so berserk they had
to tie his hands. One of my schoolmates knew of a similar case—the boy
whose mother kept him in the car, *driving* as much as possible in heavy
traffic. With both hands on the wheel at least, he was safer than elsewhere. But despite the ease of Will's light-handed ribaldry in other
matters, like so many fathers, he never once mentioned the problem of
self-help. Looking back I'm sure he considered it a pleasant part of every
boy's basic kit and felt no need to storm about it.

Still since early adolescents are more sensitive listening-devices than
anything yet perfected by the Pentagon, I collected whiffs of the culture's
severe ambivalence on the subject of what was often called self-abuse.
And again like most children, I didn't deal in shades of subtlety; my
questions were absolute. Was this department of sex all-good or all-bad?
If it was part-good, how could I tell the good half? If it was all good, how
could I stop short of utter exhaustion and death? If it was all bad, how
was I meant to bleed-off the hydraulic pressure that strained my pipes
several times a day? Was there a chart somewhere? With my luck it was
probably in another student Bible—when to start, when to stop, what
were misdemeanors, what were felonies, what led to Hell and what to
nothing much worse than a one-room tacky house, not right in Heaven
but on the outskirts? Again a joke of the time is relevant. *Mother*: "Son,
stop that! It'll make you go blind." *Son*: "Aw Ma, can't I just do it till
I need glasses?"

The Boy Scout Handbook, in the edition available to me, was vague
but discouraging in its brief reference to the subject—I seem to recall the
claim that it caused pimples, at the very least, and "lassitude" and that
frequent cold showers were imperative. I'd found an adult sex-manual
in Will's underwear drawer, beneath the perpetually replenished box of

condoms (one of Elizabeth's nephews was a Marine who managed a nearby PX, a bonanza-source in rubber-rationed wartime). But my children's dictionary was little help in understanding the Latin into which the author broke at key moments—*glans, labia, fellatio.*

A careful scan indicated that the Bible took a grim view, with its Mosaic rules for purifying the body from befouling "issues" of blood and semen. And again I had no older friend, not even a Chester-the-Molester-type scoutmaster, to ask. There was a neighbor boy, cheerfully ready to share in private contests of sexual speed and stamina. But however delightful, he was no help in the department of ethics and metaphysics. What could I do but, in the words of the hymn, "Take it to the Lord in prayer"? I asked him, more than daily, but with no audible results.

Portnoy's Complaint mined out the laughter and woe of my male generation's bondage to that brand of self-reward, self-torture. Roth's account is so dead-accurate and hilarious that it may be worth remarking that, while Portnoy's adult laughter at his adolescent self is earned, it obscures the agonized search of some three millennia of pre-Rothian Judeo-Christian males for answers to a question that impinges directly on sanity. It's hard to remember that today's blizzard of information about teenage sexuality is new. Any knowing reader of newspapers and diaries of the generations before mine can add appalling evidence— suicides, self-castrations and other maimings, many of them in demented obedience to Jesus' dark command, "If your right hand offends you, cut it off and cast it into the fire."

Till the late 1960s in America then, the frantic questions survived; and they survive now in homes beyond the reach of tolerant popular psychology and rock music's obsession with the subject. And you don't have to be religious to agonize; you just have to be a child set up suddenly in the observation booth of a hormonal eruption as unstoppable as melting plutonium.

With no outside help, and with no brake on the pleasure-pain, I sped through the jangled suburbs of early anxiety. For whatever lucky reason I was spared the darker terrors that others report. But I was just puritan enough to think that anything so enjoyable had to be harmful in excess, and I attempted personal limitations. My homemade controls though amounted to no more than a gentle foot-drag on this force that ran in mountainous torrents, a sandbag levee on the Peedee River in floodtime. So while I was not quite the haunted wraith with purple eyes, described in textbooks as the abject onanist, I was troubled.

Mother was always urging me out of my self-sufficiency, my book-and art-worm tendencies, "Go get some fresh air. *Play* with somebody." But I had the best playmate of all—attached, a virtual Siamese twin. The shut-door Eden that my growing body offered was dangerous precisely because it held me back and in. It made me like myself too much (though God knows I had few enough reasons for self-regard in those years). So without abandoning my personal facilities, I tried to police their action. But success was elusive. I'd have three days of soaring abstinence and begin to think I'd broke the hold of habit, but then some breeze would ruffle my shorts, and I'd collapse into a week-long orgy. And all my prayers went unanswered.

Maybe the fact that, by sixteen, the worry had dissolved was the answer to my pleas—that and the fact that I didn't become the Tar Heel Raskolnikov, crazed by strangled forces and driven to crime. But in case the reader feels that, in a look at religious beginnings, I've lingered embarrassingly on a trivial or irrelevant subject, I'd insist that those years of erotic confusion pressed me to learn as much about soul-searching and attentive meditation as any earlier trouble, even the fear of Will's drinking or my own torment in Warrenton. And all that boyish questing—in search of help for my rebellious but inescapable body and in the presence of what I took to be God—was the next decisive factor in the hunt.

The apparent silence of God, before the most baffling and repeated moral question of an innocent, taught me early a principle that any seeker must imbed in his foundation—all prayer is answered but a pregnant silence is often the answer. The principle was a long time coming. Meanwhile with a man's body but a boy's mind, I wrestled in darkness till a pale sun dawned. In it, I came to see that I'd been asking the maker and keeper of the farthest million galaxies an awfully small question, "Is this an offense in your eyes?" And his silence had simply said "Is it? You choose." Whether a child, or a seasoned adult, can continue to face God in the teeth of such turned-back questions is only one more of the endless tests that divide believers and suicides or those inscrutable billions who choose to steer entirely blind.

When I moved out of my trees-and-rocks mysticism into my years of church religion, it took me awhile to see that I'd done two sizable things. One was good; one was ultimately bad. Again I didn't think my way through the discovery clearly; but after a few years in churches, I knew. The good was a slow discovery that my early sense of the connection, the union, of all things could lead me to a serious error. Tempting as the notion of that union was, when I stood in the presence of a suncapped peak or an Ansel Adams photograph of the peak, I ran a grave risk in thinking that all things were not only *one* thing but that each thing contained its rightful portion of God the maker. I'd almost believed we're made out of God, and that's as risky an error as any.

For if I'm in any sense God, then I'm tempted to make the rules of my own universe, my home and family. And when I step outside my home, I'm all the more tempted to try imposing my rules on you, who understandably think you're God also. As I moved on a little in time and quantity of experience, the sights of nature and my widening knowledge of human beings renewed my awareness that all things are conscious and blessed. With the exception of my fears for Will's sobriety, I had very few unhappy hours before the age of eleven. As a child's angle of vision, that understanding was useful; it kept me wide open to life. But my long tour of churches, and my delayed exposure to human enemies and hatred, began to tame and amend the insight.

In Raleigh I heard Howard Powell's long series of sermons on Paul's hymn to love in First Corinthians 13 and began to learn the endless duties and complexities implicit in God's command, which Christ repeats, *I will have mercy and not sacrifice*. At the simplest level I saw that yes, everything is made by a single maker; but I am most surely not he. I can work to know him—I must. The work will be endless though and cannot succeed, not fully, not this side of death at least. What I can know is a ceaseless duty to love creation.

The eventually bad thing, in someone of my bent, was that for years I surrendered my lone mysticism and submerged myself in the most punishing error of Protestantism. The error was, and is, simple and may yet prove fatal. Catholic and Orthodox churches are centered on an altar that daily bears the flesh and blood of Christ; Temple Judaism was poised on the Holy of Holies, that small veiled room which once a year the High Priest entered to stand before God in his dwelling, the Ark. Both institutions then were mere shelters, fragile tents, for small but utterly central physical places that stood for the locus of human awe—*Look here: your God.*

But in their architecture and their avoidance of ritual, most Protestant churches center on a pulpit with one man, talking. The more eloquent or merciful the man (or now woman) may be, the greater the danger of that pervasive cult of personality that poisons so much else in American life. For years in my mid- and late adolescence, I leaned my spiritual hunger on a single splendid man—Howard Powell, the Methodist pastor I've mentioned. I joined his church at fifteen, I think; and for three years to come till I left home for college, I worked through him.

Those years were no mistake, far from it. My luck held strong again in having Howard Powell so near the center of my life for such an impressionable time. I learned much more from him than the complexities of all kinds of love. To set by the example of my father, he gave me the chance to watch at close range one more sane strong man who nonetheless heard a calling voice and answered it, moment by moment—hard or easy. Though he was not a highly trained student of theology or church history, he knew the texts of his faith by heart. If he was no wielder of threat and fear, he was equally no deodorized mouther of candybox comfort.

He knew that, over and beyond God's hope of mercy, there is still real evil, before us daily. We are expected to know its face and to try to refuse—that easy, that hard. And the sinew and verbal command of his sermons sent me back to his texts with new expectations and degrees of attention. Best of all, when I drove him to a few of his pastoral commitments around the state—sermons, sickbed visits, meals with the hungry or bereaved—I learned from Howard Powell, more deeply than from anyone yet, the coming necessity in my writer's life for superhuman grades of patience if I meant to understand the human mind in the infinite disguises of its desperation.

Still in learning to trust so much of my mind in another's hands, I surrendered too much of my own priesthood, my own proven access to the center of power. Like millions of others in all Protestant sects, I pressed so hard on another man—and a particular church behind him—that I risked my own collapse, if that man failed me. The error was mine, not Howard Powell's. And lucky again, I'd never stopped my private worship, even forms of devotion that I kept fully secret, like the rosary. So the old lines stayed live in my hands, if sometimes neglected in my churchly years.

Midway through high school, I began to notice a deep old stain on the fabric of Christianity in America, especially the white South. In the late 1940s, ninety years after the Civil War and the Emancipation Proclamation, white Protestant churches still ignored the continuation in our midst and *by us* of the virtual enslavement of the Negro race. No fact about Southern Christianity, in most places down to the present, is more baffling than the rigid racial division of believers and the tacit or active support by the white church of racist attitudes and laws. Like most children I accepted the facts of my culture as unchangeable. But with one more keen irony, as I entered my churchly years, that childhood acceptance began to crack under the weight of evidence from my maturing eyes.

All my life I'd heard my well-meaning, blind white kin grant that black Christianity had an enviable bone-deep sincerity, but even Will and Elizabeth were likely to smile at the exultant melodrama of black services and to point to that raucous enthusiasm as one more barrier in the path of any suggested merger of races or faiths. Even though country white churches then were a lot less middle-class-polite and comfortable than they've since become, they were still too self-conscious to permit unbridled displays of rapture or grief. Heaven was assumed to be as peacefully separate-but-equal as the Warren County schools.

Actually no one I knew believed in separate-but-equal. They were sure that we got what we'd earned, industrious and god-fearing as we were. Black people got the same. It took me no time at all to see that they'd got the absolute heel of the bread. But when I once asked why the streets weren't paved in black neighborhoods, Will said "Because they don't pay taxes, darling." He honestly believed it.

I'd gone with Will and Elizabeth to visit several black churches. If we were close to a particular cook, she might say shyly one evening "We having a meeting at church all weekend; wish y'all could come." Of course she couldn't come to our church, a fact we never mentioned or silently entertained; but if we had time to go, we'd be ushered to seats of honor in hers. The visit I remember most clearly was, at Mary Lee's invitation, to a revival service at Mount Zion Church in the country near Macon, about 1940.

Maybe wrongly I see the small interior as gray unpainted wood. I know that down front, facing the pulpit, was the Mourners' Bench, pronounced "Moaners." There sat six or eight young souls in light-colored, boiled, starched and ironed summer clothes. They had not "got religion" yet, were hopeful of doing so and meanwhile bemoaned their state in deep dead-earnest. They were harangued by the pastor, the renowned Cager Mingie; they were sung at, clapped at, prayed over, wept over. All eyes were fixed on them with a scared but tender apprehension—*scared* that the Spirit of God would suddenly descend with its tongue of flame and *tender* with hope that it would, this instant. Tears poured from most eyes. And the moaning, singing, preaching and cries from the pews rolled on in the heat till one-by-one—unless their hearts were hardened by sin—the mourners were snatched upright by the Spirit and flung into fits of actual possession. It could throw them to the floor in agonized writhing as Satan himself was torn from their soul (hence the story of the old preacher who, when women rushed to raise a new-saved mourner, cried out "Leave her lay where Jesus flang her!"). Or else—and this happened as we stood there—the Spirit could send them all but levitating, over pew-backs and sisters' stiff straw-hats, toward the open door and the graves outside (marked with nameless white fieldstones) and the starry sky.

Old-fashioned black services never obeyed the packaged sixty-minute rule of white churches. Like church in the old Plymouth colony, they were floating free-form events whose participants fell in and out as the Spirit, or some irresistible body-need, moved them. Revivals could go on more or less without stop for days, just occasional pauses for food on the grounds or to haul out a brother stunned by heat. But we spent the better part of an hour at Mount Zion.

Toward the end a stout young woman we'd known for years, as friendly and funny, suddenly "shouted." Speaking in tongues was uncommon in white Warren County and was audible only in especially heated moments of a Holiness Church service up near the box mill. Among blacks "shouting" was the principal gift of the Spirit to souls already saved, and its manifestations were similar to the signs of salvation itself—bodily ecstasies of wild exhilaration or racking sobs of grief. Seeing our gentle friend Azelle hurled to the floor in loud cries of "Jesus!", I was all but horrified.

But I wasn't. I watched hungrily. A central fold in my mind registered the sight as another revelation, almost as useful as my first at the pine tree only one year before. They were right, these people with whom I felt safe—Azelle's transaction was just this important (never for a moment, wild as things got, were we ever scared in a black church service). Whatever the Spirit of God might be, and a seven-year-old white boy had recent proof it was real as fire, this howling fit in a gentle woman was a much more convincing sign of its presence than the lightly scented air I breathed on white Sunday mornings, with nothing to watch but old ladies dozing and dive-bombing wasps.

And for the remains of my childhood and after, I wished our pallid and pasteurized rites could acknowledge a truth that then—in our social class at least—was reserved for blacks (poor-white Holiness churches shared many of the black rites and signs, though they'd have rather died—or killed you—than admit it). In another grand way that night at Mount Zion, I was shown how this despised people surpassed us.

I discussed the discovery and its growing implications with my parents; they listened with some sympathy. But kind as they were, they were snared to the ears in the racial system and couldn't take my feelings seriously, "That's their way of doing it, son. And God understands. But it wouldn't work for us. You finished your geography lesson yet? Then tell me the principal exports of Asia." For years I accepted such answers calmly. But always near me, black men and women were silently pressing their endless case. So my feelings endured—our churches were wrong, wrong deep down to the bone. By the time of my loving Pat Cowden and our shared addiction to "the beauty of holiness," those seismic feelings knocked holes through the cool crusts above them and began to burn me. Wasn't I part of an evil world that I could change?

At first I kept the thoughts private, in spiritual impotence. Eventually

I took them to Howard Powell and a few of my teachers. In truth I don't recall their separate reactions. I know that some of them agreed with me; but the consensus was, there was nothing to be done—not here, not now or for ages to come. The races had grown apart for so long, they could never be merged till all hearts changed, if God so willed. Even then, each people would lose its finest traits in the other.

I never conveyed to Howard Powell, fair as he was in his daily world, a thing that pained me to know. With all I told him of my own needs, I never said that the cry for justice to all black people should start in church; forget the *cry*, the *deeds* of justice. A decade later it did start there. But to the undying shame of the churches of my race, it didn't begin with us. It began in Alabama when a brave woman, the seamstress Rosa Parks, refused to surrender her seat in a bus; and it quickly spread through the thronged black churches of all the South in the hands of black preachers and their long-denied flocks.

For more than three centuries, in good conscience, white Christians had taught their religion of eventual love and mercy to slaves. Bereft of their own gods, their homes and their languages, the slaves took a God who promised justice (and who suffered to save us). In their churches, their songs, sermons and prayers, they tunneled through that distant God to unprecedented depths and heights of understanding and fervent poetry till they found in him a way-station that offered them the strength and the dignified elation of a tragic fate, a fate apparently limited to this brief Earthly life, with hope beyond.

In the end that hope—in the fire of its peaceful heart—proved the death of one evil; it burnt out the floor of the racial system. For though neither the prophets nor Jesus denounces the widespread slavery of their own times, the gathered weight of all they say at last proved undeniable— *God loves all human creatures equally; so must the creatures.* What accepted that truth however was not the white churches. Lyndon Johnson and the U.S. Government forced the law, and slowly the country began at least to repair its wrong.

Past too late, a pitiful few white Southern churches tried to join the rebellion; but the vast majority dug in and quailed, cobbling together atrocious tin-roofs of by-law and argument to forestall black members. I know of two local redeeming acts. First, the courage of Bishop Waters who integrated the Catholic churches and schools of the Raleigh diocese before the Supreme Court decision of 1954. At Elizabeth's Methodist Church in Macon, when the stewards met to consider their response if a black should ask for membership, our friend Clarence Thompson, Ida's next-door neighbor, carried the day with his simple question, "What would Christ do?" Twenty-five years later, I'm told, no black has applied. And almost all the churches I knew in childhood are white to this day.

Even for a witness as young as I in the 1950s, bitter as it was, that general refusal was no surprise. Since the entry of slaves into Jamestown, Virginia in 1619, white Protestant churches were the strongest pillars beneath the evil. Christ had foreseen the awful blindness ages before in Matthew 25 when he tells what the King of Heaven will say to all the wicked at the Last Judgment—

> *"You are cursed. Leave me and go to perpetual fire, built for the devil and his angels. For I was hungry and you gave me nothing to eat. I was thirsty and you gave me no drink. I was naked and you gave me no clothes, sick and in prison and you never visited me."*
>
> *Then they will answer, "Lord, when did we see you hungry or thirsty or a stranger or naked or sick or in prison and did not help you?"*
>
> *He will answer them "Amen I tell you, when you failed to do it for the lowest person, you failed to do it for me."*

Nearly two decades lay between my finding for myself that vast hole in the hull of the church and the ensuing flood of national protest. Again, in the meanwhile I was mostly silent—except for a few ineffective questions, a single high-school story and poem and continuous tries in my early fiction at understanding both races and their plights. I've examined my motives—fear, despair at the strength of the system and an inbred instinct to spy on the enemy's core and learn his ways for the future writing, which would be my action. And again I've said, all these years late, that my silence offends me.

What's more relevant here though is to say that my slow discovery of the evil—caused as it was by my boyhood revelation, by the force of black friends and my years in the church—was powerful among the reasons that drew me out of the church. For the rest of my high-school years, and through my four years of college nearby, I continued as a member of Howard Powell's church; and I went on learning from his friendship (he told me, for instance, never to be far from a place—a wall or an album—where I could study the faces of those I loved).

But by the time I left home in 1951 for the rest of my life, I'd begun to know more than one reason why I was leaving all the churches I'd experienced. I went on attending the non-sectarian but white university chapel for a while. And I took more than one course in religion (I also studied anthropology with Weston La Barre, the most learned atheist on campus, a brilliantly nimble lecturer and writer). Even in the blast of his mind though, I don't recall that my own faith staggered. The further I moved from organized worship, the more the God of my childhood meant to me—and the Christ that I thought I discerned in the warring pictures of the gospels, which may yet be the only face we have for him.

I didn't discuss my withdrawal with anyone, surely not with Howard Powell or my parents. To my churchly contemporaries I didn't defend my action or try to persuade them to follow, and I never in any way openly condemned them. My silent mind knew however, no question or qualm, that in churches I felt increasingly blocked from my best means of understanding. I'd come to believe, and still do, that those means were my own inquisitive eyes and conscience, watching intently for the motions of the spirit, and my study of the ancient texts of the Bible. And though this reason was less important, I'd found that my best gift felt useless in such a world, the gift I hoped I had for "tongues." I would use that gift in my own way—in poems and stories, plays and essays. I'd teach the young, as I'd been taught.

They were sober conclusions, too gleaming and stiff with the excess dignity and self-regard of early manhood. Yet beaten and limbered as they've been by time, they've got me to here through decades no smoother than most—still watching, still speaking, still sure of the core. More than a few men and women, some of them priests and pastors, have assisted me strongly. I've visited churches many times, for lone worship, for the chance to share the wine and bread that stand for Christ and for other chances to use that gift I'd once thought useless in pulpits, near altars—the use of words to try to convey a wordless knowledge of the core of light. But I've never yet stayed; I still withdraw. At least till now I've kept good faith with the child I was and may always be.

If you could reel the decades back to 1939 and find the boy mystic, roaming alone but tranquil and glad through the peaceful woods of central Carolina, the relics of Indian braves at my feet, me tasting the vibrant hearts of trees while all of Europe and most of Asia hunkered to bear the madness of war—if you could still find him and show him the scenes of his life to come, the tolls he'd pay and the gifts to follow, he'd have given his tombstone-size front teeth for one more sign, on the spot that moment—that he mattered by name to the perpetrator of so much splendor and its still-concealed anguish. Show him death, show him pain. What was pain to him? He was always famished for more, more— more light, more life, more answers *now*. He'd have begged for the whole gift, then and there. Try to tell him he'll get it.

Will and I on vacation with Elizabeth, Bill, Marvin and Ida, June 1952—our last photograph alone together. We kneel in White Lake, a spring-fed body of crystal water in southeast North Carolina. I'm nineteen, full of my first year at Duke and growing a goatee. Will is fifty-two, with twenty months to live and, as always, wears his glasses in swimming—prepared for all but the death rushing toward him.

8

A FINAL SECRET

WILL PRICE

WILL PRICE was a devoted provider, apparently a faithful husband, a generous companion who delighted in friendship; and of all the comedians I've watched, he was third-best after Chaplin and Keaton. By world standards, he was a brilliant mimic and quick-change deceiver in domestic pranks. Rich and long though his laughter was, like many comedians he was also fear-ridden—haunted by the steady knowledge that disaster hung just over the heads of all he loved. He seldom let any of us leave him for more than a few minutes without a serious recital of all possible dangers, from constipation to a four-car collision.

I realized early that, when we left on longer trips without him, he saw us off with surface calm but also with a gravity fit for ultimate farewells. A part of his fear was realistic. Life, even in less hostile times and places, is unspeakably fragile and threatened by the moment. But most of us barge through, oblivious of danger or at least agreeing to the necessary lies of daily life. Will wouldn't lie. Safe in the midst of his family, he could manage to laugh toward the end of most days; but far too much of his energy leaked off in useless anxiety. Granted, he feared mostly for his three main dependents, all younger and weaker than he; but he was also a maddeningly inventive hypochondriac.

Again his mother's contagious fears bore down on him, every day of his life to age twenty-seven. And in her shadow, he began his long struggle with drink. So some of his fear came naturally. Once he was sober though, in what might well have been the midst of his life—age thirty-six—he had good reason to lower his guard and to try a bolder thrust at the world. And at first, deep into the hole that was left as liquor vanished, he poured a welcome new brand of diligence and trustworthiness. All his kin and friends rejoiced in the return of the spirit of the openhearted boy he'd been before his addiction (his face and body kept a drinker's heft). But as his sobriety strengthened through the latter 1930s, Elizabeth began to notice in him a burgeoning tendency to monitor his body for the least sign of trouble. This pimple was surely cancer, this after-dinner indigestion was a bleeding ulcer, and his heart skipped beats as if it might stop any instant. If you entered a quiet room and found Will there alone, he would often be feeling his pulse. By the time I was five, he was haunting the offices of a long chain of doctors (like all hypochondriacs, he switched doctors as soon as one belittled his fears).

Elizabeth and her good-natured family and his own tart sisters tried to tease him out of an obsession that sapped his peace, his wallet and his strength; but their breath was wasted. I recall Mother telling him more than once "Will, what you need is a useful *hobby*." Her own brothers and nephews at least played golf or puttered in home workshops. And while Will was supervising the building of our Asheboro house, she gave him a nicely equipped tool box in hopes he'd build the odd shelf or shed. He barely drove a nail, and the nice box rusted. His intricate body—like all bodies, capable of sudden treason—was his true consuming hobby. Far more than his job, Will's health was his calling.

Worse, he lived in a time when little was known of the benefits of good nutrition and exercise or the harm of smoking. So he lived like a normal man of his time and income—overweight, sedentary and a heavy smoker. His approach to illness was a ceaseless watch and preventive medicine—mostly because, on a certain night in his early middle age, he'd heard his doom announce itself.

Since we were living in Ethel Cranford's apartment house in Asheboro, it must have been 1943. I was ten, Bill was two, Elizabeth thirty-eight and Will forty-three. The ceiling light had burned out in the living room. Will stood on a chair to change the bulb; and while his arm was stretched overhead, something happened in his chest. A flood of hot pain; his face went pale, he stepped down at once and said "Something broke in my heart. I felt it bleed and miss some beats."

Elizabeth and I assured him that it was only a pulled muscle; but nothing would stop his going downtown at once to the Barnes-Griffin Clinic for the opinion of a man he'd see often in coming months, Dr. Dempsy Barnes. The doctor, a soothing tactful man, took Will seriously.

Once he'd examined him that night though, Barnes told Will that there was nothing wrong with his heart—"Something muscular happened" (the heart is a complex muscle, to be sure; but Will didn't know it). In the hope of accepting the reprieve, Will repeated its terms hundreds of times in his remaining eleven years, "Your heart's as good as a new steam-engine." He even kept a studio photograph of Dempsy Barnes above our main radio the rest of his life.

But Will couldn't believe a reassurance for more than ten consecutive minutes. For the last decade of his life, he was convinced that his heart was failing. And since his work soon required him to spend four nights a week on the road, he fully expected to die in his roadhog Buick or, worse, in one of the country hotels he frequented in eastern North Carolina before the days of bright air-conditioned motels. The endless crossroad-cafe meals, all breaded and deep-fried in lard, were aimed with lethal precision at the bravest heart or stomach.

He often told us of whole sick nights spent staring out the window down east in, say, Swan Quarter where a canal ran through the middle of town and mosquitoes fat as sparrows assailed his rusty window-screens or of waiting up with his tricky heart all night in a hot tile lobby, just to be near the six other salesmen playing poker till dawn (he never had the patience to learn card games, and he passed that refusal to me).

Antacids alone were a substantial item in Will's budget. So sure was he of cardiac ambush that a bottle of spirits of ammonia was always in his pocket, for reviving sniffs. And he never left home without a full-sized Gladstone bag devoted entirely to medications. Our neighborhood druggist was cheerfully generous and had outfitted Will with one of every major item in the pharmacopeia of the 1940s and '50s, regardless of need or legality. Among dozens, the salient items were nitroglycerin for chest pain, mild opiates for diarrhea and toothache and one bottle each of the newest fad, antibiotics (including strong penicillin lozenges which we all sucked like gumdrops at the first sign of a scratchy throat). Yet Will's mother's remedies were what he leaned on—soda, witch hazel, ipecac, smelling salts, liniments, embrocations and the battery of ballistic-strength laxatives that were common to all members of his bowel-obsessed generation. And again by the forties he was so secure in his abstinence that he carried a four-ounce bottle of bourbon, in the event of palpitations or snake bite.

At home he bore his worries with a dignified creased brow and no other physical quailing; but he still moaned "Wolf!" so endlessly that, by the time I left for college in 1951, we'd all lost sympathy with the central fear of his life. We'd long since half-comically agreed that Will Price was bound to outlive us—in which case, he had genuine worries. He couldn't make so much as a cup of instant coffee, and on no single work-day had he ever selected his own tie or socks. Dozens of times we heard him half-seriously beg Elizabeth not to remarry at his death. Her response was always laughter and a plea that he remarry on the *day* of her funeral—she wouldn't have him starve for lack of a cook or leave next morning in the clashing colors of green and blue.

And since he flourished in a time when smoking was not widely implicated in lung cancer, and a modest plumpness was seen as a sign of vigor, Will's perennial medicine bag was the joke of family gatherings—he was obviously hale; calm down and enjoy it. After a little sheepish grinning, he'd join their mockery and tell the story of the night when he was waiting out Elizabeth's delivery of Bill on a January afternoon and night in 1941.

That was long before fathers were welcome in the delivery room, so Will kept going outdoors in the dark and circling the clinic to listen at the window through which Elizabeth's screams poured. (Here he would mimic a lengthy delusion in which she yelled for their friend Gale Hightower to climb down off his high-tension pole before he got electrocuted.) Eventually terrified in the dark and guilty for again conspiring to force his wife through such an ordeal, Will drank a straight slug from what he thought was his pocket-bottle of nerve-soothing ammonia, a remedy generally taken in water. In haste he'd somehow brought the wrong bottle and swallowed instead a scalding dose of camphor. Much affectionate laughter—when the joking listeners quieted though, none of them balked at accepting in private the nameless pill or the bitter slug of whatever Will prescribed for their ailments.

His only recurrent organic disease was pneumonia. From boyhood he had a weak chest; and considering that he was well over forty before internal antibiotics reached America, Will's immune system must have been superbly armed. Yet no winter passed without a week's siege of something chesty, that year's flu or a touch of pneumonia. No parent reveled more grandly than he in the misery of illness and the paraphernalia of cures—vaporizers, atomizers, heating pads, mustard plasters. And no husband was more grateful for the enveloping care that Elizabeth offered or for mine and Bill's visits.

Even now I recall the stertorous breathing of his sick nights (he seldom permitted a closed door) and the messages he'd whisper as I stood on the doorsill, "Don't come in, darling; you'll catch this mess. It's awful this year, bad as 19-and-18."

I'd hear him out, with clucks and sighs; then leave in the family's certainty that no germ invented had Will Price's number.

It wasn't a germ or even a virus. But when I was a junior at Duke, a half-hour west, I returned to my room one night to find a bleak note from the Information Desk (student phones were unheard of), "Call home soon as possible." It was dated the same day, late January 1954. I'd been home for Will's fifty-fourth birthday dinner on the tenth; and then he was a little low with the early outskirts of what seemed flu. He'd even urged us not to kiss him, a sure sign of infection in a man as committed as he to the outward confession of love; but I hadn't heard a word of further trouble.

I know now how chilled I was at the sight of the penciled words. As I waited my turn at the only pay phone in our huge dormitory, I even suspected that tonight would mark the end of my basic American love affair with the telephone. It was about to do something awful to me. Deeper still, with the never-mentioned sympathy which this reserved gentleman and I always shared, I knew that this was no trivial summons.

By the time I won my five minutes in the wooden booth, I was praying that the voice would be Mother's. Any male veteran of college in the 1950s will remember the odor of those booths—the peculiarly powerful odor of whatever substance early phone-receivers were made of and, overriding all, the traces of a constant procession of love- or money-lorn college boys in pajamas, undershorts, towels or month-old dungarees. I held my breath against both the odor and whatever came next; I deposited my nickle and placed a collect call to Raleigh, TEmple 2-3285.

It was past eleven but Will answered and accepted the charges.

"Hey, Dad, I just got the message. How's everything?"

"Darling, I can't seem to shake this pneumonia. Seems like I keep getting weaker." He didn't sound weak but the overtones were boxy and old.

I said "Have you seen Dr. Brian?"

"He stopped by this evening, said my chest sounds better."

"Are you back at work?"

"That's the whole point, Preacher. I'm needed down there, with the big meeting just two weeks away."

I tried for the upper hand and assured him of the last thing an aging adult wants to hear, "They'll get by without you. You rest till you're well."

He thanked me, impatient as ever with any hint of my coming maturity. "When you coming home?"

"Unless you need me, probably not till my birthday." That was February 1st, some ten days off.

He only said "Aw" in his patented way, quick as a wild thing, not prolonged to a wail.

"You want me sooner?"

He thought his way through it. "You'll come when I call—if I need to call—won't you?"

"Say the word, Dad, and I'll be there."

"Your money holding out?"

"Doing all right, sir. You'll be the first to know."

"Go on to sleep then, son. You need your rest. Did you get that mouthwash?" He'd written to thank me for my birthday visit and had added lightly at the end, "*Son, I noticed you had a little breath problem there. I'm enclosing $5.00—go buy you some mouthwash.*"

"Yes sir, I bought it and I smell like a rose. I've got a test tomorrow and will be up till three."

"Don't ruin your health, darling. It's the main thing you've got." I've said that Will never stinted on expressions of love for both his sons. And awkward though the endearments of his manly baritone may have sounded to other boys in our adolescence, we never silenced him or dodged his embrace.

I assured him I was fine and then we concluded. I was all the way up-stairs, back in my cherished single room, before I realized we had not mentioned Elizabeth. Was Mother there with him? Why hadn't she answered? She was the calming go-between in all Will's health scares but not tonight.

It was some weeks later, and Will was dead, before I could ask her. "Where were you that first night he called me?"

"Sitting beside him," she said.

"Why didn't you answer or speak to me anyhow, when he and I finished?"

She said "I'd watched him wait for you. I saw what he needed, and I left it to him. I knew he had to do it."

I said "And what was *it*?"

"Son, he needed to hear you say you'd come when he called. He finally suspected the time was at hand. He'd need you soon, no foolishness about it."

"Yes ma'm but who was I to him?"

"You tell me. You know more than I."

I didn't entirely, not then.

And till now, though I've worked at the meaning in my thoughts and in fiction, I can't claim to know all my father meant in the coming rush of days. What I could understand in the silence after the long storm was that something large—some hard but congruent reaction to the action of Will's death—was at work deep in me and would shoulder its huge way up, when it ripened. It took nearly two years, and I was four thousand miles from home, but that runs ahead of the story itself.

The weekend after our phone conversation, I went home for Saturday night. Meanwhile Will had seen Dr. Earl Brian again; and an X-ray had shown a dark patch on his right lung. He'd had a chest X-ray only a month earlier, in a life-insurance examination; and his chest was clear. The new finding probably meant pneumonia or, at worst, a touch of TB. He was sent home with a prescription for penicillin and orders to return on Monday for another look. I stayed less than twenty-four hours, time enough to see how weak he was on his pins. Except in his comic skits, he always moved with deliberation; but now there was hesitance and

Elizabeth and Will across from our home at 2311 Byrd Street, Raleigh, in 1950. The last photograph of the two and an honest record of their late contentment.

wavering. And privately Elizabeth said to me "Look at his hands. All of a sudden they look so old." He had enormous hands—even now his wedding ring is several sizes too large for my finger—but that day they were taut and yellow.

On Sunday morning he asked me to go to Five Points Pharmacy and rent him a pair of crutches. When I left for Duke that afternoon, he saw me off as always from the front porch, fully dressed but propped this time. Elizabeth and Bill were beside him (Bill had just turned thirteen and was watching him closely); and the sight struck me hard. Since he'd powdered his hair, that night eighteen long years ago, I really hadn't thought what his aging would mean for me. If he died soon I'd still be in college or graduate school. My present scholarship was ample, and the prospect of another was good, but how could I be a man that soon?

I went back a few days later for my twenty-first birthday dinner. He and Mother gave me a pair of engraved gold cufflinks, and we all huffed to pump the usual life into a festive evening. But Will still hadn't returned to work, his legs were weaker; and the second X-ray had shown the spot in place, unaffected by penicillin. That left TB and cancer as explanations (Elizabeth told me all I knew; one of the strange new facts was Will's silence on the subject of his health). He'd enter Rex Hospital for further tests on Wednesday. So the evening was edgy for us all. Yet oddly Will was calm. In the past he had never concealed his worries. But now that a known unknown hung overhead, he entered on a slow serenity that was almost more unsettling for us than visible anxiety.

The next Friday I returned to my college room in late afternoon to find another call-home note. This time Elizabeth answered; the worst was certain. When blood and sputum tests failed to identify the lesion, Will's right lung was inspected in a painful bronchoscopy—a wide-awake procedure that called for the insertion, down the throat and into the lung, of a lighted optical instrument. It saw no tumors but the fluid pumped from the lung swarmed with cancer cells. When Dr. Brian told Elizabeth, he could offer only two courses—remove the entire lung and radiate or do nothing and wait for Will to suffocate. If that large a man survived the loss of half his respiratory system, the chance of a five-year survival was twenty percent. Will hadn't been told. Confessional as she was, Elizabeth had managed for now to keep her own counsel; but she couldn't hold out. Could I get over to Raleigh by dark? Dr. Brian would meet us in Will's room and tell him.

I was there when the doctor appeared, a kind man from our neighborhood, about Will's age. He was pleasant for two minutes, with questions about my studies. Then he stood by the bed—Will was lying down—and spoke in a quiet voice. "Will, the pathology report shows a malignancy in that right lung. It doesn't say how big it is, or what we'd find if we go in there. I've showed the results to Dr. Sinclair, and we're in firm agreement. The next thing we can do is take out the lung. I recommend it to you. It's a serious procedure, maybe four hours long. I don't expect you to say yes or no, right here tonight. A few days more won't make any difference. Talk it over with Elizabeth and the boys. And if you want another doctor's opinion, I'll fully understand."

My experience thirty years later—at almost the same age as Will but with doctors less knowing in the humane conveyance of dreadful news—helps me guess his first response. There was surely an absolute blanking of thought, as if he'd fallen instantly to sleep or were hearing the price of grain futures on the radio or had flat-forgot the meaning of words. I recall that he looked out the window; and when he spoke, he faced nobody but the night sky. "What are my chances?"

Brian said "If you come through the surgery well and we give you some X-ray—twenty percent."

"What if I just go home tomorrow?"

"Will, I can't really guess—maybe two more years."

The next night I was back in Raleigh for the meeting Will convened in his room. He'd called his three sisters from sixty miles away; and they joined me and Elizabeth—Will had asked that Bill stay home. In our last year in Warrenton, he'd quarreled with his sisters; and relations ever since had been strained. No question now though, he needed their presence and advice. Not only were they all he had, in calling distance; he was also insuring that, if things went wrong, they wouldn't blame Elizabeth or me. So once the family news was disposed of, he laid out the choices he faced; and he told it fairly, in Dr. Brian's terms. Then he asked for advice—that straight, this man who'd run a jagged course for so long.

Mary Eleanor and Lulie were older than Will and spoke first; it was awful news but surgery looked like the only choice. Then Martha Reynolds, who shared Will's daily certainty of doom, said she understood his hesitation; but as long as there was a whisper of chance, by all means take it.

I'd already cast my vote; so I kept quiet, thinking how odd but welcome it was to meet this level realism after so much bafflement. In happier times when these sisters were packed together in too-small a house, they'd made spiky company; but now the scars of their own lives made them an apt and credible chorus. Not one of them insulted the occasion with dismissals of its weight or with empty assurance, and none was lugubrious or pitying. In their presence, for the first time, I realized a fact of vital importance to the remainder of my life and to my continuing stock of knowledge as a writer—how glad I was to have such open-eyed minds behind me. Elizabeth's family, to whom we'd naturally gravitated, were deeper-breasted and more open-hearted; but logic could quickly desert them in a crisis. It was from this night that I set myself to know my Price kin better.

In the wake of their votes, Will faced us again and said he'd obey. I know he used the word somehow, "All right, I'll obey." I wanted to move and cover his mouth, to cancel the sound. *You're not our child. Don't obey. Choose and then we'll follow.* Either way, he'd chosen and he never looked back.

On Sunday after lunch Will made a choice that may have been harder than the gamble on surgery. Dr. Brian had come by his room in the morning and said that, since the day was so fine, Will might like to take a ride after lunch. Will didn't leap to answer at once, and I knew not to push him, but after lunch he said "Let's ride home." Then he dressed himself and, since he'd mysteriously recovered strength in his legs, he walked to the car. Though it was mid-February—Valentine's Day—the short drive down St. Mary's Street, across Glenwood and down our Byrd Street was all in sun, a pale twin light. At our house, 2311 Byrd, he also walked inside unaided. Bill hadn't seen him for several days and was at the door, ready with his gift for raising the tone. But at once Will seemed like a stranger in his own house, a formal guest. And his slow, almost delicate movements showed he felt the strangeness.

We'd eaten at the hospital, so there was nothing as merciful as food to help us through the time. The overstuffed chair in the den was his, but he went nowhere near it. Now he sat in a striped chair in the living room and tried to fabricate a normal interest in Bill's school news. After a few minutes of that, he quietly moved to the sofa and lay down. Elizabeth sat on the brocade chair, reading the paper and trying to bring him up to date on the neighborhood news.

Bill and I scattered to more bearable parts of the house; but we strictly avoided one another, a contact that might have bred whispers or grief. We'd always known that Mother endured, in her own childhood, the deaths of her parents. And Bill and I were veterans of more than one family funeral—mostly ancient great-uncles—but we were new to this fresh matter of absolute gravity plunged down among us in our own tame rooms. So we chose to bear alone, twelve feet apart, an unbearable thing— it was surely our father's last time here.

What lurked in the air that mild afternoon of false spring to tell us the truth, when the doctors were giving us one chance in five? Through the years till now, however anxious Will was, we other three had struggled to keep hope flying on the mast, most days at least. From earliest childhood Bill and I had learned the means of easing his enormous fears. We'd tell him school tales, show him our drawings or ask him questions about some fact in the radio news. But now, without a shared look, we knew that a life was ending among us. Whatever made the chance a fact in our minds—Will's weakness or his mute unprecedented calm—weighed on us by the minute. And though our father was free here till dusk, before a full two hours had passed, he called us downstairs, "Preacher, let's roll."

He made no final tour of the premises, no fondling of objects, no word of advice. His favorite miniature portrait of his mother was near the sofa, but he never glanced toward it. He kissed Elizabeth and Bill, the usual dry brushes on the lips; and we all walked slowly out to the car.

Then Will and I got in as if we were driving to the post office; and when I pulled out into the street, he didn't look back or wave. He'd had his last sight of the only house he'd come near to owning, the only house in which he had more than two consecutive years of solvent adult happiness (we'd been there nearly seven years). He'd seen the last of his younger son, the one who bore his name, who resembled him most and in whom he took special delight. And with the little insurance he'd been able to afford, he knew he was leaving it all to a wife who'd need an immediate job, though she'd never worked a day outside the home.

Through the ten-minute ride, and the slow climb back up the hospital steps, he didn't speak. I can guess his reason; I was sure of my own. With all the ringing heroic rites I'd met in my reading—and the funeral march in Olivier's *Hamlet*—I hated the silence of the whole transaction. The car itself should have sounded a chord of grateful pomp. Nothing but the bump of tires on asphalt. And I, for all my poems and tunes, knew better now than to trust myself with anything as armed and punitive as words.

I've lost the reasons but, with tests and visits from doctors, Will waited through two more days for surgery. I spent Monday at Duke attending classes, but I drove to Raleigh that evening. Elizabeth and Will's local friends had the room full of talk. I planned to visit him on the night before Wednesday morning's surgery, but I thought I'd sleep at home with Bill and Mother.

Before I left Monday night however, when Will and I were alone together, he said "Preacher, will you please stay in here with me tomorrow night?"

I said I'd be glad to and that I'd ask about getting a cot rolled in.

"I've already asked and they say no, but they won't object if you sleep in that easy chair."

The chair was barely easy, but I told him that one night in a chair would be no hardship.

He let those words settle carefully in the air. Then he said "If it's more than one night, you'll stick with me, won't you?"

I said he'd stuck with me twenty-one years; any number of nights would be my privilege. By then we really did talk like that, as if we were Grecian chiefs in armor on the dark beach at Troy or friends in a tale by Henry James, saying precisely what we meant in words that were hopeless to bear our weight.

Only as I opened the door to go did Will bring us down. He said "You sure that coat's big enough?"

Old as I was, I'd only that week bought my first sport jacket without either his or Mother's advice—a brown Harris Tweed for forty-eight dollars on sale, size thirty-eight. He was right; it was more than a little trim. But I said "Rest easy. It fits like a glove."

He nodded. "Don't wait too late to change it." And as always leaving no mischance uncovered, he said "Even if I can't ask you, you'll know if I need you and you decide. Don't let anybody run you off. I'm paying good money for a private room, so tell them I want you."

For reasons I didn't examine but that filled me again with solemn elation, I never mentioned the request to Mother. Even I, though, couldn't imagine the depth or crushing centrifugal power of the vortex I'd unthinkingly vowed to enter.

When I turned up the next afternoon with my books, my shaving kit and a change of clothes, Elizabeth had the grace to show no surprise. She left at six to cook supper for Bill, but she said she'd be back before bedtime.

In an unusually firm voice, Will told her no—to stay at home, keep Bill company and go to sleep early. He'd hope to see her in the morning before the orderlies came at 6:30 to wheel him out. All the years I'd known the two of them, all our time together in the triad, I don't remember an earlier occasion when he took such a firm tone; it was certainly the only time I'd seen Elizabeth assent with no fight to a brake on her wishes. But that night she took it with a smiling nod.

Will ate a light, mostly liquid supper. I ducked out quickly to the sandwich machine; and when I got to Will's room, the best friend of his youth, whom I've called Alec, was there. They'd been inseparable next-door neighbors from birth; and one of my early pleasures was hearing them relive their boyhood japes, imaginative in small-town inventiveness but epic in daring to a boy as quiet as I'd been.

For instance they once built a steam calliope from an assemblage of tin cans, and it played admirably till they pushed their luck in striving for more volume. The boiler exploded and scalded their friend and co-builder Pat Hunter. Pat survived to become the physician who delivered me; but with third-degree steam burns in 1912, he required leg grafts of "sheep skin." Will and Alec swore that the skin grew wool and had to be shorn for the rest of Pat's life.

Any of their recollections ended in hilarious accounts of the endless quest of boys under Prohibition, the hunt for a safe and reliable bootlegger (bad moonshine could blind you). Will's monumental thirst began in those harmless-sounding days; and the laughter lasted right through his and Elizabeth's wedding when Alec, as the drunk best man, sobbed so loudly at the altar that Elizabeth would always claim "I'm not that sure we really are married—I never heard the vows; Alec sobbed so loud."

Will had seen almost nothing of Alec in recent years. Before we moved back to Warrenton in the forties, Will had great hopes for reviving the friendship. But the years, and the fact that Will had had better luck than Alec in halting the runaway thirst of their youth, had cut an unbridgeable gap between them. So the hometown reunion amounted to little more than occasional street encounters and Will's being called in one night by Alec's mother when Alec was raging against his wife.

Yet here he was now, the last visitor before what might be a fatal operation. Alec was famed for a learned and outrageous wit, and now he strained to cheer his old friend with the tag-ends of their riotous youth. Alec even broke new ground, for me, with allusions to willing country girls and their fathers with buckshot. He even risked veiled hints of romantic relations between another friend of theirs and a live chicken. But loud as he was, after an hour Alec was at least sober enough to realize that his jokes were failing, were unnerving Will, and he left with a bluff farewell.

As soon as he was out the door, Will called me over. "Son, look at this." In the elbow crease of his right arm, a firm blue knot had appeared, big as a bird egg.

I said "When did that happen?"

"Just now, I guess—since supper anyhow."

We called an intern, who studied it slowly, obviously didn't know what it was but said it was nothing to worry about.

Will had reached a point where even a thing that alarming was normal for the course he'd accepted. He pulled his sleeve down and never looked again.

I suggested that we watch television. It had entered Will's, and most of America's, life only recently; and like the rest of the country, he'd welcomed it gladly.

But I'd hardly made the proposal before he said "Not yet" and told me to get out paper and pencil from my bag. Then with firm clarity he gave me practical instructions—the details of his meager assets, his few debts, the style of his tombstone, the names of his pallbearers: "I wish it could just be Grant." He even stipulated that I choose his funeral music. Then he said "That's all for now. See you don't lose it."

I dreaded what came next. Though he was generally august in his self-possession, I've said that he never found it hard to make frank statements of love, thanks or go-to-hell contempt. And now I feared he was near to speaking about our relations through the years, my special standing as his pledge to God.

To be sure I'd known of the fact for years, but Will had never mentioned it (and his only warning against liquor came as I joined a college fraternity; shortly after, when he and I were alone together, he remarked off-hand, "You know that the men in your family were never too good around liquor?"). I'd never questioned that he loved and honored me, yet we shared few interests outside the home, and his innate reserve had kept us formal. Tonight I feared that, if he broke the code of two decades and made a declaration or exacted a further vow, I'd lose my hold on this new strength that I'd never tried before and was not sure I owned.

He only said "Now watch your TV."

I said "It's not mine. I thought you might enjoy it."

"I might. Turn it on."

So for two hours more, we watched the flickering black and white programs of those live early days. I forget which programs; I was grateful for them all. I recall being drowned in the shows and barely thinking to check Will's face. When I did, he'd be watching as intently as I. Only then would I think of the morning and what we must do. On balance till now, I can say that I've had a much less fearful life than Will's. But I know a strange fact about myself—the night before my own first surgery for cancer, I lay alone in my hospital room and watched with absorption and pleasure a two-hour televised history of *Giselle*, the ballet and its most famous performers.

I can hope that Will found similar distraction in what we watched. Anyhow it was he who called bedtime. The doctors and nurses had made their last calls; he'd taken the standard-issue sleeping pill. We brushed our teeth and settled in the darkness. All his adult life, he abhorred shut doors, shut rooms. When I was fourteen and went with him on a business train-trip to Ohio, his claustrophobia made him leave the door of our sleeping compartment ajar; and I was humiliated as only an adolescent can be. But there in Rex I plainly remember we had the door shut and Will didn't object.

He probably asked if I'd said my prayers. I can't find in my memory that he followed his lifelong habit of kneeling by the bed for his last devotions; his legs may have been too weak. I know that we read no Bible verses and we didn't pray together (we never had). His private untalkative faith was something he knew I shared, though I often wondered how well it served him in fearful times. He'd have probably said he couldn't have made it this far without a certainty that he was known and watched with care by God. But beyond half-amused debates on minor points of doctrine, I doubt we spoke a hundred words about it ever.

Interrupted only by a night nurse making routine checks, we both managed more sleep than I'd expected. Nothing had touched Will's snoring power; and when I woke briefly a time or two, he was grinding it out in torrents. But we were both awake well before six. I had time to wash my face; and when a black orderly came to shave Will's chest, I took ten minutes to go for coffee and toast. By the time I was back, Elizabeth was there.

Always tender-hearted in an earned unsentimental way, in these last days Mother had managed to steel herself surprisingly and could show an attentive warmth but no tears or empty cheer. She had known this man twelve years before my birth; and as she was finally to tell me, they shared exchanges that I never knew (days later in a near-trance of exhausted grief, she was to tell me that they'd made love a last time, there in Will's toilet).

Anyone who's undergone radical surgery or seen a friend through it will supply here the desert clarity of the stale air that fills a room in those last private minutes. If the patient knows that his condition is grave, that his hopes are severely limited, then both he and you are visible in your dire helplessness as never before. You hang in a narrow space with miles of distance between him and you, and you meet each other's eyes like partners in a killing or victims about to be shot at the edge of a ditch they've made you dig all night.

No firing squad can thrust you out of warmth and safety onto the windy ledges of mortality quicker than the arrival of two orderlies in surgical green with a rolling stretcher. The patient is either trying to pray or is grappling in silence with doubts, real fears and the need to show heroic calm. The friend is also trying his version of similar needs. And the line dividing the two is paper-thin—one is the victim, today. The friend is wild with a thanks he must not show, a thanks that freezes if he's realistic and knows he's next.

Then before you've mastered your face and voice, the orderlies start their urgent work. Your last exchanges lapse into code, never "Goodbye" or "Thanks" but empty promises of meeting—"I'll be right here when the ether wears off. Don't give away any state secrets now." The patient remembers the wedding ring he's forgot to take off. He hands it to you; you wear it for safety. Then the stretcher rolls and at last you see with scalding newness how near to lost any loved one is, racked out flat under taut white sheets; how lost you'll be when your day comes.

I've sunk the memory of what Will said as Elizabeth and I walked by the stretcher as far as they'd let us or whether he spoke at all. In narrow straits he mostly went silent, though his eyes were wide. I do know that when we reached the swinging doors at the turn-back point, my father was watching me with gray eyes that could fix me as still as an owl's. Elizabeth clasped his hand for an instant; I must have as well. I know I waved but he only kept his eyes on me.

I'd give a lot to know what he thought as the doors closed between us. Or maybe I wouldn't, now that I'm older than he was then and can make a fair guess—*That's it. So long. It goes so fast. I was scared of this and now—Lord God—I'm calm and ready.*

I know I suspected he'd die before noon.

We waited in his room. A friend or two joined us for the vigil; I can no longer see who. But I could draw an accurate police portrait of the surgeon when he thrust through the door at eleven. Till then Dr. Sinclair had seemed a compact powerful man, maybe forty. Now he was shrunk, ashen and drained. He looked as exhausted as if he'd been beat by strong assailants for the last three hours. It was my introduction to the way so many doctors manage hard meetings, *Set your face on a spot near their eyes, and start with the worst.* We faced him with transparent hope.

With no prelude, he set his face and said "I couldn't save him. I got the lung out. But he's got tumors strung on up in his neck, the size of hen eggs—no way to get at them."

Elizabeth sat down stunned and said "No." If a human voice could turn the tide, her single word would have locked the east coast.

I thought he was saying that Will was dead.

But he said "Mrs. Price, you can go to him now. The nurse will take you to Intensive Care."

Mother looked to me, speechless.

So I asked if I could go with her.

Sinclair nodded. "But nobody else."

To this day, it was the worst sight I've seen, in life or on film. In a large room of groaning supine bodies in all stages of waking, Will was strapped to a stretcher on a gray rubber sheet. His chest was bare except for a huge white dressing on the right. My memory also sees a lot of blood. I doubt that now but a catheter tube ran down to a bottle with a dark inch of piss. Fixed to his mouth was what I see as a red rubber breathing-bag the size of a softball; it collapsed and filled as he struggled to talk. If this had been a prison in Paraguay, I'd have known they'd found the perfect way to torture Will Price with his terror of confinement, his passion for air. My memory sees nothing of his eyes or expression, but I know his hands were struggling against the straps to touch us, and his head was flailing. Around the black mouthpiece, he was managing to ask over and over where Bill was.

Elizabeth told him "Safe at home."

Then he said "I nearly died."

I know that I thought "Do. Die now." There was no way this pitching ruined body could ever be reconstructed to live.

But each of us touched his arm, so he managed to free the powerful right hand and reach it toward us. When we gave him our hands, he seized them fiercely and blared his gray eyes to search our faces, "Where is *Bill?*"

I said "At home, waiting. Bill's fine; you rest." I was telling the truth; Will had insisted that Bill be kept from sights like this.

But one more time Will counted our faces; one of us was lost. Then he fixed on Elizabeth a look of such need and expectation that I thought it might kill her, *Save me now.*

I think she didn't speak, but she bent to their joined hands and kissed him there. I was no part of it.

A nurse came up and asked us to leave. We told him we'd see him back in his room.

He made no effort to keep us.

Nearly died. We didn't say so but, when Mother and I faced each other, we had to think death would come in minutes, the only mercy.

I also had an instant to think how amazed I should be that—seeing a man I honored like him, turned on God's hot spit like a carcass—I was upright and working in place. In the past year or two, as I'd moved forward more nearly on my hope to be a writer, I'd felt deprived of a chance to fight in a war. I saw how crucial war had been for Tolstoy, Hemingway and the young American writers then emerging before me. But there by Will, I knew I was living through worse than war and was still upright; still stronger than Mother, who ate down a terrible sob as we went. I was wrong in the latter, as she was to prove with years of lone strength; but at twenty-one I believed myself proudly.

By midafternoon Will was back in his room—the cored-out body; the mind was never fully conscious again. We'd requested a private nurse; and from here on she was a steady presence in the room, a fine-looking fortyish woman of swift competence and kindness whose name I've lost. I told her at once that I meant to spend the nights with Will. In those days, hospital rules would bend; and often whole families camped out for weeks by a kinsman's bed, subsisting on peanuts and bottled drinks. And the nurse saw no problem in my sleeping on the easy chair—she'd be busy with his care and would have no time to rest.

More even than elsewhere, it's necessary that now I not invent useful memories. So I have to say that I don't remember clearly a single word exchanged between me and Will from the awful minute in Intensive Care right through his death. I remember one sentence he said to the air. And I know there were rare exchanges between us, one of which I've tried to sketch credibly. I know that I left the room only to eat; and on Wednesday and Thursday, Will had lucid times; but I've kept no more than peripheral and silent details—that when I helped him hold the chromium urinal, for instance, I registered the irony of my handling the pitifully reduced genital that, in stronger days, had issued one of the two first cells of my body.

There were quick moments, after cold machine-snacks, when I'd sit in a side room off the lobby because a powerful statue was there, carved in Italy. It was Christ in white marble, his chest half-bare, his open hands extended in welcome and the offer of healing—what the gospels call his "streaming power." Elizabeth had told me more than once that the statue was given by an old beau of my grandmother Price and that it had stood in the old Rex building downtown. She also said that Will had sat by it when I was wheeled off for an emergency tonsillectomy at eighteen months.

There was dense brown air in the room in the evenings, when Elizabeth would stop in for a few minutes before going home to be with Bill— no other visitors now allowed. Surely Will acknowledged her presence; yet I recall no talk between them, only his obvious wish that she leave, that she not stay long. Mother and I agreed to believe he was worried that she might witness a disaster, a sudden hemorrhage from the stump of his lung. I know I was glad she showed no sign of minding his wish for my constant presence. And since her emotions were as clear as spring air, I know she was what she said—grateful. Someone at least was doing some good; the family at least was represented, whatever was rushing toward him in the dark. I know I'd nod and see her to the door. I know I felt brave and grown at last, horrified and far more helpless than at any other time in my life, even in my own body's later trials.

I do have three more keen recollections. The surgery took place on Wednesday morning, the 17th of February. Late in the night on Friday, past midnight really, Will grew wildly restless. He couldn't breathe easily, and he began to thrash in bed. The nurse asked him if he'd like to try sitting up—Dr. Sinclair had authorized it. Will nodded yes fervently. So she and I heaved him slowly upright, to the edge of the bed with his white legs dangling.

At first he wavered; it took him a minute to adjust to the position. Then he drew the deep breath he craved and it calmed him. But soon his eyes were searching the dark room frantically.

I said "Is there something you want?"

Will could only shake his head; did that mean no? Two minutes later his left hand flew to his bandaged right side, and a look of dark astonishment flooded his face. He made no sound but at once fell back, crooked on the pillows. His eyes shut and his chest barely moved.

The nurse reached for his pulse, then told me to stand by; she had to get the doctor.

My guess was that something had torn loose in his chest. The omen he guessed at—changing a light bulb, years ago—had finally struck. I'd seen the incision that evening when the nurse changed his dressing—a huge reversed letter C that jagged from his breastbone downward, then up nearly to his right armpit. It was sewed with black knots of what seemed barbed wire. Or had other organs collapsed into the cavity left by the missing lung? More than anything else, another of this lifelong claustrophobe's worst fears seemed realized—he was now unbearably crowded. I was holding his wrist and feeling a light pulse, so I knew he wasn't dead. But again I thought this was it, a matter of minutes.

The nurse returned to say that Dr. Bonk, Sinclair's partner, was on his way from home. In the waste time she and I stood on opposite sides of the bed and watched. Something forced me to see each moment; I didn't look up, even to ask her what had happened. And when Will and I were alone in the room, though I held his hand, he never spoke and his eyes never opened. All his force was aimed at breathing—awful, torn-out shallow breath.

Twenty minutes passed before Bonk arrived, an anxious-looking young man who'd plainly dressed fast (open-necked, no tie). He listened to Will's heart and called to him strongly, "Mr. Price. This is Dr. Bonk. Do you hear me?"

Will's eyes were open but he gave away nothing.

My next memories may not sound feasible to anyone with knowledge of medicine in the 1950s; but I think I saw Bonk strip off the dressing, then pull an enormous hypodermic syringe from his bag. It looked two inches in diameter and eight inches long, with a needle like a skewer; and I thought of the pump for an enormous football. I also thought he'd plunge it now into Will's chest and reinflate whatever had collapsed.

At the sight I fell into the trap set for the innocent by the visible mystique of medicine. The tools themselves are so new and bizarre that they bestow an illusory magical competence upon their users, a power that excludes us. I thought whatever this was would surely work. Nothing so weird, employed so swiftly, could possibly fail. And so at that moment I wondered if my presence was legal—I know I thought *legal*, not *permitted* or *wise*.

As if he heard me, Bonk turned and said "Wait in the hall."

Like a child expelled from adult secrets, I had no choice but obedience. With no word to Will, I went out, shut the door and sat on a bench nearby in the hall. Many empty hours seemed to pass, floated on the regulation noises of a surgical ward in the dead of night—sighs, gurgitations, outcries cut down as if by knives, the occasional clear set of words launched into air with the reckless certainty of a god-seized sibyl. I recall one cry because I wrote it down. A man's clear strong voice said "I've asked you why and you have not answered me. Goddammit, say why." But he never said who he challenged to speak; and in all the time I sat there, he never spoke again. Through it all ran the buoyant murmur of student nurses planning their weekend, the clothes they'd swap.

For nearly three weeks I'd been a man, a certified adult. With good public schools behind me, and now in my third year at the university, I'd read my way through the Greeks and Romans, the Old and New Testaments; the classic novels of Russia, France, England, America and a good deal of history. And like most innocent children who have the mixed luck to grow up in stable (if not peaceful) families, I'd feasted my mind on a fresh diet of imaginary horrors. I'd learned from books, movies and radio of the dangers of life—a cousin's raving madness and the hurtful bafflements of so many more kinsmen, Agamemnon's murder, Medea's slaughter of her sons, the death of Tolstoy's Ivan Ilyich, Eliot's stare at the black heart of life and the newsreel pictures of Dachau and Belsen— skeletons lightly tarred with skin and, on every mouth, the frozen ghost of a smile. More than a few million cells of my mind were watching myself with a wild exhilaration.

The inward pacific boy I'd been, a target for the love and hate of others, was standing at last in the white-hot eye of ultimate flame and— look—I was lasting, faithful and dauntless. What else could a father be for but this, to teach such skills? My youth and the terrible weight of the time forbade my seeing the self-regard in the midst of the thought or of thinking mainly on the man hid from me, a generous father. But even now, hard as it sounds, my finding has a kernel of truth—*All their lives they teach us life. Before they go, parents must teach us the final skill or they fail us badly.*

I also knew that, any instant now, the door would open and Bonk would walk toward me with the news, "Your father is dead." A burning pall would pull back off me, but another would settle—I would now be the man to a baffled widow and a boy thirteen.

But when Bonk appeared, he seemed in a rush and only said "You may go back in."

Obedient again to the power most doctors possess to cancel our questions, I nodded, stood and entered the room. The overhead light must have been on; but from here to the end, all my memories see Will only, as if he lies in a pool of light on a wide dark field. I could hear him breathing, still fast and shallow; but he seemed asleep—sealed off at least. And as the nurse worked to arrange the sheets, I sat and tried to rest again.

I must have managed short naps; but mostly I was awake with the knowledge that, whatever I dreaded in childhood and youth, here now was a trial like those in the worst nightmares—a story in which I truly couldn't move, to flee or to fight, but was forced to watch in the knowledge that any instant the cause of this danger might seize and devour me too.

Bad as the time was, I was fueled by an even higher burn of my thoughts in the hall. Will had asked for no one but me. I've mentioned how often he told Elizabeth to go on home and see to Bill. I had then, and have till today, no serious doubt that Will and I hewed silently to a wordless plan. And we understood it clearer than if we'd discussed it— in this plain room we were enacting, under torture and in the space of a few days, a lifetime of the necessary roles that would end Will's life and certify mine.

We were father and son, bound in blood duty. He'd guarded my life for two decades. I guarded his death and, in it, he taught me the final lesson of life—how, hard as it is, death is no whit harder than the long trek toward it. And both things, the trek of life and death's wide mouth, can be endured with dignity anyhow (the self-possession and open kindness with which you've borne yourself each day through eighteen sober years). Both life and death can be endured when love, laughter and consciousness itself have been stripped off like the last three leaves, if you've worked to bear yourself with the daily care that exudes a grace too fine to forget.

We were also shadows of Abraham and Isaac. Will was the father who recklessly vows to God; I was the son who's all but sacrificed; then rescued at last, forever marked by the risk. If we played the other last roles that I—with my reading—might have expected, it was in deep silence and with utmost mercy: Oedipus killing his father at the crossroads, then marching for Thebes and his waiting mother; or the aged Lear as he begs full pardon from a grateful child.

Because Will couldn't speak to ask for life and because I couldn't help with so much as water, I longed again for the only rescue. Painful as the finding was, I was helped by knowing—again from books—that the wish was common. There are hundreds of states far worse than death, and choosing the instant to beg for an end is a choice hard as any. Maybe if I'd watched by an agonized child of my own body, I'd have felt something more, even the will to suffer in his place. I was young though; my blood beat strong in my ears, untried and eager. Seeing my father, gone past saving but held down here by the misplaced hope of doctors, I know I thought of Bach's noble song—"*Komm, süsser Tod.*" *Come, sweet death.*

Till dawn I ran its lines through my mind, always in the unanswerable voice of Marian Anderson, dark as our walnut dining table, the table of Will's mother's childhood home, the bearer of food to ease the pain of five generations and serving still. *Come, come soon; silent and sweet.* I didn't consider that, in Will's own head, he might be oaring another way, *Spare me please, with more good life.* And my only justification was that, though he'd fought death back for years, now he gave the signs of readiness.

Somewhere in those late hours too, I realized that—not for a moment in the night's ordeal—had I thought of phoning Mother. Will asked for me; I promised him. It didn't taste like jealousy of her or a selfish territorial claim. She'd had the most of a twenty-seven-year marriage; now Will wanted me. Coming now so late, my chance to serve felt right and it does today. With the punishing courage of children and fools, I'd cling to this till they hacked me free.

By the time Elizabeth arrived on Saturday morning, Will's breathing was even more labored. And for whatever reason, he was nearly comatose with few signs of recognition. When Sinclair passed on his early rounds, he took a slow look, then motioned us out. In the hall he didn't say what had broken in the night, and neither I nor Mother asked. When you've had body blows by the moment for days, you dodge when you can. He said that the good lung was proving insufficient, and the only thing that might ease Will's breathing was a tracheotomy. That would involve returning him to surgery, full anesthesia; then the insertion of a silver breathing-tube through the soft pit at the base of his throat, below the Adam's apple. It would give him more air, but he wouldn't be able to speak unless we covered the hole with a piece of gauze. Did we authorize that?

Mother looked to me.

In the night under darkness, I'd have surely said no. But in daylight, in a crowded hall in the midst of healthy people, I nodded yes. I knew I'd condemned my father to further pain—anesthesia and its oblivion were terrors for Will—but I didn't yet know how to sign a death warrant. And I've kept no memory of which of us told him what came next nor of what he may have said or signaled.

Will was back in an hour, with the hole in his neck. I searched his eyes for a trace of blame, but by now he was past human judgments. Within an hour an orderly entered and installed an oxygen tent. Before the advent of compact respirators, an actual tent with clear plastic walls was pitched over the patient's head—a small confinement cell, as if he weren't already far enough from the world of life. In his rare moments of clarity now, since he was mute, Will must tap on a wall of the tent to get my attention. Then I reached under, pressed a pad on the silver hole; and he croaked out his need—water or a question like "How is Bill?"

Beyond those brief requests, I think he said nothing. In life he'd hardly

been a big talker till called upon, but his silence now was the surest sign
of transformation. He never asked a question about what had happened
in the first surgery or the subsequent alarms. He never inquired about
anyone but Bill, certainly no word about my stamina or Elizabeth's, no
further plans or instructions—he counted on our lasting him out, whatever. Or maybe we'd left his mind completely. He was almost a thing
now, honored and watched but all the same a nearly posthumous thing
with a few last needs but nothing more—no thoughts, fears or human
affections that we could see.

—*That* I *could see*. If Will's mind gave him pictures, they didn't mark
his face. It was blank of every sign of feeling, only a fixed deep concen-
tration. On what, I never knew. I wish I could say, as others have at death-
beds, that Will Price gave signs of glimpsing a new world of contentment,
a place where his failures were forgiven and all his dead loved ones
awaited his coming. After the tracheotomy I never saw him agonized or
fearful again. I saw him intent but if he saw bliss, it was his last secret.
He never told me.

Before they stopped his voice, he had talked in his sleep, the common
snatches of urgent-sounding surreal thought. Of many such speeches, I
remember only one. On Friday night when he and I were alone in the
room, he cleared his throat to speak; but what he said was "Don't forget
to give Jack Rowan one of those puppies." Jack was Elizabeth's nephew,
and she'd raised cocker pups in the 1940s, but that was years ago and
Jack never wanted one.

All day Saturday and into the evening, Will's heart continued. Elizabeth stayed mostly in the hall or lobby, with friends and family. She and
Will had been as closely wed as any two mates I've known; but helpless
now, she would enter, study his face, touch his cheek or hand, say a word
or two, get no response, smooth his cover and leave the room to me.

Again my service was stripped back to that of a helpless witness. I'd
occasionally help an orderly swap oxygen tanks; but since Will now took
intravenous water, I couldn't even hold his glass. And since he was
catheterized again, there was no more urinal holding. I'd sat in the room
now nearly four days and was already far into that numb trance hospitals
induce, in the sick and the healthy. I couldn't think. I could barely feel

and all other conscious functions were suspended. I only knew I wanted him to end; but because I'd sworn, I meant to be here. I'd read of astounding feats of endurance in the Second War—children bearing their wounded kin over frozen mountains. I thought I could last many days like this. I was already some cause of wonder to my kin, none of whom had seen me perform as a man.

When Dr. Sinclair looked in at supper time, he noticed my presence and asked how long since I'd had a full night's sleep.

"Monday," five days ago.

He said "Your father's heart is strong as an ox; it could keep him going for weeks like this. Get yourself home, wash up, sleep a night."

My mind was nearly too shut to hear, but I wanted to believe him. Will was unconscious; I couldn't ask permission. But Mother was there and she took the same line—I'd gone too far; I'd be needed worse later. Two of her nephews were coming in an hour. They'd stay with her and anyhow, she'd call me the instant there was news. I made her swear and then I left. Guilt was much too human a feeling for a mind tired as mine. At home I took time to talk with Bill, whose smiling world was also sinking. But by eight o'clock I was deep asleep, still no blame and no trace of dream.

Just after daylight the phone rang at home. It was Mother, "Come on back please; he's asking for you."

I could reproduce the color of that Sunday dawn, a uniform dull pewter. Even the Sunday-schoolers weren't out on the streets as I drove toward Rex; there was even a choice of parking places in the hospital lot. Will's room was on the front of the building, first floor left; and his window showed light. As I walked uphill I suddenly knew I was twenty-one years and twenty-one days old. All my life, numbers had played these solemn games in code round my head; surely Will was dead or would die today.

When I got to the room though, he was under the tent, calm and awake. His eyes caught me as I entered the door.

I went straight to the bed and touched his right hand. He was losing weight but otherwise he looked no worse for the night behind us.

I said "It's Reynolds, sir. I'm back."

I think he nodded but he gave no sign of pleased relief or of wanting to speak; then he shut his eyes.

Elizabeth was there with her two nephews. They said Will had waked several times in the night, demanding me with rising impatience. Each time, they said I would be back shortly. Finally at dawn he woke again. With me still absent, he finally raved—digging at his tubes, clawing at the tent and scrambling to rise. Only the promise to call me and an extra shot of Demerol had calmed him.

Is it plain by now that I'd be glad of the news or, more nearly, exultant? What son wouldn't have felt rewarded? There can be only one or two other things for which a young son hopes as strongly. The news blanked any sense of blame at leaving him. At the first sign of consciousness, I'd thank him and swear not to go again. I've said that I had no sense, then or since, of breaking a promise when I left for the night. Is that because in general I was self-forgiving or because I knew that I'd reached a beginner's breaking point?

Anyhow Will had seen my return. After that, he lay on his back through the short dark day, growing calmer and stiller till sleep imperceptibly merged into coma. Again friends came and went in the hall, and one by one his sisters entered briefly. None of them touched him.

I felt no regret at missing a final chance to speak. It would only have been a one-sided moment, for my sole purpose. Even in his drugged and departing mind, I doubt Will blamed me. I saw his eyes that one last moment; they were not condemning. And my own later weeks of hospital confinement told me that, in the bleak blind-alleys of desperate need, the trivial grievance-counting of daily life instantly vanishes. You take what you can get and are glad of it.

There in sight of Will's peaceful body and his utterly mysterious mind, I was far from guessing what we'd transacted in these five days. But I dimly knew that, however tragic in its brevity and speed, what we'd made was a healing, maybe even a last-hour rescue for us both. A bond like ours, armed through two decades to kill us both, had been silently tried a final time and found to hold.

Thirty-three years later I can say no less. I can't imagine freeing myself, on my own recognizance, from the debt I owed my father without a last chance to guard his death, the chance he'd somehow known he should give me. For his own reasons and fearful of and for me, Will withdrew himself from the habit of drink, that had been so precious for so many years. And with no sign of grudge, he bore the rest of his life cold sober, caring for a wife and two sons with all the strength he could spare and more. Since I was the first new thing he helped make, I got the most of that sacrifice. In the end he gave me the chance to pay for it. I found the stamina that final week; and with two defaults (the tracheotomy, the night away), I paid all I had. When his heart chose to stop, I could leave his side with one whole page of debits cleared.

Late that evening the nurse went out to get his next shot. I stayed in the room with Pat Cowden, the neighbor with whom I'd spent a good part of the past seven years in close affection and whom Will admired. We sat in chairs by the bed at Will's left. My hand was under the sheet, on his wrist. The pulse had long since ceased to pound; it was only a ragged thread of motion, as if the heart he feared so long had forgot all else but how to stop.

Then it stopped. My finger knew the instant and pressed round to hunt—nothing: pure stillness, warm dead flesh. We heard a high moan, an eerie whistle, and looked to his face. His head was starting a final act, a powerful last response to the halt or a desperate try at starting again or a purge of the final volts of life. His skull pressed deep into the pillows. The eyes stayed shut but the skin of his face turned purple, and the hard wave rolled downward from mind to feet. It was plainly as real and irresistible as what drives the surf. I've never seen its like again; and if asked, I'd have to say that it moved on through him, through the wall of the room and outward.

But before it was gone, Elizabeth opened the door to enter. I knew she couldn't have heard his moan; I only knew she shouldn't see this. I said it firmly, "Mother, go back"—maybe even "Get out." I doubt I'd given her an outright order since infancy. Struck and afraid, her face froze white but she quickly obeyed. I didn't consider my motive then—I hope I meant to spare her the sight—but now I think I wanted this instant to myself, not shared with anyone else who loved him. I thought he'd have wanted it exactly this way; I also thought I'd earned it.

Close behind Mother came the nurse with his shot. By the time she was there, the convulsion had run its course and gone.

I asked her only what caused the wave.

She was already folding the tent back off him, smoothing his hair and hands, composing the sheets. She said "I've seen it a few times before. I guess the body just doesn't mean to die."

I thought she was wrong; I thought he'd all but begged for death since Wednesday noon. Pat took my hand; we stood and held one another close. I leaned to my father and kissed his brow; it felt no different from all the million times I'd touched it in my past life.

Then Pat and I went out to Mother, her nephews and Will's sisters in the hall. They stood as I came, and I guessed I was tall by the slant of their eyes. My father had led me to do a large thing, the first I freely willed to try. Together we'd done the hardest deed. And while I thought the word *love* could cover our years before the hospital—we'd never once quarreled; he'd never laid an angry hand on me, and we'd steadily worked for one another—as I told them the news, I discovered a whole new fact for myself: Will Price meant more to me than anything else.

Late that night I drove the twenty-two miles back to college, to get a few clothes and sleep in a room he'd never known—a neutral space seemed necessary. I made the rounds of a few friends' rooms, informing them and arranging volunteers to replace the blood Will had used. I also collected the awe they clearly showed at my strength, the first such admiration I'd had. Then I was back alone but near the humming live dormitory dark, lives young as mine but still untried. As I entered the zone this side of sleep, the place where secrets reach us, I began to feel a slow change in the room.

The air itself was being packed. Something had sealed the chinks in my space and was filling it, pound by pound, with pressure. It was already painful to my eyes and ears, and I suddenly knew it was somehow Will. He'd followed me here in his new changed life but was far too huge for this small room. I'd heard of ghosts and spirits since childhood but always in stories. In my common-sense families, I knew of no one who claimed to have seen or heard a ghost. In the stories ghosts were either confused, shut out and sadly hunting a home; or they meant real harm.

And the room kept filling with my father's return. I didn't think he intended harm, I didn't expect a voice or touch, but I knew I'd die if all of him entered. So I said the word "Go," the actual word to the air above me. Whatever was there—my dread, the guilt at my failure to save him, my bitter longing for what I'd lost or some form of Will—the pressure halted and began to subside, leaving so slowly that I was asleep before it finished. I'd dream of Will for years to come.

I'd generally be at a crowded party; and suddenly there across the room, Will would stand, hale and laughing in a ring of strangers. I'd freeze and think "But I saw him die." It sometimes took me a stretch of time before I gathered my nerve, approached him and proved that yes, it was he, strong and happy, though somehow changed. I've known many people with similar dreams of a dead loved one. Maybe the mind is that unwilling to grant a death; or are some minds that deeply sure of death's only momentary hold on life, with a newness beyond? I underwent a number of trials, then and later, to deal with his absence; but I never felt my father's palpable presence again nor another such uncanny manifestation of a lost friend.

It took me years to restore what I could of the strength I spent in those days, to tame the pictures that haunted my nights and to learn to use the strength I'd won. First I had to experience, alone in England some two years later, a harrowing internal contest between what I'd learned at Will's dying side and what I hoped to believe. I had to find a way to proceed. I was then twenty-two; but with all a young man's taste for life, I already knew what few Americans learn till much later—what waits ahead, a grinding agony, then a death and some immeasurable aftermath. Death was no longer a word, the cause of much poetry; for me now it was thousands of pictures of one good man dying.

In Oxford the outward signs of my struggle were an obsessive conviction that I also was afflicted with cancer and a longing to rush home to die. There was unquestionably a lump in my left side, big as a bird egg. There was no question that, after a banquet one night in November, I vomited blood. I took my proof to the college doctor; he sent me to a surgeon who took my symptoms seriously enough to order a series of barium-swallow X-rays—no sign of organic trouble. The surgeon suggested that the lump was a nodule of newly acquired fat. He went on to

My freshman year at Duke University, Kilgo Quad, in 1951. I'm gone from home a matter of weeks and think I'm free.

suggest that, as a newcomer to the bread and potato-swamped British diet of those postwar years, I was undergoing a bad attack of "carbohydrate shock," a phenomenon he'd observed in liberated concentration-camp victims who gorged too quickly on starch.

I couldn't believe him of course, and my death-devoted plans continued. I canceled the few English promises I'd made (trips to London and Stratford and Christmas in Italy, all with friends); and I secretly looked into the ways-and-means of transporting a corpse to America. But in a few weeks more of self-inflicted punishment, self-dramatization, I was ready to be reprieved. I returned to the surgeon, who examined me patiently again. Then with admirable insight he referred me to a wise old family-practitioner in Long Wall Street. He also felt my knob of fat, studied my X-rays, listened to my story of Will's ordeal, proclaimed me sound, suggested long walks and urged me to live.

It would be thirty years before that fear was enacted in my actual body; so after a few more dodgy days, the slow convivial rhythms of Oxford began to work. And they brought me through, with the added blessings of requited love and the start of a lifetime's gratifying work. I believed my doctors; apparently I was going to live. I went to Stratford for phenomenal performances of *Macbeth*, *Twelfth Night* and *Titus Andronicus* with Laurence Olivier and Vivien Leigh. In London I saw Margot Fonteyn dance *Cinderella*, and I began to mine the staggering riches of Oxford itself. I went with a friend to Florence and Rome and sat bare-armed in the Coliseum on Christmas day. And by early spring I'd lain well back onto love and work.

Unquestionably those days with Will were a fulcrum of my life, the point on which youth tilted into manhood—a long plateau and then the slope down. Freud said that the most important day of a man's life is the day of his father's death. In a way that Freud may not have meant, I entirely agree. As I settled into the tranquil flow of life in a country that then honored privacy and the lone mind's prerogative above all else, I began to see a hard paradox, a truth at first bitter to taste. I saw that the kindest thing Will Price did for me was to die when he did, when I stood on the doorsill of maturity in an America that was already starting its lethal commitment to the prolongation of youth.

I was more than ready to grow; and there in the generous absence of my father's huge presence, I began to move into that grown life I'd suddenly won—a life in which I could learn and then write what I needed to know and say about my home, the far-from-simple people who'd trained me there and the world beyond them. The power of witness and duty that Will awarded me on his deathbed was an integral part of what I knew and must live to say. The only block in my path was me, my own fear and blindness, everyone's block always.

The memories recorded here, good and bad, show how thoroughly I failed to bury them. When I woke in my domitory room, the first morning without him, and rose to head back home for his wake—the tears, the music, the laughing memories of all who'd loved him (memories that live in the minds of children unborn when he died)—I suspected I'd learned a durable share of all I needed to stand into life. So many fathers are cruel or cold, lions in the road yet transparent and impalpable. I had the daunting gift of a brave and good, scared, hilarious man who won the two pitched fights of his life, though the second fight killed him.

It was long years later in another grief, for my own maimed body, that I knew what was maybe the final gift of those winter days in 1954. Will Price had wanted me at his bedside, serving a body that had mostly shrunk from my childish hands; and he wanted me for a conscious purpose. Needlessly fearful as he'd always been, he was wild to show me, not only the blood rites of duty but a last and larger thing—the secret I'd need when my own end came: the naked reckless hunger to go.

AFTERWORD

CENTENARIANS ARE ASKED the secrets of their endurance; and they sometimes answer with useful advice, *Rub your ankles with cider vinegar* or *Never let the wife wear her false teeth to bed*. As I write this page, I'm fifty-five, a year older than Will lived to be. Though I hope to last longer, in working order, a man who watched his early life as closely as this book suggests might be expected to have boiled his findings to at least an interim essence, ten absolute warnings or a sentence of wisdom—*This too shall pass away*. And I do have a list of stalwart truths that I'm prepared to share with friends, on demand only now; I seldom volunteer.

But if I'd written this far in a memoir at thirty, I'd have had a long list ready for the end, an ice-water recipe of ways and means to live a useful life. Even more than most young men, I had a solution for every question this side of the calculus. I believed in watching the world closely, as I've said—the things and people in range of my senses. Then I told those people the truth I thought I'd found, the fruit of my clear vision and merciful judgment. Hatred, evil, even household confusions would dissolve in truth; and I more than guessed I knew it.

One of my findings was that life begins its wrecking action on American men in the midst of their thirties. With my good sense, I planned to dodge it. And I had what seemed fine omens before me. My books were successful, my teaching job was firm and rewarding, beautiful and brave people were giving me love and accepting mine. A month before I was thirty-two, I bought a spacious house of my own, in the open country. And though I stayed there mostly alone, life seemed good. I thought I was home.

But four months later, Elizabeth died after years of pain. Though I hadn't lived in the family place for fifteen years, and had been happy elsewhere, the roomy house on its green lot in Raleigh, with the creek behind, was there safe to visit, all its old meanings propped around my mother's gallant ending. That May afternoon, home vanished in an instant when an artery blew in her brain. One of her nephews, Ida's middle son, was sick upstairs and staying with Mother. She was on the phone to his doctor in Durham; and a neighbor happened to be there with her when she said the thing such victims often say, "I've got a terrible pain in my head." The neighbor helped her lie on the floor, called an ambulance and then called me to say they'd rushed her to Wake Memorial. I was walking out the door of my house when the telephone rang.

I rushed through the twenty-odd miles in a lightning storm. When I reached the hospital, she was still alive; her hand was warm. But she gave no sign of knowing me and she never rallied. In a loaded exchange, I asked the doctor if there was any hope. He held my eyes very closely and said "If I were you, I'd hope there was not." I must have looked baffled. He said "She could live for years like this, but her brain is already badly damaged." So I nodded agreement; I wouldn't hope.

Her heart beat on till nearly dawn. She'd made it to sixty, older than her parents. Bill was married by then but was floating somewhere off Cuba, in the Navy; he was back in two days, and we buried her by Will. We'd expected such a fate for years—she often joked about the time bomb in her skull—but the sudden disappearance of the woman who made you, in whom you actually lived and grew for nearly a year, is not a change you can brace to meet.

I say that home ended instantly. I'm speaking of all the meanings of *home*—the cradle, nursery, school, hearth, the ruin and health of most human lives. Another hidden meaning was involved. Whatever steps a grown human being takes toward building his or her own hearth, in a central part of his mind, he's a child till his parents are dead. Only then, with no backer behind him or shield in front, must he really face the reality of death—*You are next in line.*

For months after Elizabeth's funeral, the dead-hearted house sat empty, adrift in wild grass and packed with the cargo of four lifetimes. Since Bill and I never planned to live there, it would have to be sold. So while he completed his stint in the Navy, which took him finally to Vietnam, I managed the end of our old campaign through the middle seaboard, a restless band, closer for the roaming. With Bill's wife Pia to help me, I dismantled our unimaginable hoardings. True to her orphan's dread of loss, Mother had saved nearly forty years of worn clothes, rusty toys, miles of magazines, every scrap of paper a loved one had marked and a hundred jelly glasses. We sorted them all, divided the good things amicably, discarded truckloads and sold the rest for a ludicrous pittance to the kind of junk dealer who leans on your panic to cut and run. Then we put the house up, *"Priced to move,"* and sold the only home we'd had to a family as close as we'd been, refugees from Hungary.

Dazed by the loss of the source of more than half my knowledge, and driven by folly to find quick shelter in the lives of others, I trusted the reading of what I thought was a true inner compass; and soon my lifeboat was snagged on a shoal. I had a bona fide old-fashioned breakdown, like the ones in Chekhov that send you to the country or the brand of failure endured by my kinsmen who paradoxically couldn't leave the homes that tortured them. My sight was blocked, I couldn't see forward, I couldn't work. The house I'd bought only deepened my torpor.

So I took a friend's advice and sat for weeks on the porch of a house by a broad deep river and watched the barges fifty yards off and the fat hedgehogs between me and water. I rose and dressed and grinned at callers, none of whom guessed. But at any pressure, my stamina buckled; and careful not to flinch in public, I went to my room and memorized another few yards of ceiling. I never consulted a doctor or priest. I waited in stillness and tried to hope that, somewhere beneath, there were nets to catch me if the fall continued. With the patience of friends and with calls for help to the light I trusted but could nowhere see, one more slow time the long fall slowed and turned. By the first cold weather, I was more or less back—a different man but able to work.

The given and taken scars of that decade are charted, at an unsafe distance, in the novels, stories and poems of those years. I may yet write about the time directly, but now is too soon. Hard as the years were on me and my friends, they constituted the second test (Will's death was the first) that tried me for the third. That came years later with the news which was brought to me and Bill as I waited on a stretcher in a hospital hallway crammed with strangers—something lethal had lain in my spine for years and was growing.

As it turned out, I lasted, partly through the heroic care of friends and the skill of my doctors but largely through grace, the unseen gifts that arrived as needed—hope, then healing; then a thirst for new life, which meant new work. But I'd shamefully deny the legacy of Will, Elizabeth, Ida, my Price aunts, Mac, Grant, Flora and all my other teachers if I didn't acknowledge that down in my cellarage, below any frost line, were stone piers driven by selfless people too strong and good to fail.

Long before, Howard Powell had advised me not to venture far from a place where I could study the faces I thanked and must not betray. He kept his pictures on separate pages of a book that he leafed through in prayer each day. When I'd bought a house, I took his advice. I covered a wall beside my bed with familiar faces, the people who've trusted me past my due, some of whom have done the unthinkable favor of lending me their warmth to hold against me.

Toward the end of that second test, I lay down numbly, through long afternoons and watched their faces. I thought they watched back. And partly because of the gifts and trust they'd lavished on me, they saw me once more attempt a life on the old groundwork they'd laid in the dark, when they had no notion of what was to come. Till now that new life has been all the sweeter for the memory of their daring gifts. And they've watched ever since, through the deeper fall that was not of my making.

Also late in the second test, a friend thrust a dead-straight finger to the core of one of my confident monologues-in-guidance. He said "Some people are rumor mongers, Reynolds. The trouble with you is, you're a truth monger. You see a little; you think you understand it and can say what it means. Then you say it all night." I've mentioned priding myself for my eyes, the constant witness I learned from my kin. But I've also valued that friend's true thrust, precise as a laser, searing and cleaning. Before the third test, I was working at repair.

In daily life and all later work, I tried to see clearer, steadier, deeper.

No human being sees much. Our eyes don't begin to exhaust the spectrum of light; rooms may swarm with angels twining their limbs in a robust saraband our ears can't hear, though the old dog may or why's he shivering there on the hearth? But I try to go on seeing more. Then I hope to say what I see, as plainly as possible with a minimum of comment, blame or counsel.

If I have an aim for whatever time is left to my faculties, it may be the oldest aim of all, to go on being a picture maker. From early childhood I tried to make safe alternate worlds—elephants, movie stars, gleaming heroes, clean block-cities: handmade joy. Now I concentrate on offering scenes, people in rooms or God in hearts. The scenes can be called back from memory, as here, or laid out fresh by a copying mind, like a still life of pears in the waning moon of this long night, near the shortest day. In every picture, I work to clarify the salient faces and whatever sign of unseen power is pressing from inside with love or havoc, which may also be love, to move the things apart or nearer.

For a man trained from birth by unbroken relays of knowing witnesses, the aim sounds easy—to watch the world in all directions and say what he sees to patient hearers with no bigger stake in who I am or what I do than the cost of a book, and to say it in a language as ready as any on Earth to serve. With age I'd hoped for "the gift to be simple." At the age I am now, this is what came.

REYNOLDS PRICE

Reynolds Price was born in 1933 in Macon, North Carolina, a village surrounded by cotton and tobacco but split in the midst by the Seaboard Railway, the Raleigh-to-Norfolk line. His father, a salesman, led the family to various small towns in search of work toward the end of the Depression. A few days after the opening of the Second World War, he began grade school in Asheboro, N.C. School at once became the best place in a generally happy childhood; and it fostered his first great avocation, drawing and painting. When he was in the second grade, he was joined in the family by a welcome brother, his only near relation.

In 1944 the family returned to Warrenton, the county seat of its homeplace, Warren County. There for three years he met the farm children who, a decade later, would be the prototypes of his early fiction. He continued to encounter splendid teachers—in the seventh grade, a woman who taught him hundreds of lines of poetry and, in the eighth, a woman who had published a short story in the O. Henry Prize Stories of 1931. He had long been fascinated by books; by adolescence he was addicted, a craving which his insolvent parents freely supported. By the age of thirteen, he had made a start at writing his own.

When the family moved to Raleigh in 1947—his thirteenth move in fourteen years—he met other fine teachers and began the serious writing of plays, fiction and poetry. The luck continued through four years as a student of English literature and history at Duke University and three years at Merton College, Oxford. There as a Rhodes Scholar, he studied John Milton, Italian Renaissance criticism and Greek drama with such guides as W. H. Auden, David Cecil, Nevill Coghill and Helen Gardner. He traveled widely in Europe and spent a perilous amount of time writing fiction and poetry. But at last he completed a thesis and received a B.Litt. degree.

He returned to Duke in 1958 and began the teaching which has occupied a satisfying third of his year ever since. In the ensuing thirty years, while pursuing his own work, he became James B. Duke Professor of English and has witnessed the early fiction and poetry of such writers as Fred Chappell, Anne Tyler, Josephine Humphreys, Charlie Smith and David Guy.

After his gypsy youth, through the past three decades, he has been firmly anchored by a country pond in Orange County, North Carolina—the home also of fish, a winter clutch of mallards, hawks, herons, a snapping turtle the size of a tub, muskrats, foxes, copperheads, blacksnakes, chipmunks, raccoons and a noble though ravenous herd of deer.

In 1984 an astrocytoma in his spinal cord resulted in paraplegia. Since then he has completed four novels, a collection of poems, a collection of thirty-three years of essays, and four plays while continuing to teach at Duke. A list of earlier books appears at the head of this one. His fiction has been translated into sixteen languages.